POLITICAL SOCIOLOGY
A Comparative/Historical Approach
Second Edition

POLITICAL SOCIOLOGY
A Comparative/Historical Approach

Second Edition

Berch Berberoglu
University of Nevada, Reno

GENERAL HALL, INC.
Publishers
5 Talon Way
Dix Hills, New York 11746

POLITICAL SOCIOLOGY
A Comparative/Historical Approach
Second Edition

GENERAL HALL, INC.
5 Talon Way
Dix Hills, New York 11746

Publisher: Ravi Mehra
Composition: Graphics Division, General Hall, Inc.

LIBRARY OF CONGRESS CATALOG CARD NUMBER: **01-34644**

ISBN:1–882289–70–6 [paper]
1–882289–71–4 [cloth]

ISBN 1-882289-71-4

9 781882 289714

Manufactured in the United States of America

Contents

PREFACE TO THE SECOND EDITION

During the course of the twentieth century, the state has come to play a central role in modern society. And with this role, there has emerged a renewed interest among scholars in the study of politics and the state. Discussions and debates on the nature and role of the modern state have grown and spread across many disciplines. Together with the analysis of class structure, the state has taken center stage in social analysis in such disciplines as political economy, history, anthropology, and comparative politics, as well as sociology.

Although political sociologists have long tackled the question of the state and its role in society, interest in the state has now become a central feature in the study of politics and society. As a result, the relationship between class and state has become more obvious than before, and some important conclusions have been reached regarding the class nature of the state and politics in contemporary capitalist society.

I hope that this book will make a significant contribution to the field of political sociology and will help clarify the links between the state and society in general and the class basis of the state, power, and politics in particular.

This second edition of *Political Sociology: A Comparative/Historical Approach* has been completely updated and revised, providing the latest data available on much of the information conveyed throughout the book. The material at the end of Chapter 4 and data in Chapters 5 and 6 have been thoroughly updated, while an account of developments in China, the former Soviet Union, and Eastern Europe in the 1990s have been added to Chapter 7 to bring the analysis up to the present.

Much has changed since this book was first published in 1990, but much has remained the same in politics and the role of the state over the course of the past decade. Thus, much of the substantive arguments originally made in this book some ten years earlier remain the same in this special second edition.

1

Despite all the turbulance and upheavals of the past ten years, societies around the world have shown remarkable resilience in their resistance to change. The Soviet Union is no more, yet the old Soviet republics function much the same as before under a new national identity within the framework of the Commonwealth of Independent States (CIS). The former Eastern European socialist states have over the past decade moved in a capitalist direction, yet communists have won important victories in recent elections in Poland, Hungary, and other countries in Eastern Europe during this period. Some have declared the death of socialism and communism in the East and the decline of class politics in the West, yet China has been making great progress under the banner of "socialism" and "communism" that it claims to uphold, while the class struggles have been intensifying in France, Italy, Germany, and other advanced capitalist states in the West where socialist and communist forces are vying for power through the electoral process. In South Africa, apartheid has been officially abolished, yet the white power structure and Afrikaner capital has flourished under the leadership of Nelson Mandela and the African National Congress (ANC). The "Evil Empire" has been defeated, as some have happily proclaimed, yet another has been substituted to take its place as the sole superpower as we enter a new century. Some have declared "the end of history" with capitalism triumphant, but the contradictions of capitalism are surfacing everywhere once again and are bound to intensify with the economic and political crises that are in the making.

The world is rapidly changing as centers of power shift from one region to another, but the unfolding contradictions of global capitalism are forcing its chief protagonists to build new alliances to maintain their power in response to these changes. We have seen the fierce competition and rivalry between the leading capitalist powers in the economic sphere over the past few decades. The political/military rivalry and confrontation between the competing poles of capital that are in turn bound to develop in the next period will be a reflection of changes in the economic base of global capitalism that the capitalist states will inevitably face on a worldwide basis. Thus, the cyclical fluctuations that have threatened the stability of the capitalist system from within its economic conditions to this day, will now lead the system to a new plane where gradual quantitative changes will of necessity lead to the resolution of its fundamental contradictions in a qualitative way, such that the continuing rivalries between the chief capitalist powers will soon evoke open conflict between the main antagonistic classes—labor and capital—within each capitalist society and lend themselves to new (revolutionary) political and social transformations in the coming period.

As we enter the twenty-first century, class conflict will emerge as a primary feature of struggles within and between the major capitalist powers as they attempt to dominate the global political economy in the post-Soviet world order. As we leave behind the Cold War rivalry between the U.S. and the U.S.S.R.—a rivalry which kept the U.S. labor movement in check for decades—the rapidly developing contradictions of global capitalism will soon prompt the working class in the United States and elsewhere to take charge of its own agenda and interests and confront the power of capital and the capitalist state head on, and put up a determined fight in the ensuing class struggles that are bound to come in the years ahead. Thus, the twenty-first century promises to be an exciting century that will affect all aspects of life in a new and most decisive way. The next big fight between labor and capital, between the forces of progress and reaction, may be upon us sooner than many have been led to believe, as the all-round contradictions of capital and the entire capitalist system unravel in front of our eyes in the period ahead.

As in any human activity involving social thought or action, the ideas expressed here are the result of a collective process. Thus, the assumptions made, the concepts utilized, and the approach adopted in this book have been developed over many years of reflection and analysis, involving many people who have addressed the pressing issues concerning the state, and politics in general, and the centrality of *class* in analyzing political institutions and affairs within a comparative-historical framework—a process that is enriched with the highest level of cumulative scholarship that is embodied in this work.

Much of the intellectual debt I owe ultimately goes to working people and their struggles throughout modern history; together with the giants of social thought in the late nineteenth and early twentieth centuries, who helped interpret *and change* the world from the standpoint of the working people, they have provided the framework of analysis presented in this book.

Within the academic community, mentors and colleagues have played an important role in the formation and transformation of my thinking during the course of my intellectual development. First and foremost, I am grateful to Larry T. Reynolds for introducing me to the tools and framework of social analysis that I have come to adopt in my studies on politics and society. His teaching and seminars have played an important role in influencing my thinking on critical questions of our time. I would also like to thank Blain Stevenson for his part in setting me on a most valuable political and intellectual journey during my early college years through my graduate studies, for without his guidance, my work would not have taken the direction it has today. Similarly, I thank James Petras for making a powerful impact on my thinking through his writings and during my graduate studies at the State University of New York at Binghamton in the early 1970s. His influence continues to enrich my thinking more than quarter of a century later.

The consolidation of my ideas on society, especially political sociology, began to take place at the University of Oregon where I studied for my doctorate under Albert Szymanski in the mid 1970s. In his provocative seminars on social theory, class analysis, and political sociology, I began to formulate many of the ideas I had wrestled with in my earlier studies. My intellectual development came to a head and began to bear fruit at the conclusion of my studies at Oregon. For all I learned from Al, and for his role as friend and mentor, I express my deep appreciation and gratitude.

I would also like to thank Walda Katz Fishman, Alan Spector, Julia Fox, Marty Orr, Gianfranco Pala, Carla Filosa, Dave Harvey, and Johnson Makoba for their participation in discussions or comments on some of the major political issues addressed in this book.

I would like to thank my students in my undergraduate and graduate political sociology classes and seminars who discussed and debated the class nature of politics and the state in capitalist society. Their valuable insights and input have made an important contribution to the shaping of the second edition of this book.

Finally, I would like to thank my wife, Suzan, and my sons, Stephen and Michael, for their love and support, without which this book could not have been written.

Needless to say, the ideas expressed in this book—dependent as they are on those of countless others—are nevertheless mine; any errors in facts or interpretation thus remain mine alone.

Berch Berberoglu
August 2000

INTRODUCTION

Nearly three decades have passed since the Poulantzas-Miliband debate on the nature and role of the modern capitalist state, yet interest in the state continues to grow and spread across disciplinary and paradigmatic lines. As the state plays an increasingly central role in modern society and takes center stage under advanced capitalism, scholars and observers across the political spectrum have developed an interest in the study of the current structure and future direction of the state and its role in society. Thus, while conservative analysts have intensified their antistate rhetoric, combined with "free market" advocacy against state intervention in the economy and society and liberal academics have focused on the question of bureaucracy and attempted to develop a "state centered" theory of the state, scholars on the left have continued their discussion and debate around the class nature of the state, its structural imperatives, and its role in the age of globalization.[1]

Central to the study of the state and its role in society is an analysis of its nature and structure, as perceived by observers from different perspectives. Thus to the question "What is the state?" pluralist, elite, and Marxist theories have provided alternative answers and have reconceptualized the relationship between the state and society.

In Chapters 1 and 2, I discuss and criticize these alternative views of the state at length, but it is important here to lay bare my own approach to this key question, for an understanding of one's theoretical and methodological approach to the state is essential to an understanding of the nature, development, and transformation of the state in different comparative and historical settings.

In this context, it should be pointed out at the outset that this book is not a text in conventional political sociology, as the field is

5

traditionally defined, for it does not deal with established main-stream political parties or electoral politics; nor is it a book of political theory as such, though various theories of the state and politics are discussed at length. Instead, this volume goes to the heart of the nature and role of the state in society and examines the *linkages between class and state* in different comparative and historical settings, for as the state has increasingly taken center stage in social life, these linkages, taken together, constitute the very foundation of the modern state as the central political institution of the twentieth century.[2]

"When talking about the state in any society," writes R. B. Sutcliffe, "we have to ask several questions: firstly, who (what social class, group or alliance of classes) controls or wrestles for the power of the state? Secondly, we must ask how great is the power of the State? This depends upon how powerful are the groups or classes which control it."[3] In discussing the state, "the first question must always be which class is dominant in a given social formation," argues Leys; "since this dominance must be enforced by the state, the class character of the state is given by this relationship."[4] The central question regarding the nature of the state, then, is the character of its relationship with the prevailing social forces in society.

In examining the origins and development of the state, as I do in Chapter 3, it becomes clear that this question can be answered only through a historically specific analysis of the laws of motion of different modes of production lodged in a particular social forma-tion. The failure of attempts to construct a universal, abstract model of state behavior across societal lines demonstrates the correctness of this observation. Yet debates over the nature of the state at the general, theoretical level rage across various disciplines and within particular perspectives as well. Thus, while historians, political scientists, sociologists, and other academics ponder over the bound-aries of state rule in civil society, debates within Marxism on the structural imperatives of the capitalist mode of production on state policy, and the class-fractional relationship in this context, continue to occupy center stage of discussion and debate on the state.

The central argument of this volume is that class structure and class relations are the major determinants of politics and the state, and that class conflicts and class struggles lie at the center of social and political transformations, for it is only through such struggles that state power is attained and the will of the victorious social class(es) is imposed over society—although the dialectics of the class struggle permits the state, from time to time, to become "relatively autonomous" of the contending class forces and their fractions and *appear* to favor neither of the two main antagonistic classes. Thus I opt for a historical-materialist conception of the state as the chief superstructural institution that is a direct product of the social-economic base, or mode of production, which sets the political parameters of the social formation in question.

I argue that efforts toward the conceptualization of the state outside the base-superstructure problematic are doomed to failure, as the political (or more broadly, superstructural) institutions of society (of which the state is the chief component) are a reflection of the social-economic base which the state itself subsequently acts to complete its dialectic. Far from a mechanical, reductionist interpretation of state determinations as a product of the productive forces shaping the relations of production, my interpretation of the base-superstructure problematic is lodged in a *social* (not technical) acceptance of the *primacy of production relations* that define the nature and structure of social classes, class struggles, and struggles for state power. It is within this context of the class basis of political power that the productive forces must be understood, notwithstanding the fact that the productive forces themselves have long ago set the initial parameters of the social conditions leading to the development of social classes, class conflicts, and the formation of the state.

Chapter 3 provides an analysis of the role of the state in different types of societies in the historical process and traces the origins and development of the state from earlier times to more recent periods. It shows that with the division of society into classes, the state arose to serve the interests of the wealthy and privileged sectors of society.

Chapter 4 examines the development of the capitalist state in its transition from medieval feudalism, beginning in the sixteenth century. The transformation of the feudal state began with the growth of a merchant class that came to possess immense wealth through overseas trade. Gradually, with the rise to prominence of merchants and manufacturers during the subsequent mercantilist era, the state came to reflect the interests of the rising bourgeoisie, who swept aside competing class forces in the struggle for state power. This chapter takes a closer look at the state as it developed in Europe, and then shifts to the United States to trace the development of the U.S. state since its founding in the late eighteenth century. Through a careful examination of the Constitutional Convention, its participants, and proceedings, this chapter lays bare the class origins and nature of the early U.S. state, which set the stage for its subsequent transformation into a capitalist state following the Civil War, and ultimately into an advanced capitalist state in the early twentieth century.

Chapter 5 takes up the task of examining the crisis of the advanced capitalist state in the United States in the latter part of the twentieth century and provides data and analysis on some of its fundamental contradictions. I argue that the crisis of the late capitalist state in the United States is a product of its global expansion, i.e., a consequence of the globalization of U.S. capital on a worldwide scale.

Chapter 6 examines the nature and role of the state in the Third World and outlines and discusses the variants of the capitalist state in different historic and geographic settings. Here, I discuss the origins and development of the state in Latin America, Asia, Africa, and the Middle East within the context of the world political economy. I argue that the state in the Third World is by and large an organ of local landowning and capitalist interests tied to foreign capital. This neocolonial relationship explains the class nature of the state in the Third World and at the same time reveals its most fundamental contradictions, which often have led to civil wars and revolutions.

An alternative path against capitalism and the capitalist state has led to the formation of socialist states in a number of important regions of the world. In Chapter 7, the former Soviet Union and China, two classic examples of the socialist state, are taken up for study. Providing a historical account of the development of the socialist state in these societies, I examine the twists and turns of the development process in the postrevolutionary period and lay the basis for a discussion of the contradictions involved in the transition from capitalism to socialism and beyond.

Finally, Chapter 8 provides a concluding analysis on the nature, origins, development, and role of the state and examines the relationship between class, state, and power in society, informing our inquiry into the politics of change based on the dialectics of class relations, class struggles, and social transformation.[5]

Notes

1. In the pages that follow, I discuss the major competing perspectives on the role of the state and politics in classical and contemporary social-political theory.

2. I explore the relationship between class and state, as well as the state and nation and other related issues at length in my forthcoming book *Class, State, and Nation* (Westport, Conn.: Greenwood Press, 2001).

3. R.B. Sutcliffe, *Industry and Underdevelopment* (London: Addison-Wesley, 1971), p. 285.

4. Colin Leys, "The 'Overdeveloped' Post-Colonial State: A Re-Evaluation," *Review of African Political Economy*, No. 5 (1976), p. 44.

5. For an extended analysis of the class basis of social relations and social transformation, see Berch Berberoglu, *Class Structure and Social Transformation* (Westport, Conn.: Praeger Publishers, 1994).

CHAPTER 1

THEORIES OF THE STATE:
PLURALISM AND ELITE THEORY

This chapter presents an analysis of the two major contending perspectives in mainstream political sociology: pluralism and elite theory. After an examination of the fundamentals of each of these theories and their variants, Chapter 2 provides an overview of classical and contemporary Marxist theories of the state. Thus the stage is set for an analysis of the origins, nature, and development of the state in different comparative and historical settings, an analysis presented in the remainder of the book. We begin our survey with the most prominent mainstream academic theory of politics and the state in the United States: pluralist theory.

Pluralism

Until recently, the predominant approach in mainstream American political sociology has been pluralist theory. Claiming that society is made up of a multitude of conflicting interest groups balanced by the state, pluralists see these groups as equally influential in their impact on government policy and major institutions in society.[1] "Political power or influence in the United States," writes Arnold Rose,

> is distributed over as many citizens, working through their associations, as want to take the responsibility for power. . . . Through the voluntary association the ordinary citizen can acquire as much power in the

community or the nation as his free time, ability, and inclinations permit him to. . . .[2]

Society, according to pluralists, consists of many diverse groups and associations (e.g., business, labor, and professional, religious, and other organizations) and constitutes a conglomeration of dissimilar and often conflicting interests—no one of which plays a singularly dominant role—that, through a process of "democratic competition," determine the nature and direction of society.[3] Hence, "It is . . . multiple memberships in potential groups based on widely held and accepted interests that serve as a balance wheel in a going political system like that of the United States."[4]

State policy, which the pluralists argue flows out of the pressures of these groups, is seen as the result of bargaining and compromise among the groups in the state's pursuit of achieving equilibrium in society. In this view, the state serves neither its own interests nor those of any single group or class; instead, its primary task is to balance the interests of a multitude of competing groups. Thus, "A major preoccupation of government is the policing of conflicts of interest."[5]

"Pressure," writes Bentley, a prominent American pluralist, "is always a group phenomenon. It indicates the push and resistance between groups. The balance of the group pressures is the existing state of society."[6] Thus,

> In governments like that of the United States we see these manifold interests gaining representation through many thousands of officials in varying degrees of success . . . while "special interests" make special use of officials, rising in other spots to dominate, using one agency of the government against another, now with stealth, now with open force, and in general moving along the route of time with that organized turmoil which is life where the adjustments are much disturbed....[7]

According to pluralists, the political process is made up of social groups, and policy outcomes are a result of group processes. Being essentially "autonomous" and "democratic," and each reflecting its special social situation, these groups, claim the pluralists, play a key role in charting the course of societal development.[8] The "push and pull" and "cross pressures" resulting from the competitive struggle between "veto groups" work to ensure a mutual resolution of problems in favor of all parties concerned and thus guarantee the stability of the political system.[9] In this way, the state is able to institutionalize its rule and maintain order in society.

In a manner similar to pluralist reasoning, functionalist sociologists such as Talcott Parsons and Neil Smelser have also characterized the modern U.S. state as a democratic institution whose primary function is to promote harmony within the system to secure equilibrium and order.[10] Representing the interests of society as a whole, the state coordinates the other major institutions of society—the economy, education, religion, and so on—and advances both the general social welfare and that of individuals within it. Thus, for functionalists, while the state provides strong, effective leadership and represents institutionalized power and authority vis-à-vis the citizenry, its rule nevertheless reflects the widespread and diverse interests that exist in society—interests that, the functionalists claim, are well represented within the state. As the supreme guardian of representative democracy in modern society, the state thus fulfills its role in carrying out its social tasks while ensuring its democratic control by society.

"Power," according to Parsons, "is a generalized facility or resource in the society":

> It has to be divided or allocated, but it also has to be produced and it has collective as well as distributive functions. It has the capacity to mobilize the resources of the society for the attainment of goals for which a general "public" commitment has been made, or may be made. It is mobilization, above all, of the action of persons and groups, which is *binding* on them by virtue of their position in the society.[11]

Thus the state maintains an autonomous role for itself as the sole public authority and at the same time assures the equal distribution of power across competing political groups in society. "This tension in functionalist thinking on the state between a view of the necessity for a strong, modernizing, central co-ordinator on the one hand, and a relatively equal distribution of social powers on the other," observes one critic, "reflects the cross-pulls from two allegedly functional pre-requisites: the need for autonomy and the need for integration."[12] By distributing its control among a broad range of social groups and preventing its monopolization by any one group, the state, according to the functionalists, thus paves the way for political competition and pluralist democracy.[13]

The pluralist and functionalist notion that in America power resides with many diverse and equally powerful groups reflecting the interests of the vast majority of the population—a notion advanced in the mid-nineteenth century by Tocqueville in his *Democracy in America*—has come under strong criticism in recent decades. In the late 1950s, critics, led by C. Wright Mills, began to provide a powerful critique of pluralism and Parsonian functionalism that set the stage for subsequent debates within political sociology.[14] Expanding this effort during the 1960s and early 1970s, Grant McConnell, G. William Domhoff, Richard Hamilton, and Michael Parenti, as well as numerous others, were instrumental in widening the attack on pluralism and thus breaking its decades-long monopoly over political theory.[15]

In brief, these critics pointed out that very few people in the total population belong to a multitude of voluntary associations, and those that do are often members of social, cultural, youth, church, or other groups whose primary interests are often *not* political. Also, most of the associations that people belong to lack any democratic control by the rank and file, such as trade unions, political parties, and religious organizations; these organizations are bureaucratically structured, which prevents direct individual participation in decision making.[16] In addition, the disproportionate power of different associations rules out meaningful compromise and the balancing of conflicting interests among these groups.[17] More specifically, "Voluntary associations are asymmetrical in the amount of power they wield per member":

> For example, the AFL-CIO, with over 15 million members, does not have as much clout as the Council on Foreign Relations (the leading business group dealing with foreign affairs), which has only about 1300 mem-

bers, because of the tremendous economic power and
the political connections of the latter group. Business
people and corporations are far more organized, politically conscious, politically active, and able to influence
politics through money, connections, and prestige. . . .[18]

As a result, pluralism in American society turns out exists among
the most powerful and wealthy business interests and groups, not
among broad segments of the population.[19] In this context, the
policies of the state reflect the interests of the most powerful
economic groups in U.S. society—owners of the means of production and distribution, or capitalists—while the structural imperatives of the capitalist system over state policy (i.e., the basic
operating principles of capitalism within which policies are formulated and implemented), result in the institutionalization of capitalist
class rule.[20] Thus the pluralist claim that the modern U.S. state is an
arbiter of conflicting interests of many divergent groups in American society and that this represents "pluralist democracy" has been
shown to be far from reality; critics have argued that this claim to a
large degree is a reflection of the preoccupation of pluralists with
analyzing *formal* political institutions, and have criticized them for
confusing how politics is *supposed to* work with how it *actually*
works under capitalism. They have further pointed out that claims
regarding the prevalence of pluralist democracy in America have
served as an ideological rationale for the maintenance and continuation of prevailing capitalist social relations.

Another variant of pluralism, commonly referred to as "elite
pluralism," attempts to redefine pluralist democracy in the light of
the prominence of elites in modern society. Seymour Martin Lipset
is the best-known proponent of this version of pluralist theory; other
pluralists, such as Robert Dahl, have arrived at a similar conception
of power and politics in their later writings.[21] In this elitist reformulation of the pluralist position, the meaning of democracy is changed
from one of direct popular rule to that of competition among elites
to control the state. Conceding that the masses do not govern themselves through popular rule, the "elite pluralists" have thus developed the idea of "competing elites" as the main contenders for
political power. As Martin Marger points out, "Modern pluralists
have synthesized the reality of elite rule with the view of a pluralistic

elite structure, a characteristic that presumably assures a form of democracy." [22] Such pluralistic competition takes place *among elites*, however, *not* between diverse and equally powerful groups in the larger society.

Corporatism, proposed by some as a remedy for interest-group domination of the state, is viewed by its proponents as a necessary corrective to the complexities of modern industrial society where the clash of group interests now threatens the very survival of society.[23] In this reformulation of the pluralist problematic, the state enters into the political equation as the supreme organ responsible for organizing and leading society under its own directives. Defined as representing "the common good," the state is viewed here as the guardian of order and moral authority that can bring about class harmony and national unity.[24] The corporatist state thus takes on the responsibility of leading the nation by taking an active role in the major institutions of society, including the economy.[25]

But critics point out that this intervention by a strong central state in capitalist society, growing out of the state's continued control by the capitalist class, actually results, at best, in the consolidation of capital's power in the advanced capitalist polity during "normal" periods[26] while preparing the groundwork for the rise of the authoritarian state in crisis-ridden, less developed formations of the Third World[27] and, ultimately, providing the material base for the emergence of fascism in response to economic and political crises of advanced capitalism, as was the case in Italy and Germany earlier in this century.[28] Thus, corporatism, a more sophisticated form of elite pluralism, incorporating into the power structure the direct intervention of the state, can be seen as a political form designed to protect the interests of monopoly capital under both "normal" and crisis conditions.

Given the convergence of the two views, the elite pluralist and corporatist conceptualizations of power turn out to be much closer to the classical elite theory than the theory of pluralist democracy. Hence, it is to the fundamentals of elite theory that we now turn.

Elite Theory

The second major approach that attempts to explain the nature of the state and politics in society is generally referred to as the *elite theory*. This theory consists of two distinct versions: classical (aristocratic) and contemporary (radical). At the center of classical elite theory lies the work of Vilfredo Pareto, Gaetano Mosca, and Robert Michels. Together their work on elite formation and oligarchic rule constitutes the core of the classical bureaucratic elite theory of politics.

Classical elite theory maintains that all societies are ruled by elites, and that the state is the political instrument by which the vast majority is ruled. This is so, according to this view, because the masses are inherently incapable of governing themselves; therefore, society must be led by a small number of individuals (the elite) who rule on behalf of the masses.

An understanding of the historical context in which Pareto and Mosca developed their theories is important and instructive, for they formulated their approach in reaction to socialist currents in Europe at the end of the nineteenth and beginning of the twentieth century. "In the world in which we are living," wrote Mosca quite bluntly, "socialism will be arrested only if a realistic political science succeeds in demolishing the metaphysical and optimistic methods that prevail at present in social studies. . . ." [29] Mosca's particular target was Karl Marx and his theory, historical materialism:

> Now one of the doctrines that are widely popular today, and are making a correct view of the world difficult, is the doctrine commonly called "historical materialism."
> . . . The greatest danger that lies in the wide acceptance of the theory, and in the great intellectual and moral influence which it exerts, lies on the modicum of truth that it contains. . . .
> The conclusion of the second assumption of historical materialism, and indeed of the doctrine as a whole, seems to us utterly fantastic—namely, that once collectivism is established, it will be the beginning of an era of universal equality and justice, during which the state will no longer be the organ of a class and the exploiter and the exploited will be no more. We shall not stop to refute that utopia once again. *This whole work [The Ruling Class] is a refutation of it.*[30]

The "realistic science" that Mosca wanted to develop, and that Pareto, Michels, and others in different ways helped to further, was thus intended primarily to refute Marx's theory of power on two essential points:

> first, to show that the Marxist conception of a "ruling *class*" is erroneous, by demonstrating the continual circulation of elites, which prevents in most societies, and especially in modern industrial societies, the formation of a stable and closed ruling class; and secondly, to show that a classless society is impossible, since in every society there is, and must be, a minority which actually rules.[31]

The fundamental idea that Mosca wanted to express in his major work, *The Ruling Class*, was to clarify his systematic distinction between "elite" and "masses," and to develop a new (anti-Marxist) *political* theory of power. He divided all societies into essentially two classes: the ruling class (the elite) and the class that is ruled (the masses). The ruling class always enjoys a monopoly of political power over the masses and directs society according to its own interests:

> Among the constant facts and tendencies that are to be found in all political organisms, one is so obvious that it is apparent to the most casual eye. In *all* societies— from societies that are very meagerly developed and have barely attained the dawning of civilization, down to the most advanced and powerful societies—two classes of people appear—a class that rules and a class that is ruled. The first class, always the less numerous, performs all political functions, monopolizes power and enjoys the advantages that power brings, whereas the second, the more numerous class is directed and controlled by the first, in a manner that is now more or less legal, now more or less arbitrary and violent. . . .[32]

This is not merely so with every known society of the past and the present; *all* societies *must* be so divided. Herein lies Mosca's argument for the "universal necessity" and "inevitability" of class rule:

> Absolute equality has never existed in human societies: Political power never has been, and never will be, founded upon the explicit consent of majorities. It always has been, and it always will be, exercised by organized minorities, which have had, and will have, the means, varying as the times vary, to impose their supremacy on the multitudes.[33]

Mosca attempts here to establish "the real superiority of the concept of the ruling, or political, class," to show that "the varying structure of ruling classes has a preponderant importance in determining the political type, and also the level of civilization, of the different peoples."[34] Hence it is the *politics* of a particular ruling class—not the economic or class structure in society—that determines the nature and movement of society and societal change. At one point, Mosca writes that "the discontent of the masses might succeed in deposing a ruling class"; he immediately adds, however, that "inevitably . . . there would have to be another organized minority within the masses themselves to discharge the functions of a ruling class."[35] As Mosca viewed the specific "functions" of ruling classes in universal terms, he could not envision a state and society *at the service of the laboring masses*, not the alleged "ruling class" or "organized minority within the masses." His tautological arguments regarding the "inevitability" of elite rule cast a heavy shadow on Mosca's work and call into question the accuracy of his "realistic political science."

Perhaps one of Mosca's more important (though certainly not original) contributions was his emphasis on the importance of organization. He explains the ruling power of the minority over the majority by the fact that the former is organized:

> . . . the dominion of an organized minority, obeying a single impulse, over the unorganized majority is inevitable. The power of any minority is irresistible as against each single individual in the majority, who stands alone before the totality of the organized minor-

ity. At the same time, the minority is organized for the very reason that it is a minority. A hundred men acting uniformly in concert, with a common understanding, will triumph over a thousand men who are not in accord and can therefore be dealt with one by one.[36]

To this, Mosca adds that this minority is usually composed of "superior individuals" and that this superiority serves, in turn, to further the legitimization of elite rule:

> . . . in addition to the great advantage accruing to them from the fact of being organized, ruling minorities are usually so constituted that the individuals who make them up are distinguished from the mass of the governed by qualities that give them a certain material, intellectual or even moral superiority; or else they are the heirs of individuals who possessed such qualities. In other words, members of a ruling minority regularly have some attribute, real or apparent, which is highly esteemed and very influential in the society in which they live.[37]

Although there are major theoretical similarities between the arguments presented by Mosca and Pareto, the latter's theoretical formulation of "the governing elite" and his conceptualization of elite rule need to be clarified: "So let us make a class of the people who have the highest indices in their branch of activity, and to that class give the name of *elite*."[38] By the term elite, Pareto meant to stress the superior (psychological) qualities of the ruling minority. As one of his students, Kolabinska, put it:

> . . . the principal notion conveyed by the term "elite" is that of superiority. . . . In a broad sense I mean by the *elite* in a society people who possess in marked degree qualities of intelligence, character, skill, capacity, of whatever kind....[39]

But above all, Pareto's interest was the study of the "governing elite." In fact, the main part of his major work, *The Mind and Society*, was devoted to it:

> For the particular investigation with which we are en-
> gaged, a study of the social equilibrium, it will help if we
> further divide that class [the elite] into two classes: a
> *governing elite*, comprising individuals who directly or
> indirectly play some considerable part in government, and
> a *non-governing elite*, comprising the rest. . . .
>
> So we get two strata in a population: (1) a lower
> stratum, the *non-elite*, with whose possible influence on
> government we are not just here concerned; then (2) a
> higher stratum, *the elite*, which is divided into two: (a)
> a governing elite, (b) a non-governing elite.[40]

Within this framework, the fundamental idea set forth and
developed by Pareto was that of the "circulation of elites." By this,
Pareto meant two diverse processes operative in the perpetual
continuity of elite rule: (1) the process in which *individuals* circulate
between the elite and the nonelite; and (2) the process in which a
whole elite is replaced by a new one. As Pareto put it: "Aristocracies
do not last. Whatever the causes, it is an incontestable fact that after
a certain length of time they pass away. History is a graveyard of
aristocracies."[41] Hence the decay and renewal of aristocracies constitute a central part of Pareto's concept of the circulation of elites. But
explicating this phenomenon still further, he adds that "the governing class is restored not only in numbers but—and that is the most
important thing—in quality, by families rising from the lower
classes. . . ."[42] A failure in the circulation of elites thus described
increases instability in the social equilibrium so much that "the
governing class crashes to ruin and often sweeps the whole of a
nation along with it."[43] In Pareto's reasoning, a "potential cause of
disturbance in the equilibrium is the accumulation of the superior
elements in the lower classes and, conversely, of inferior elements
in the higher classes."[44] In short, Pareto's explanation of the nature
and dynamics of elite rule and their circulation is in terms of the
psychological characteristics of persons in both elite and nonelite
segments of society.

Robert Michels, the third influential classical elite theorist,
stressed that the source of the problem of elite rule lies in the nature
and structure of bureaucratic organization.[45] He argued that the
bureaucratic organization itself, irrespective of the intentions of

bureaucrats, results in the formation of an elite-dominated society. Thus, regardless of ideological ends, organizational means would inevitably lead to oligarchic rule:

> It is organization which gives birth to the domination of the elected over the electors, of the mandataries over the mandators, of the delegates over the delegators. Who says organization, says oligarchy.[46]

At the heart of Michels's theoretical model lie the three basic principles of elite formation that take place within the bureaucratic structure of political organization: (1) the need for specialized staff, facilities, and, above all, leaders; (2) the utilization of such specialized facilities by leaders within these organizations; and (3) the psychological attributes of the leaders (i.e., charisma).

Michels argued that the bureaucratic structure of modern political parties or organizations gives rise to specific conditions that corrupt the leaders and bureaucrats in such parties. These leaders, in turn, consolidate the power of the party leadership and set themselves apart from the masses. This is so, goes the argument, not only with the so-called democratic organizations of bourgeois society but with socialist parties as well. Michels, a one-time "socialist," thought that if socialist parties, dedicated as they were to the highest egalitarian values, were undemocratic and elitist, then all organizations had to be elitist. "Even the purest of idealists who attains to power for a few years is unable to escape the corruption which the exercise of power carries in its train."[47] For Michels, this pointed to the conservative basis of (any) organization, since the *organizational form* as such was the basis of the conservatism, and this conservatism was the inevitable outcome of power attained through political organization. Hence, "Political organization leads to power, but power is always conservative."[48]

Based on this reasoning, one might think that Michels was an anarchist; he was not. He insisted that *any* organization, *including those of the anarchists*, was subject to the "iron law":

> ... anarchism, a movement on behalf of liberty, founded on the inalienable right of the human being over his own person, succumbs, no less than the Socialist Party, to the

> law of authoritarianism as soon as it abandons the
> region of pure thought and as soon as its adherents unite
> to form associations aiming at any sort of political
> activity.[49]

This same phenomenon of elitism/authoritarianism, argued Michels, also occurs at the individual level. Hence, to close the various gaps in his theory, Michels resorted to human-nature tauto-logical arguments: Once a person ascends to the leadership level, he becomes a part of his new social milieu to the extent that he would resist ever leaving that position. The argument here is that the leader consolidates his power around the newly acquired condition and uses that power to serve *his* interests by perpetuating the mainte-nance of that power. In order to avoid this and eliminate authoritarianism, which comes about in "associations aiming at any sort of political activity," one must *not* "abandon the region of pure thought"! Herein lay the self-serving conservatism of Michels, who in the latter part of his life turned to the cause of Italian fascism.[50]

Max Weber, who normally is not included among elite theorists, is nevertheless viewed by many as a proponent of a theory of bureaucratic organization similar to that developed by Michels. I argue, however, that while Weber's analysis of the nature of the state, bureaucracy, and power contains elements of classical elite theory, it is also distinct from it. Having arrived at the conclusion that economic relations (i.e., class relations based on wealth and income) lie at the source of power and politics, Weber shifts his analysis to focus on a *manifestation* of class power exercised through the state—thus his focus on the bureaucracy. What distinguishes Weber's analysis from that of Marx, in particular, and leads to an affinity with elite theory, is Weber's attempt to assign a quasi-autonomous role to the state in which state bureaucrats appear to be serving their own interests and the bureaucracy appears to be a power unto itself, with more and more permanent features. Operating at this secondary, institutional level, "bureaucracy," writes Weber, "is a power instru-ment of the first order," and he adds that "where the bureaucratiza-tion of administration has been completely carried through, a form of power relation is established that is practically unshatterable."[51] Moreover,

> The individual bureaucrat cannot squirm out of the apparatus in which he is harnessed. . . . In the great majority of cases, he is only a single cog in an ever-moving mechanism which prescribes to him an essentially fixed route of march. . . .
>
> The ruled, for their part, cannot dispense with or replace the bureaucratic apparatus of authority once it exists. . . . More and more the material fate of the masses depends upon the steady and correct functioning of the increasingly bureaucratic organizations of private capitalism. The idea of eliminating these organizations becomes more and more utopian.[52]

The key question then becomes one of determining *who* controls and directs the complex bureaucratic machine. Unlike Michels, Weber does *not* believe bureaucracy, in essence, to be an autonomous power unto itself; rather, it is a tool or instrument *of* power: "The consequences of bureaucracy depend therefore upon the direction which the *powers using the apparatus* give to it." [53]

It is not surprising that most contemporary Weberians have separated Weber's analysis of bureaucracy from his generalized theory of class and power in society, and thus have managed to give a conservative twist to his otherwise controversial analysis. Viewed within a broader societal context, however, bureaucracy and power to Weber are the *manifestations* of the real material forces that dominate the social-economic structure of modern society. Thus, to give primacy to the analytic strength of these concepts would mean one is dealing with *surface* phenomena. This is clearly evident, for example, in the works of (most) contemporary theorists of complex organizations, where power is consistently located *within* the structure of specific bureaucratic organizations, while bureaucracies are given a logic of their own and are conceived in terms of their special power and dynamics. Distortions such as these have brought confusion to the interpretation of the works of Weber, so much so that even otherwise critical and progressive intellectuals like C. Wright Mills have failed to avoid essentially elitist interpretations of Weber's conceptualization of bureaucratic power in the analysis of dominant institutional structures in contemporary capitalist society.

In contrast to the classical (aristocratic) version of elite theory, which views the masses as apathetic, incompetent, and unable to govern themselves, and for whom, therefore, elite rule is both necessary and desirable, the contemporary (radical) version of elite theory views the masses as manipulated and exploited by elites and takes up a position highly critical of elite rule.

The most influential proponent of the radical version of elite theory is C. Wright Mills. In his pioneering work, *The Power Elite*, written at the height of McCarthyism and the cold war in the 1950s, and at a time when pluralism enjoyed a monopoly over political theory, Mills advanced the position that American society is governed by a small but influential power elite consisting of the top layers of the three most important institutions of modern society: the economy, the state, and the military.[54] Referring to the power elite, Mills wrote:

> They are in command of the major hierarchies and organizations of modern society. They rule the big corporations. They run the machinery of the state and claim its prerogatives. They direct the military establishment. They occupy the strategic command posts of the social structure.[55]

In a manner similar to classical elite theorists, especially Pareto, but also Mosca, Mills characterized the elite as those holding the highest positions in the key institutions of society. Broader in scope than Mosca's political elite and more restricted in size and extent than Pareto's multitude of elites across many institutions and professions, Mills's work focused on the three institutions he identified as the centers of power in modern American society. In this sense, Mills's approach is an integration and reformulation of positions advanced by classical elite theorists, informed at the same time by the bureaucratic organizational formulations of Michels and Weber, on the one hand, and Marx's class analysis approach, on the other, while rejecting the essentially conservative political implications of the classical elite model and advancing in its place a radical critique of the theory and practice of elite rule.

Mills's intellectual struggle against conservative political interpretations of classical elite theory opened the way to a new approach in political sociology, prompting scholars like Floyd Hunter to undertake studies on the national power structure and on important policy-making groups and institutions.[56] Hunter's findings supported Mills's contention regarding the existence of a power elite composed of individuals situated in the government, the military, and the business sector—the latter, representing corporate interests, emerging as the dominant institution. Extending beyond the established academic circles, Mills's pioneering work informed the thinking of a new generation of critical scholars, such as G. William Domhoff, who have contributed to the popularization of Mills's approach through "power structure research." [57]

Domhoff, going beyond Mills, reconceptualizes the power elite in class terms. He argues that there is in the United States a corporate *upper class* that owns major business assets and controls the bulk of the wealth of the country.[58] Domhoff shows that this class, by virtue of its economic power, also controls and influences important departments and agencies of the state, and in this way becomes a "governing class." For Domhoff, the governing class is

> a social upper class which owns a disproportionate amount of the country's wealth, receives a disproportionate amount of a country's yearly income, and contributes a disproportionate number of its members to the controlling institutions and key decision-making groups of the country.[59]

Domhoff goes on to show that this upper class controls the major banks and corporations; major newspapers, radio, television, and other mass media; elite universities; foundations; important private advisory groups and organizations, such as the Council on Foreign Relations and the Committee for Economic Development; as well as the executive branch of government, the cabinet, the judiciary, the military, and the regulatory agencies.[60] Thus, through an analysis of the linkages between the upper class and the personnel occupying posts in major private and public institutions of American society, Domhoff confirms the prevalence of a dominant power elite, which he identifies as "the American business aristocracy." [61]

While Domhoff's detailed empirical work on the American governmental and institutional structure and linkages of the upper class to the state has contributed much to our understanding of the mechanisms of control of the U.S. state by the "corporate upper class," the fundamentally institutional focus of this stream of thought has generally turned attention away from a class analysis approach based on wealth and power as lodged in relations of production and exploitation.

Whereas the locus of relations between elites and masses, for both the conservative and radical versions of elite theory (except for Domhoff), is political rule by elite functionaries over the masses in society, the Marxist approach focuses on economic power based on the ownership and control of the means of production as the source of political power and control of the state. It is to the analysis of this approach that we next turn.

Notes

1. See Arnold Rose, *The Power Structure* (New York: Oxford University Press, 1967); and Arthur Bentley, *The Process of Government* (Cambridge, Mass.: Benklap Press of Harvard University, 1967).

2. Rose, *The Power Structure*, p. 247.

3. Ibid.

4. David Truman, *The Government Process* (New York: Knopf, 1964), p. 514.

5. V.O. Key, *Public Opinion and American Democracy* (New York: Knopf, 1964), p. 150.

6. Bentley, *The Process of Government*, p. 258.

7. Ibid., p. 453.

8. Nelson Polsby, *Community Power and Political Theory* (New Haven: Yale University Press, 1963).

9. David Easton, *The Political System* (New York: Knopf, 1971).

10. Talcott Parsons, *Societies: An Evolutionary Approach* (Englewood Cliffs, N.J.: Prentice-Hall, 1966); and idem, "On the Concept of Political Power," in T. Parsons, *Sociological Theory and Modern Society* (New York: Free Press, 1967); N. Smelser, "Mechanisms of Change and Adjustment to Change," in *Industrialization and Society*, ed. B. Hoselitz and W. Moore (New York: Mouton, 1963). For an extended critical analysis of the Parsonian approach, see Berch berberoglu, *An Introduction to Classical and Contemporary Social Theory*, 2nd. ed. (New York: General Hall, 1998), Chap. 10.

11. Talcott Parsons, *Structure and Process in Modern Societies* (New York: Free Press, 1960), p. 221.

12. Roger King, *The State in Modern Society* (Chatham, N.J.: Chatham House, 1986), p. 15.

13. S.N. Eisenstadt, ed., *Modernization: Protest and Change* (Englewood Cliffs, N.J.: Prentice-Hall, 1966). Cited in King, *State in Modern Society*, p. 15.

14. C. Wright Mills, *The Power Elite* (New York: Oxford University Press, 1956); and idem, *The Sociological Imagination* (New York: Oxford University Press, 1959).

15. See Grant McConnell, *Private Power and American Democracy* (New York: Knopf, 1966); G. William Domhoff, *The Higher Circles* (New York: Random House, 1970); Richard Hamilton, *Class and Politics in the United States* (New York: Wiley, 1972); Michael Parenti, "Power and Pluralism: The View from the Bottom," *Journal of Politics* 32 (August 1970); and idem, *Democracy for the Few*, 6th ed. (New York: St. Martin's, 1994).

16. Mills, *The Power Elite*.

17. Martin N. Marger, *Elites and Masses: An Introduction to Political Sociology*, 2nd ed. (Belmont, Calif.: Wadsworth, 1987). See also George A. Kourvetaris, *Political Sociology: Structure and Process* (Boston: Allyn and Bacon, 1997).

18. Albert Szymanski, *The Capitalist State and the Politics of Class* (Cambridge, Mass.: Winthrop, 1978), p. 5.

19. Herbert H. Hyman and Charles R. Wright, "Trends in Voluntary Association Memberships of American Adults," *American Sociological Review* 36 (April 1971).

20. Szymanski, *The Capitalist State and the Politics of Class*.

21. See Seymour Martin Lipset, *Political Man* (Garden City, N.Y.: Doubleday Anchor, 1960); Robert Dahl, *Who Governs?* (New Haven: Yale University Press, 1961). In his later book *Pluralist Democracy in the United States: Conflict and Consensus* (Chicago: Rand McNally, 1967), Dahl introduces the concept "polyarchy," by which he means numerous elites who compete for political influence within a pluralist framework.

22. Marger, *Elites and Masses*, p. 76.

23. See Phillippe Schmitter, "Still the Century of Corporatism?" in *The New Corporatism*, ed. Frederick Pike and Thomas Stritch (Notre Dame, Ind.: University of Notre Dame Press, 1974); Alfred Stepan, *The State and Society* (Princeton: Princeton University Press, 1978); Leo Panitch, "Recent Theorizations of Corporatism," *British Journal of Sociology* (June 1980).

24. Stepan, *The State and Society*. This is, in a way, similar to labor's postwar social-democratic participation in the "corporatist" state, sometimes characterized as "the welfare state," where a compromise is struck between labor and capital under the leadership of the state which moderates the conflict and enforces the terms of this compromise. Referring to this "social-democratic compromise," Adam Przeworski writes: "This compromise consists of a trade-off between workers' militancy and capitalists' consumption. Capitalists agree to invest at a high rate and workers agree to moderate their demands with regard to profits." See Adam Przeworski, "Economic Conditions of Class Compromise" (University of Chicago, 1979), p. 32. Mimeographed. Also see A. Przeworski and Michael Wallerstein, "The Structure of Class Conflict in Democratic Capitalist Societies." *American Political Science Review* 76, no. 2 (1982).

In a quite different context, it is also possible to characterize corporatism as fascism in the advanced capitalist countries and right-wing petty bourgeois state capitalism and bureaucratic authoritarianism in the countries of the Third World.

Virtually in all cases, however, corporatism appears to emerge in response to the rise of a militant working-class movement and is instituted to preempt a socialist revolution. In the Third World, however, it may also emerge as "nationalism" in response to imperialism and internal reaction (see Chapter 6).

25. Stepan, *The State and Society*.

26. See Bob Jessop, *The Capitalist State* (New York and London: New York University Press, 1982), Chap. 2, for a discussion of the theory of state-monopoly capitalism, which, its proponents argue, is nothing but the consolidation of monopoly-capitalist control of the state, *presenting itself* and *appearing as* a "corporatist" or "welfare" state.

27. See Guillermo O'Donnell, "Tensions in the Bureaucratic-Authoritarian State and the Question of Democracy," in *The New Authoritarianism in Latin America*, ed. David Collier (Princeton: Princeton University Press, 1979).

28. See Nicos Poulantzas, *Fascism and Dictatorship* (London: New Left Books, 1974); and idem, *The Crisis of the Dictatorships* (London: New Left Books, 1976). Also see Szymanski, *The Capitalist State and the Politics of Class*, Chap. 12.

29. Gaetano Mosca, *The Ruling Class* (New York: McGraw-Hill, 1939), p. 327.

30. Ibid., p. 439, 447; emphasis added.

31. T. B. Bottomore, *Elites and Society* (Baltimore: Penguin, 1966).

32. Mosca, *The Ruling Class*, p. 50; emphasis added.

33. Ibid., p. 326.

34. Ibid., p. 51.

35. Ibid.

36. Ibid., p. 53.

37. Ibid.

38. Vilfredo Pareto, "Elites and Their Circulation," in *Structured Social Inequality*, ed. C.S. Heller (New York: Macmillan, 1969), p. 35.

39. Kolabinska, *La circulation des elites en France*, quoted in Pareto, "Elites," p. 35.

40. Pareto, "Elites," p. 35; italics in original.

41. Ibid., p. 38.

42. Ibid.

43. Ibid.

44. Ibid.

45. Robert Michels, *Political Parties* (New York: Free Press, 1968).

46. Ibid., p. 365.

47. Ibid., p. 355.

48. Ibid., p. 333.

49. Ibid., pp. 327-28.

50. In his "Introduction" to a recent edition of Michels's book *Political Parties*, Seymour Martin Lipset writes: "Michels, who had been barred from academic appointment in Germany for many years because of his socialism, left his position at the University of Basle to accept a chair at the University of Perugia offered to him personally by Benito Mussolini in 1928" (p. 33). Lipset continues: "Michels found his charismatic leader in Benito Mussolini. For him, Il Duce translated 'in a naked and brilliant form the aims of the multitude'." (p. 32). Finally, Michels "died as a supporter of fascist rule in Italy" (p. 38). See Seymour Martin Lipset, "Introduction" in Michels, *Political Parties*.

51. Max Weber, *From Max Weber. Essays in Sociology*, trans., ed., and with an intro. by H.H. Gerth and C. Wright Mills (New York: Oxford University Press, 1967), p. 228.

52. Ibid., pp. 228-29.

53. Ibid., p. 230; emphasis added.

54. C. Wright Mills, *The Power Elite* (New York: Oxford University Press, 1956).

55. Ibid., pp. 3-4.

56. See Floyd Hunter, *Top Leadership, U.S.A.* (Chapel Hill: University of North Carolina Press, 1959). For his earlier community power structure studies, focusing on Atlanta, see idem, *Community Power Structure* (Chapel Hill: University of North Carolina Press, 1953).

57. For an analysis of the contributions of scholars in this tradition, see John Mollenkopf, "Theories of the State and Power Structure Research," *Insurgent Sociologist* 5, no. 3 (1975).

58. G. William Domhoff, *Who Rules America?* (Englewood Cliffs, N.J.: Prentice-Hall, 1967).

59. Ibid., p. 5.

60. Ibid. Also see G. William Domhoff, *The Higher Circles* (New York: Random House, 1970); idem, *The Powers That Be* (New York: Random House, 1979); and idem, *The Power Elite and the State* (New York: Aldine de Gruyter, 1990).

61. Domhoff, *Who Rules America?* p. 62. See also the revised and updated version of this book for further evidence and discussion on this topic: G. William Domhoff, *Who Rules America? Power and Politics in the Year 2000* (Mountain View, Calif.: Mayfield Publishing Company, 1998).

CHAPTER 2

MARXIST THEORIES OF THE STATE

This chapter provides an overview of classical and contemporary Marxist theories of the state. After a brief examination of the fundamentals of the classical Marxist position on the origins, nature, and development of the state, we examine some recent developments in Marxist theories of the state in both Europe and the United States. This, in turn, provides the theoretical framework of the analysis of the origins, development, and contradictions of the state in the world historical process, which is presented in the remainder of the book. We begin our analysis with an overview of the classical Marxist position.

Classical Marxism

The classical Marxist theory of the state, based on the writings of Karl Marx, Frederick Engels, and V.I. Lenin, focuses on the class basis of politics as the major determinant of political phenomena. It explains the nature of the superstructure (including, first and foremost, the state) as a reflection of the *mode of production*, which embodies in it social *relations of production* (or property-based class relations). Once fully developed and matured, these class relations result in open class struggles and struggles for *state power*.

Outlined in its clearest and most concise form in Lenin's classic work *The State and Revolution*, which is based on Marx's and Engels's numerous writings on the subject, the classical Marxist theory of the state stresses that in all class-divided societies, the *class essence* of the state's rule over society is rooted in domination and exploitation by a propertied ruling class of the propertyless, oppressed class. In *The Origin of the Family, Private Property and the State*, Engels writes:

> . . . it is, as a rule, the state of the most powerful, economically dominant class, which, through the medium of the state, becomes also the politically dominant class, and thus acquires new means of holding down and exploiting the oppressed class. Thus, the state of antiquity was above all the state of the slave owners for the purpose of holding down the slaves, as the feudal state was the organ of the nobility for holding down the peasant serfs and bondsmen, and the modern representative state is an instrument of exploitation of wage labor by capital.[1]

Thus, in all class-divided societies throughout history, write Marx and Engels, "political power is merely the organized power of one class for oppressing another."[2] In our epoch, writes Lenin, "Every state in which private ownership of the land and means of production exists, in which capital dominates, however democratic it may be, is a capitalist state, a machine used by the capitalists to keep the working class and the poor peasants in subjection."[3] Thus, to accomplish this subjection, the state becomes "an organ or instrument of violence exercised by one class against another."[4]

As class relations in society are based on relations of production, which together with the productive forces constitute the mode of production, the superstructural institutions, including the state, arise from the prevailing mode and reinforce the maintenance of a social order that favors the dominant class in society.[5] As Marx writes in *Preface to a Contribution to the Critique of Political Economy* :

> In the social production of their life, men enter into definite relations that are indispensable and independent of their will, relations of production which correspond to a definite stage of development of their material productive forces. The sum total of these relations of production constitutes the economic structure of

society, the real foundation, on which rises a legal and political superstructure and to which correspond definite forms of social consciousness.[6]

For Marx, then, the *relations of production*, that is, the "relationship of the owners of the conditions of production to the direct producers," as he defines it, "reveals the innermost secret, the hidden basis of the entire social structure, and with it the political form of the relation of sovereignty and dependence, in short, the corresponding specific form of the state."[7]

Marx began his analysis of the state with a critique of G.W.F. Hegel's view of the state as representing the "social collectivity," (i.e., the common good). For Hegel, the "rational" state stood above particular groups and classes in order to preserve the social whole. Instead of placing it in its historical context, as Marx had done, Hegel conceptualized the state as "an ideal State involving a just, ethical relationship of harmony among elements of society. For Hegel, the State is eternal, not historical; it transcends society as an idealized collectivity. Thus it is more than simply political institutions."[8]

Countering Hegel's idealist formulation of politics and the state, Engels, like Marx, provides a materialist conception of history: "In modern history," he writes:

> ... all political struggles are class struggles, and all class struggles for emancipation, despite their necessarily political form—for every class struggle is a political struggle—turn ultimately on the question of *economic* emancipation. Therefore, here at least, the state—the political order—is the subordinate, and civil society— the realm of economic relations—the decisive element.[9]

Referring to earlier, idealist conceptions of the state, including that of Hegel, Engels continues:

> The traditional conception, to which Hegel, too, pays homage, saw in the state the determining element, and in civil society the element determined by it. Appearances correspond to this. As all the driving forces of the

actions of any individual person must pass through his
brain, and transform themselves into motives of his will
in order to set him into action, so also all the needs of
civil society—no matter which class happens to be the
ruling one—must pass through the will of the state in
order to secure general validity in the form of laws. That
is the formal aspect of the matter—the one which is self-
evident. The question arises, however, what is the
content of this merely formal will—of the individual as
well as of the state—and whence is this content derived?
Why is just this willed and not something else? If we
enquire into this we discover that in modern history the
will of the state is, on the whole, determined by the
changing needs of civil society, by the supremacy of this
or that class. . . .[10]

Thus, as a reflection of the interests of the dominant class, the state
in capitalist society can be identified as the *capitalist state*, for as
Marx and Engels point out, this state "is nothing more than the form
of organization which the bourgeoisie necessarily adopts both for
internal and external purposes, for the mutual guarantee of their
property and interests."[11] Hence, "the bourgeoisie has . . . conquered
for itself, in the modern representative State, exclusive political
sway. The executive of the modern State is but a committee for
managing the common affairs of the whole bourgeoisie."[12] In this
sense, the struggle of the working class against capital takes on both
an economic *and* a political content:

. . . the more it [the state] becomes the organ of a
particular class, the more it directly enforces the supremacy of that class. The fight of the oppressed class
against the ruling class becomes necessarily a political
fight, a fight first of all against the political dominance
of this class.[13]

Expanding on their analysis of the superstructure in relation to
its class base, Marx and Engels argued that control by the dominant
economic class of the major superstructural institutions in society
reveals the nature of the dominant ideas of a given epoch. "The ideas

of the ruling class are in every epoch the ruling ideas: i.e., the class, which is the ruling material force of society, is at the same time its ruling intellectual force."[14] And the state, as the supreme superstructural organ whose legitimacy is institutionalized by law, plays a key role in the dissemination of these ideas, thus ensuring the ideological hegemony of the ruling class. In this context, Marx, commenting on the Paris Commune,[15] wrote: "The working class cannot simply lay hold of the ready-made state machinery, and wield it for its own purposes."[16] He later added, in a letter to L. Kugelmann, "The next attempt of the French Revolution will be no longer, as before, to transfer the bureaucratic-military machine from one hand to another, but *to smash* it, and this is the preliminary condition for every real people's revolution on the Continent. And this is what our heroic Party comrades in Paris are attempting."[17]

Seen in this way, the centrality of the state as an instrument of *class rule* takes on an added importance, and so in examining the nature of a given state, it becomes imperative to ask the decisive question: *Which class controls and dominates the state?*

Lenin, writing in August 1917, on the eve of the October Revolution in Russia, points out both the class nature of the state *and*, more important, the necessity of its revolutionary overthrow. He writes:

> If the state is the product of the irreconcilability of class antagonisms, if it is a power standing *above* society and "*alienating* itself *more and more* from it," it is clear that the liberation of the oppressed class is impossible not only without a violent revolution, *but also without the destruction* of the apparatus of state power which was created by the ruling class and which is the embodiment of this "alienation."[18]

In an important passage in *The State and Revolution*, Lenin stresses that the state in capitalist society is not only or simply the political organ of the capitalist class; it is structured in such a way that guarantees the class rule of the capitalists, and short of a revolutionary rupture, its entrenched power is practically unshakable:

> A democratic republic is the best possible political shell for capitalism, and, therefore, once capital has gained

possession of this very best shell . . . it establishes its power so securely, so firmly, that *no* change of persons, institutions or parties in the bourgeois-democratic republic can shake it.[19]

The question remains: With the obvious contradictions and conflicts between labor and capital, and with the ever-more visible unity of capital and the state, how is it that capital is able to convince broad segments of the laboring masses of the legitimacy of its class rule and the rule of the capitalist state over society?

In explaining the *process* by which the capitalist class controls the state and secures its dominance in society, Antonio Gramsci, a prominent Marxist writing at the turn of the century, drew attention to the *ideological apparatuses* of the capitalist state and introduced the concept of bourgeois cultural and ideological *hegemony*.[20] He stressed that it is not enough for the capitalist class simply to take control of the state machine and rule society directly through force and coercion; it must also convince the oppressed classes of the legitimacy of its rule: "The state is the entire complex of practical and theoretical activities with which the ruling class not only justifies and maintains its dominance, but manages to win the active consent of those over whom it rules."[21] Through its dominance of the superstructural organs of the state, the ruling class controls and shapes the ideas, hence consciousness, of the masses. Thus:

> Hegemony involves the successful attempts of the dominant class to use its political, moral, and intellectual leadership to establish its view of the world as all-inclusive and universal, and to shape the interests and needs of subordinate groups.[22]

With the acceptance of its ideas and the legitimization of its rule, the capitalist class is able to exercise control and domination of society through its ideological hegemony at the level of the superstructure with the aid and instrumentality of the state. Gramsci, writes Martin Carnoy, "assigned to the State part of this function of promoting a single (bourgeois) concept of reality, and, therefore, gave the State a more extensive (enlarged) role in perpetuating class" and preventing the development of class consciousness.[23] As such,

> It was not merely lack of understanding of their position in the economic process that kept workers from comprehending their class role, nor was it only the "private" institutions of society, such as religion, that were responsible for keeping the working class from self-realization, but it was the *State itself* that was involved in reproducing the relations of production. In other words, the State was much more than the coercive apparatus of the bourgeoisie; the State included the hegemony of the bourgeoisie in the superstructure.[24]

Although the dialectics of the accumulation process, which involves, first and foremost, the exploitation of labor, ultimately results in class struggles, civil war, and revolution to seize state power, the ideological hegemony of the ruling class, operating through the state itself, prolongs its class rule and institutionalizes and legitimizes exploitation. The recognition of this fact by the working class, stressed Gramsci, helps expand the class struggle from the economic and social spheres into the sphere of politics and ideology, so the struggle against capitalist *ideology* promoted by the capitalist *state* becomes just as important, perhaps more so, as the struggle against capital in other spheres of society. In this way, as the struggle against the state becomes an important part of the class struggle in general, the struggle against capitalism takes on a truly *political* and *ideological* content.

Gramsci's contribution to the Marxist theory of the state, then, both affirms *and* extends the analyses of the Marxist classics and advances our understanding of the processes of ruling class domination and hegemony and the responses needed for the transformation of capitalist society.

Recent Developments in Marxist Theories of the State

More recently, beginning in the late 1960s, Gramsci's contributions to Marxist theory were reintroduced into Marxist discourse on ideology and the state, along with an extended discussion on the basic concepts of historical materialism. Louis Althusser played a key role in this effort through the incorporation of the Gramscian notion of ideological hegemony into his own analysis of the "ideological state apparatuses."[25]

In linking the political superstructure to the social-economic base, or mode of production, Althusser argues in favor of the classical Marxist position, which identifies the superstructure as determined "in the last instance" by the base: "The upper floors," writes Althusser, in reference to the superstructure, "could not 'stay up' (in the air) alone, if they did not rest precisely on their base."[26] Thus, the state, the supreme superstructural institution and repressive apparatus of society, "enables the ruling classes to ensure their domination over the working class, thus enabling the former to subject the latter to the process of surplus-value extortion."[27] This is so precisely because the state is controlled by the ruling classes. And it is such control that makes the state, and the superstructure in general, dependent on and determined by the dominant class in the base.

In his essay "Ideology and Ideological State Apparatuses," Althusser expands his analysis of the base-superstructure relationship to include such other superstructural institutions as the cultural, religious, educational, legal, and family. As the hegemony of the ruling class in these spheres becomes critical for its control over the dominated classes, and society in general, the class struggle takes on a tri-level character, consisting of the economic, political, and ideological levels. This Althusserian conception of the structural totality of the capitalist mode in its relation with the superstructure came to inform Poulantzas's analysis of classes, class struggles, and the state, and set the stage for the recent discussion and debate on Marxist theories of the state.

Developments in Marxist theorizing on the state since the Poulantzas-Miliband debate in the late 1960s and early 1970s[28] have taken three divergent paths: (1) that influenced by the Hegelian-Marxist formulations of the Frankfurt School of critical theory; (2) that influenced by the Weberian tradition, stressing a "state centered" theory of state autonomy; and (3) that arguing in favor of a class-based, historical-materialist theory of the state based on Marxist classics. All three approaches developed in the 1970s primarily in response to the questions raised in the Poulantzas-Miliband debate.[29]

Before examining each approach in detail, let us first look at the diverse views and analyses presented in the Poulantzas-Miliband debate, for it is this debate which prompted the recent renewed interest in Marxist theorizing on the state. In it one position emphasizes the direct and indirect control of the state by the dominant capitalist class, and another emphasizes the structural imperatives of the capitalist system as they affect the state and its "relative autonomy." These two views correspond to the so-called instrumentalist and structuralist positions associated with Ralph Miliband and Nicos Poulantzas, respectively. Central to the debate are questions related to the class nature of the state, the relationship between different classes and the state, and the notion of relative autonomy in the exercise of state power.

In his original formulation of the problem in *The State in Capitalist Society*, Miliband approaches the question of the state via a critique of the pluralist models still dominant in political sociology and mainstream political theory. In so doing, he provides an approach and analysis that earns his work the unwarranted label "instrumentalism." And it is in reaction to this instrumentalism that critiques of his work have resulted in the formulation of a counterposition that has come to be labeled "structuralism."

The central question addressed in the initial formulation of the instrumentalist problematic has been a determination of the role of the state in a society dominated by capitalist social relations. In this vein, Miliband's study of the capitalist state focuses on the special relationship between the state and the capitalist class, and the mechanisms of control of the state by this class that, *de facto*, transform the state into a *capitalist state*.

In contrast, Poulantzas, representing the so-called structuralist position, focuses on the structural constraints of the capitalist system that set limits to the state's autonomy and force it to work within the framework of an order that yields results invariably favorable to the dominant capitalist class. According to this view, it is by virtue of the system of production itself in capitalist society that the state becomes a *capitalist* state, even in the absence of direct control of the state apparatus by capitalists.

It should be pointed out, however, that the degree of lack of direct control of the state apparatus by the capitalist class determines the degree of the state's relative autonomy from this class. And this relative autonomy, in turn, gives the state the necessary freedom to manage the overall interests of the capitalist class and rule society on behalf of the established capitalist order.[30]

The central problem for these competing views of the state is not so much whether the state in capitalist society is a *capitalist* state— they agree that it is—but *how* that state *becomes* a capitalist state. Far more than the limited academic value, the answers to this question have immense political implications because the debates surrounding this issue originally emerged in Europe in response to the pivotal political question regarding the strategy and tactics of taking state power under advanced capitalism.

Let us briefly look at the fundamentals of the instrumentalist versus structuralist problematic and show, in the process, that the above dichotomy has been ill conceived, as both Miliband and Poulantzas ultimately, in later reformulation of their positions, basically accept the validity of their critics' conclusions.

To start with, in his initial formulation of the problem, Miliband writes:

> In the Marxist scheme, the "ruling class" of capitalist
> society is that class which owns and controls the means
> of production and which is able, by virtue of the eco-
> nomic power thus conferred upon it, to use the state as
> its instrument for the domination of society.[31]

This seemingly instrumentalist statement is expounded by Miliband through his focus on "patterns and consequences of personal and social ties between individuals occupying positions of power in different institutional spheres." [32] Concentrating on a study of the nature of the capitalist class, the mechanisms that tie this class to the state, and the specific relationships between state policies and class interests,[33] Miliband has left himself open to charges of voluntarism and instrumentalism.

In contrast, Poulantzas argues that "the *direct* participation of members of the capitalist class in the state apparatus and in the government, even where it exists, is not the important side of the matter."[34] What is crucial to understand, according to Poulantzas, is this:

> The relation between the bourgeois class and the state is
> an *objective relation*. This means that if the *function* of
> the state in a determinate social formation and the
> *interests* of the dominant class in this formation *coin-
> cide*, it is by reason of the system itself: the direct
> participation of members of the ruling class in the state
> apparatus is not the *cause* but the *effect*, and moreover
> a chance and contingent one, of this objective coinci-
> dence.[35]

In this formulation, the functions of the state are broadly determined by the structural imperatives of the capitalist mode of production and the constraints placed on it by the structural environment in
which the state must operate. Given these parameters of operation,
the state obtains relative autonomy from the various fractions of the
capitalist class in order to carry out its functions as a capitalist state.
Thus Poulantzas accepts the control of the state by the capitalist class
through direct and/or indirect means, but assigns it relative autonomy vis-à-vis any one *fraction* of that class.[36] Hence, in this
formulation, the capitalist state is the state of the capitalist class and
serves the interests of that class as a whole; and at the same time it
maintains relative autonomy from its various fractions.

Miliband, defending himself against vulgar instrumentalist interpretations of his argument, later concedes that the state can and
must have a certain degree of autonomy from the capitalist class.
Referring to Marx's and Engels's assertion that "the modern state is
but a committee for managing the common affairs of the whole
bourgeoisie," Miliband writes:

> This has regularly been taken to mean not only that the
> state acts *on behalf* of the dominant class . . . but that it
> acts *at the behest* of that class which is an altogether
> different assertion and, as I would argue, a vulgar
> deformation of the thought of Marx and Engels. . . .
> [T]he notion of common affairs assumes the existence
> of particular ones; and the notion of the whole bourgeoi-
> sie implies the existence of separate elements which
> make up that whole. This being the case, there is an
> obvious need for an institution of the kind they refer to,

namely the state; and the state *cannot* meet this need without enjoying a certain degree of autonomy. In other words, the notion of autonomy is embedded in the definition itself, is an intrinsic part of it.[37]

Elsewhere, Miliband addresses this question more directly: "Different forms of state have different degrees of autonomy. But all states enjoy some autonomy or independence from all classes, including the dominant classes."[38] Nevertheless, "The relative independence of the state does not reduce its class character: on the contrary, its relative independence makes it *possible* for the state to play its class role in an appropriately flexible manner. If it really was the simple 'instrument' of the 'ruling class,' it would be fatally inhibited in the performance of its role."[39] Miliband goes on to argue that "the intervention of the state is always and necessarily partisan: as a class state, it always intervenes for the purpose of maintaining the existing system of domination, even where it intervenes to mitigate the harshness of that system of domination."[40] Thus Miliband takes a big step toward reconciliation with the relative autonomy thesis while retaining the core of his argument in seeing the capitalist state as an institution controlled by the capitalist class as a whole.

Poulantzas, in his later writings, also moves in a direction away from his earlier position on relative autonomy. He admits that in the current monopoly stage of capitalism, it is the *monopoly fraction* of the capitalist class that dominates the state and thereby secures favorable policies in its own favor over that of other fractions of the bourgeois power bloc.[41] This situation, he adds, poses problems to the state's traditional role as "political organizer of the general interest of the bourgeoisie" and "restrict[s] the limits of the relative autonomy of the state in relation to monopoly capital and to the field of the compromises it makes with other fractions of the bourgeoisie."[42] The political crisis resulting from this fractional domination and fragmentation, argues Poulantzas, leads to a crisis of the bourgeois state.[43]

With these later reformulations of both Poulantzas and Miliband, we see a convergence of the two positions and arrive at the general conclusion that the state in capitalist society is *both* controlled by *and*, at the same time, relatively autonomous from the various fractions of the capitalist class, in order to (1) perform its functions in advancing the interests of the capitalist class as a whole; and (2) maintain its legitimacy over society—although this "autonomy," limited as it is, is rapidly being undermined by the hegemonic (monopoly) fraction within the capitalist class and, in this way, is undermining the state's effectiveness in fulfilling its political role as the "executive committee" of the entire bourgeoisie.

Critical of both the Poulantzas and Miliband formulations, and moving beyond the debate to another level of structural explanation influenced by the Frankfurt School, Claus Offe and Joachim Hirsh present two complementary views of the capitalist state in the German context. In contrast to Poulantzas's strong emphasis on ideological factors, both Offe and Hirsh attempt to explain the state through its economic role. For Offe, it is based on the necessity for capital accumulation, involving the extraction of surplus and the reproduction of capitalist relations; for Hirsh, it is based on the necessity to counter the tendency of the falling rate of profit and the contradictions that emerge from it.

Offe's initial formulation focuses on the internal mechanisms of the state in terms of its dependence on capital accumulation, which, he argues, is vital for its survival. Introducing the concept of *selective mechanisms*, Offe argues that these mechanisms work to serve a number of important functions that give the state its class character. These functions are

> (1) *Negative selection*: the selective mechanisms sys-
> tematically exclude anti-capitalist interests from state
> activity; (2) *positive selection*: from the range of re-
> maining alternatives, the policy which is in the interests
> of capital as a whole is selected over policies serving the
> parochial interests of specific capitalist groups; (3)
> *disguising selection*: the institutions of the state must
> somehow maintain the appearance of class-neutrality
> while at the same time effectively excluding anti-capi-
> talist alternatives.[44]

These mechanisms are contradictory in nature and present problems for the state in carrying out its dual role of maintaining accumulation and legitimation. Thus the capitalist state cannot effectively fulfill its essential role as an "ideal collective capitalist," notes Offe, unless it can conceal its class bias behind the cloak of the general interest and carry out the other functions relegated to it by the logic of capital accumulation. In this way, the state's promotion of the capital accumulation process also results in the reproduction of the bureaucratic apparatus, which itself depends on the continued accumulation of capital.[45]

Offe argues that in attempts to overcome these functional requisites, that the state faces its biggest challenge and falls short in fulfilling its crucial role. Hence, the state faces an emergent "crisis of crisis management," which reveals itself in the areas of a fiscal crisis, a crisis of administrative rationality, and a crisis of mass loyalty.[46] As the "selective mechanisms" begin to break down in periods of political crisis, the state begins to rely more and more on repression in order to maintain its class character; as a result, it exposes the inner nature of the state itself.[47]

Despite the fact that he comes from the Hegelian-Marxist tradition of the Frankfurt School and was once a student of Jurgen Habermas, Offe's theoretical conclusions on the political crisis of the capitalist state are actually quite similar to Poulantzas's conclusions on the crisis of legitimacy and, more broadly, of class hegemony in late capitalist society.[48] What distinguishes Offe's analysis from that of Poulantzas is Offe's insistence on the *autonomy* of the state from both the capitalist class and society as a whole and the primacy of the state in maintaining its special bureaucratic interests. Nevertheless, the structural imperatives of the capital accumulation process, with or without such autonomy, yield similar results in determining the political outcome of the state's actions, hence its class character.

Joachim Hirsh, in a manner similar to the analysis provided by Offe, derives his categories of discourse on the state directly from the accumulation process. Not particularly interested in Offe's preoccupation with the innerworkings of the state apparatus, Hirsh focuses on what he views as the state's main task of countering the tendency of the falling rate of profit. As the class struggle against capital threatens the interests of the capitalist class and affects the rate of profit (thus affecting the survival of the state), the state is compelled to intervene to reverse this trend and promote further capital accumulation. Hirsh writes:

> The bourgeois state, by reason of its essential character,
> cannot act as regulator of the social process of develop-
> ment, but must be understood in the determination of its
> concrete functions as a reaction to the fundamentally
> crisis-ridden course of the economic and social process
> of reproduction. . . . These can be condensed in terms of
> value theory in the law of the tendency of the rate of
> profit to fall, which also means that this law must be the
> conceptual point of departure for an analysis of state
> functions, to be developed out of the concrete course of
> capital accumulation and class conflicts.[49]

Although Hirsh characterizes the state as "the authority guaranteeing the rules of equal exchange and of commodity circulation,
and autonomous from the social process of reproduction and the
social classes," [50] state intervention in the economy in favor of
capital (and against labor) defines the class nature of the state (i.e.,
as a capitalist state). Contrary to the classical Marxist and recent
instrumentalist formulations, Hirsh argues that "the bourgeois state
does not originate historically as a result of the conscious activity of
a society or class in pursuit of its 'general will' but rather as the result
of often contradictory and short-sighted class struggles and conflicts."[51] Being autonomous from the production process and the
dominant classes in society, yet operating within the parameters of
a capitalist social order, the success of the state in securing its
material base, Hirsh argues, depends on its success in the promotion
of the continued and uninterrupted accumulation of capital. Thus,
like Offe, Hirsh provides an analysis of the class nature of the state
based on its economic role in mediating the accumulation of capital
and its associated crises, which are rooted in the laws of motion of
the capitalist mode of production and its logic of development.[52] The
state's response to these crises and its interest in their resolution,
prompted by its economic dependence on capital, then, by necessity
bring the state to the aid of capital and, in this way, define its class
role in society.[53]

This narrow focus on the state's economic dependence on
capital—to the exclusion of political and ideological mechanisms of
class control and domination, in the Gramscian sense—differenti-

ates the German debate (varied as it is) from earlier Marxist formulations of the class nature of the capitalist state.

James O'Connor's contribution to a theory of the capitalist state takes place at the empirical level, where he focuses on the fiscal crisis of the state and its resultant contradictions.[54] Concentrating on the U.S. state, O'Connor explains this crisis in terms of the growth and expansion of capital during this century, and with it the development and expansion of the state. Following the analysis developed by his German counterparts Offe and Hirsh, O'Connor provides an analysis of the U.S. state based on its dual functions of accumulation and legitimation. These functions lead the state to expand its role in the economy and society by way of increased public expenditures within the confines of a capitalist economy based on private profit. As the cost of these expenditures increase and as the state is unable to raise the needed revenues to balance its budget, the fiscal crisis of the state develops. The fiscal crisis therefore consists of the "gap between expenditures and revenues, which is one form of the general contradiction between social production and private ownership."[55] This central contradiction of capitalism thus becomes intensified by the fiscal crisis and leads to a broader political crisis consisting of struggles over the state budget and social policy.

Another aspect of O'Connor's analysis of the role of the state in the late monopoly-capitalist stage involves the political implications of the state's increased social spending translating into new forms of class struggle waged by state workers within the state sector. "The fusion of economic base and political superstructure in the current era," he argues, "has extended the class struggle from the sphere of direct production to the sphere of state administration, and transformed the forms of the struggle."[56] O'Connor suggests that, as a result, the class struggle increasingly takes on a political content, as an expanding segment of the working class comes to confront the state directly.

Contrary to O'Connor's expectations, such a challenge, in the absence of a strong and effective workers' party and a class-conscious workers' movement to back it, may well remain narrowly economic in nature. And while workers' struggle for higher wages and benefits at the state level may open up yet another important front in the struggle against capital and the capitalist state, one cannot assume that such struggles would readily develop into *political* struggles that would help topple the capitalist state.

Another recent approach to state theory, adopted by authors influenced by the Weberian school, has stressed the autonomy of the state vis-à-vis the dominant and dominated classes, hence seeing the state as an independent power base free from the control of contending class forces.[57]

Ellen Kay Trimberger, in her book *Revolution from Above*, attempts to synthesize this essentially neo-Weberian formulation with Marxist theory by reference to Marx's observations in *The Eighteenth Brumaire of Louis Bonaparte*, asserting that Marx, too, concurred with this analysis and observed exceptional periods when the state assumed an independent role and state bureaucrats became independent agents free of class control. Trimberger writes:

> A bureaucratic state apparatus, or a segment of it can be said to be relatively autonomous when those who hold high civil and/or military posts satisfy two conditions: (1) they are not recruited form the dominant landed, commercial or industrial classes; and (2) they do not form close personal and economic ties with these classes after their elevation to high office. Relatively autonomous bureaucrats are thus independent of those classes which control the means of production.[58]

What Trimberger fails to tell us is: (1) the class ideology of these bureaucrats (which is substantially, but not exclusively, determined by their class origin); (2) the class interests they intend to serve (which is related to the above considerations of origin and/or ideology), and, most important, (3) the structural consequences of policies pursued by these bureaucrats and their positive and/or negative impact on different classes. Ignoring such important questions, Trimberger goes on to argue that "dynamically autonomous bureaucrats enter the class struggle as an *independent* force, rather than as an instrument of other class forces." [59] If, as Trimberger contends, they held on to no particular class interests of their own (or those of other classes), it is not clear why "dynamically autonomous bureaucrats" would be "acting to destroy an existing economic and class order" in crisis situations.[60] Trimberger's general contention that "control of the governing apparatus is a source of power independent of that held by class"[61] constitutes a departure from the classical Marxist theory of the state and is, in fact, a restatement of a revised version of the Weberian position.

An extension of this line of reasoning has led some analysts in a pluralist direction where, as evidenced in Fred Block's argument, the state and state officials become "autonomous" agents; while still functioning within the framework of capitalist structures, they nonetheless acquire "autonomy" from the capitalist class and, further, determine policy over the heads of this class, including the formulation of policies that sometimes go *against* the interests of the bourgeoisie as a whole.[62]

In his controversial article "The Ruling Class Does Not Rule," Block attacks the structuralist position of Poulantzas as "a slightly more sophisticated version" of the instrumentalist thesis and proposes to replace it with his own reformulation that supposedly "corrects" this "deficiency." The underlying argument advanced by Block against the structuralist/instrumentalist problematic rests on his conception of the role of "state managers," who, according to Block, are autonomous agents functioning in their own self (or positional) interests and are *not* consciously engaged in the protection of the interests of the capitalist class. Thus, Block introduces into the debate "autonomous state managers" controlled by no one and subservient to no particular class interests other than their own—although they are forced to formulate policies within the framework of a capitalist environment that includes both bourgeois domination of the economy and class struggle between two contending class forces, the bourgeoisie and the proletariat. This becomes clear when Block states: "State managers do have an interest in expanding their own power, including their own power to manage the economy."[63] To back up this claim, Block writes: "German capitalists were reduced to being functionaries, albeit highly paid functionaries, of the Nazi state that was acting in its own profoundly irrational interests."[64]

Elsewhere, Block asserts that "the rationality of the capitalist state emerges out of the three-sided relationship between state managers, capital and subordinate classes."[65] Referring to his own theoretical formulation, and distancing himself from Marxism, he writes: "The virtue of this model is that it allows one to get away from the standard Marxist methodological tool of assuming that state policies always reflect the intentionality of a social class or sector of a class. It renders obsolete the procedure of looking for a specific social base for any particular state policy." [66] Block's so-called structuralism carries him so far away from any Marxist understanding of the nature of the state and state policy that he comments: "One can say that a policy objectively benefited a particular social class, but that is very different from saying that this social class, or sector of a class, subjectively wanted the policy or that its intentions were a critical element in policy development." [67] He concludes: "The road to analytic confusion in Marxism is paved with an exaggerated concern with class intentionality." [68]

This seemingly broader structuralist reformulation, which allows "state managers" considerable autonomy on the one hand while placing structural limitations on state policy on the other, unfortunately turns out to be a slightly more sophisticated version of the *pluralist* position (combined with aspects of the bureaucratic/political-elite theories of Michels and Mosca) than a new attempt at the construction of a Marxist theory of the state.

Others, such as Theda Skocpol, have adopted an approach similar to that of Trimberger and Block in conceptualizing the state as an independent force, and in the process have come to embrace a more elaborate "state centered" approach, rejecting the Marxist position on the class nature of the state. Influenced by the theories of Weber and Hintze, and utilizing the methodological approach of Barrington Moore, Jr., Skocpol's book *States and Social Revolutions* attempts to counter the classical Marxist position on the relationship of the state to the mode of production and the class basis of politics and the state. [69] She writes:

> In contrast to most (especially recent) Marxist theories, this view refuses to treat states as if they were mere analytic aspects of abstractly conceived modes of production, or even political aspects of concrete class relations and struggles. Rather it insists that states are actual organizations controlling (or attempting to control) territories and people. [70]

Arguing in favor of the view that the state is an entity with "an autonomous structure—a structure with a logic and interests of its own,"[71] Skocpol examines the French, Russian, and Chinese revolutions in terms of the centrality of the state's role in "acting for itself." "State and party organizations," she argues, must be viewed "as *independent* determinants of political conflicts and outcomes."[72] Skocpol sees in the state "potential autonomy of action over . . . the dominant class and existing relations of production."[73] In this formulation, the state is divorced from and opposed to social classes and acts in accordance with its distinct interests in society—interests based primarily on the maintenance of internal order and competition against external forces (i.e., other states) threatening its survival. "The political crises that have launched social revolutions," writes Skocpol, "have not at all been epiphenomenal reflections of societal strains or class contradictions. Rather, they have been direct expressions of contradictions centered in the structures of old-regime states."[74] To understand better those processes where the state has taken the center stage of history, Skocpol suggests "the need for a more state-centered approach" in studying states and social revolutions.[75]

Contrary to the Trimberger, Block, and Skocpol formulations, one could argue that although the state can, and sometimes does, gain limited autonomy from the direct control of main class forces in society (especially during periods of crises), this autonomy by no means implies the class neutrality of the state and its agents, that the state and state officials are "above class." This was made clear by Marx in *The Eighteenth Brumaire of Louis Bonaparte*, which is, ironically, often cited in support of the "state autonomy" position. Here, in no uncertain terms, Marx writes: "Bonaparte would like to appear as the patriarchal benefactor of all classes. But he cannot give to one class without taking from another."[76]

> Under the absolute monarchy, during the first revolution, under Napoleon, bureaucracy was only the means of preparing the class rule of the bourgeoisie. Under the Restoration, under Louis Philippe, under the parliamentary republic, it was the instrument of the ruling class. . . .[77]

"Only under the second Bonaparte," writes Marx, "does the state *seem* to have made itself completely independent."

> And yet the state power is *not* suspended in mid air. *Bonaparte represents a class*, and the most numerous class of French society at that, the *small-holding [Parzellen] peasants*.[78]

Moreover:

> As the executive authority which has made itself an independent power, Bonaparte feels it to be his mission to safeguard "bourgeois order." But the strength of this bourgeois order lies in the *middle class*. He looks on himself, therefore, as the *representative of the middle class* and issues decrees in this sense. . . . As against the bourgeoisie, Bonaparte looks on himself, at the same time, as the representative of the *peasants* and of the people in general, who wants to make the lower classes of the people happy within the frame of bourgeois society. . . .
>
>   But above all, Bonaparte looks on himself as the chief of the Society of December 10, as the representative of the *lumpenproletariat* to which he himself, his entourage, his government and his army belong. . . .[79]

"This contradictory task of the man," Marx continues, "explains the contradictions of his government,"

> the confused grouping about which seeks now to win, now to humiliate first one class and then another and arrays all of them uniformly against him. . . .
>
>   Industry and trade, hence, the business affairs of the middle class, are to prosper in hothouse fashion under the strong government. The grant of innumerable railway concessions. But the Bonapartist *lumpenproletariat* is to enrich itself.[80]

A careful reading of Marx's account of the class content of the Bonapartist state would reveal its petty-bourgeois character. Representing the general interests of this class, the state, under the leadership of Bonaparte, sides with all sections of the intermediate strata against the landed aristocracy and acquires a certain degree of independence in relation to both the bourgeoisie and the proletariat. But since this is to take place within the framework of the bourgeois social order, the basic mode of production and social organization remains *capitalist*. The Bonapartist mission here is to safeguard that order and perfect it through a series of reforms: the confiscation of the estates of the landed aristocracy and their conversion into productive capital, the safeguarding of peasant smallholdings to assure subsistence, the extension of aid to the bourgeoisie to expand accumulation, the granting of concessions to the petty bourgeoisie to raise and consolidate its position, and the expansion of employment and public works projects to assure the full participation of the proletariat in the capital accumulation process. All these things, wrapped in benevolent phraseology and nationalist ideology, would make Bonaparte *"appear* as the patriarchal benefactor of all classes," Marx pointed out. "But he cannot give to one class without taking from another."

Clearly, Marx's analysis of the Bonapartist state supports my contention that even in exceptional circumstances, the state cannot be seen in terms distinct from class forces and the class struggle in society. However independent it may at times *appear* to be, the state, as the supreme superstructural institution in society, is in the final analysis a reflection of the underlying mode of production defined by definite relations of production that characterize the class nature of that state. This understanding of the materialist dynamics of history lies at the heart of Marx's class analysis. And only through such an approach can a more complete understanding of the relationship between the state and society be obtained, and the real nature of politics and the state be revealed.

In contrast to both Hegelian-Marxist and neo-Weberian formulations of politics and the state, Goran Therborn and Albert Szymanski provide an alternative historical-materialist approach to the study of the state. Advancing a class-based view of the state, and combining instrumentalist and structuralist conceptualizations, as well as incorporating some of the important Marxist theorizing of the 1970s into a theory of the state based on a class-analysis approach informed by the dialectics of the class struggle, Therborn and Szymanski have made an important contribution to the resurgence of historical materialism, bringing back into the debate the invaluable analyses of the Marxist classics. Thus, after a brief pause during the early 1970s, when theorists associated with the Frankfurt School had a dominant influence in state theorizing, the efforts of Therborn, Szymanski, and others in the late 1970s set the stage for the resurgence of Marxist analysis grounded in the historical-materialist conception of class, state, and society.

"This renaissance of Marxist political analysis in the 1980's," writes Therborn, "will appear unexpected":

> The irony is that while many former protagonists and adherents of various "schools" of neo-Marxism are now proclaiming a post-Marxist, beyond-class stance, a new, vigorous self-confident class theory of politics and the state is being launched, impeccably dressed in the best clothes of modern empirical social science, while making no secret of its inspiring commitment to the working-class movement. . . .
>
> There is, then, still a contingent of scholars arguing, that states are a function of classes, rather than the other way round.[81]

To his credit, Therborn's contribution to this renaissance has led to a flood of studies in Marxist political economy and class theory of the state in the 1980s.

The origins of this new wave of Marxist theorizing on the state, however, go back to the late 1970s, when Therborn and a number of other Marxist intellectuals set forth their class theory of the state,[82] setting the stage for the subsequent emergence of works bringing back into the debate questions of paramount importance originally formulated by Marx, Engels, and Lenin.

In his book *What Does the Ruling Class Do When It Rules?* Therborn argues in favor of an alternative historical-materialist conception of the state and politics. He writes:

> In the present theoretical and political conjuncture, I think it appropriate to bend the stick in the other direction: to attempt to develop a formal, comparative analytical model of the class character of the state apparatus. . . .

> In my opinion, such a model should start not from
> the functionalist problematic of the role of the state in
> the reproduction of capital, but from the relations be-
> tween antagonistic classes, as determined by the forces
> and relations of production.[83]

The aim of such a theoretical model, argues Therborn, "is to show
that different types of class relations and of class power generate
corresponding forms of state organization, and to elucidate the way
in which the class character of the state apparatus is determined and
revealed." [84]

> According to the axioms of historical materialism, class
> and state condition each other: where there are no
> classes, there is no state. In class societies, moreover,
> social relations are first and foremost class relations.
> Thus, by definition, every state has a class character,
> and every class society has a ruling class (or bloc of
> ruling classes). In other words, Marxist discourse does
> not pertain at all to the subjectivist debate on whether
> there exists a ruling class. If it seeks to identify the ruling
> class and the class character of state power, it does so in
> order to discover the characteristic social structures and
> relations which are promoted and protected above all
> others by the material force of the state; and in order to
> determine the conditions under which they may be
> changed or abolished.[85]

Contrary to Hegelian-Marxist and neo-Weberian notions of
"state autonomy" and "state centered" theories that assign primacy
to the state and superstructural institutions in society, Therborn
reintroduces into the debate the "base-superstructure" problematic,
interpreted in a new light—one that avoids economistic
conceptualizations of politics on the one hand while rejecting
eclectic "codeterminist" notions of class and state on the other. Basic
to Therborn's analysis of the relationship of the economic base to the
political superstructure is the role of the class struggle engendered
by the dominant mode of production. "In very general terms," writes
Therborn,

the character of state power is defined by the two
fundamental processes of determination of the superstructure by the base—processes which in reality are
two aspects of the same determination. One of these is
the systemic logic of social modes of production, that is
to say, the tendencies and contradictions of the specific
dynamic of each mode. The other is the struggle of
classes, defined by their position in the mode of production. These two forms of determination by the base are
logically interrelated in the basic theory of historical
materialism, and serious distortions of an "economist"
or "politicist" nature result from their dissociation. The
former determination constitutes the structural fit of
state and society; the second the manner in which it is
actively experienced and fought out by the ruling and
ruled classes.[86]

In this formulation, the state is no longer viewed simply as a
passive recipient of directives from the dominant class but is
actively involved in the reproduction of the dominant relations of
production. "Invariably the state enters into the reproduction of the
relations of production by providing the latter with a stabilizing legal
framework backed by force." [87] Moreover, "Social relations of
production are framed by legal rules which define relations" between dominant and subordinate classes, although "the range and
modality of state intervention in the economy vary greatly according
to the nature and stage of development of the mode of production." [88]

To sum up Therborn's position:

The economic base determines the political superstructure by entering into the reproduction of state power and
the state apparatus. . . . It shapes the character of state
power by, among other things, providing the basic
parameters of state action and structuring the population into classes. . . . By definition, the ruling class
exercises its ruling power over other classes and strata
through the state—through holding state power. Consequently, two relationships must be ensured. The state,
particularly its commanding personnel, must *represent*,

that is to say, promote and defend, the ruling class and its mode of exploitation or supremacy. At the same time, the state must *mediate* the exploitation or domination of the ruling class over other classes and strata. In other words, it follows from the irreducible material specificity of the class state that it is simultaneously both an *expression* of class exploitation and domination, and *something more* than a simple expression— something other than the non-state ruling-class apparatuses necessary to support these relations.[89]

Viewing the class-state problematic in these terms, Therborn bridges the gap between structuralist and instrumentalist formulations of the state and provides a dialectical analysis of the relationship between base and superstructure, thus advancing the debate through a fresh look at historical materialism as the basis for a new, resurgent Marxist theory of the state.

Albert Szymanski, in his book *The Capitalist State and the Politics of Class*, makes a similar case in favor of the historical-materialist approach to the study of state and society.[90] Citing the works of Marx, Engels, and Lenin on the state, Szymanski argues that the state plays a central role in society and that "a Marxist political sociology must thus give careful and detailed consideration to the nature of the state."[91]

Examining the nature and role of the state in class-divided societies in general and capitalist society in particular, Szymanski writes:

> The state is an instrument by which the exploitation of the economically subordinate class is secured by the economically dominant class that controls the state. . . . The social relationships and the social order that the state guarantees are thus the social relationships of inequality and the order of property and exploitation. The historically specific manifestation of the state is always a product of the means and mode of production prevailing in society. Thus in capitalist society we speak of *the capitalist state*. . . .

> The state in capitalist society is a capitalist state by
> virtue of its domination by the capitalist class *and* in that
> it functions most immediately in the interests of capi-
> tal.[92]

Moreover, "The state must operate within an ideological, economic,
military, and political environment structured by capitalist relations
of production."[93] This means that the logic of capitalist economic
relations, reinforced by capital's ideological hegemony, dictate the
policies the state must follow, which are formulated within a very
limited range of options allowed by the capitalist mode of production. Thus the state in capitalist society is controlled by the capitalist
class through both direct and indirect mechanisms that foster the
interests of this class.

Far from providing a simple instrumentalist view of the state,
Szymanski reveals the full range and complexity of the state's
actions in response to the ensuing class struggles in society: "Political outcomes are the result of the relative size, social location,
consciousness, degree of organization, and strategies followed by
classes and segments of classes in their ongoing struggles."[94] He
goes on to point out:

> No one class or segment of a class is ever able totally to
> control all aspects of society. State policy is always
> influenced to some extent by the various classes, even
> while it is normally under the domination of the class
> that owns and controls the means of production, and
> even when other classes have no formal representation
> in the organs of government. The ruling class must take
> into account both the demands and likely responses of
> other classes when it makes state policy. If it does not it
> may suffer very serious consequences, including social
> revolution.[95]

"The degree of relative autonomy of the state bureaucracy from
direct capitalist-class domination," writes Szymanski, "can either
decrease *or* increase drastically during an economic and social
crisis":

A state that is too directly dominated by the majority bloc of the capitalist class may be unable to handle such a crisis, because the narrow-minded self-interest of this bloc prevents the state it dominates from adopting the policies necessary to save and advance the system. Domination of the state by these groups also tends to discredit the state, which because of such control is obviously not alleviating an economic crisis. The legitimating function of the state thus comes into increasing conflict with direct capitalist-class control.[96]

Providing an empirical path out of the structuralist-instrumentalist problematic, Szymanski argues that some states are dominated principally by direct mechanisms, while others are dominated by indirect mechanisms, and still others are dominated by *both*.

Commenting on the question of relative autonomy, David Gold, Clarence Y. H. Lo, and Erik Olin Wright make a similar argument when they point out that such autonomy "is not an invariant feature of the capitalist state":

> Particular capitalist states will be more or less autonomous depending upon the degree of internal divisiveness, the contradictions within the various classes and fractions which constitute the power bloc, and upon the intensity of class struggle between the working class and the capitalist class as a whole.[97]

In Europe, for example, given the differential political development of some European formations (e.g., France, Italy, Spain, and Greece) where strong socialist and communist parties and movements have developed and flourished, it has been difficult for capital to maintain direct, exclusive control of the state apparatus and yield results always in line with its interests. In these formations, the state has been shaped not only by the various fractions of the capitalist class but also by the representatives of rival opposition forces, including the socialists and the communists, contending for state power. This situation has invariably been effected through the presence of opposition forces within the very organs and institutions of the state. As the power and influence of these parties have increased disproportionately vis-à-vis that of the capitalists, a resurgence of the class struggle and struggles for state power have occurred—sometimes leading to the possession of political power by socialist and communist forces in key state institutions, such as the parliament or the presidency and cabinet posts within the executive branch, as in Spain during the latter phase of the Republic in the late 1930s and, more recently, in Spain, France, Italy, Greece, and Portugal, as well as elsewhere in Europe at various levels of government in local and national politics.

In the United States, in contrast, except possibly during crisis periods (such as the Great Depression of the 1930s) when there has been a resurgence of class politics, the state has been completely dominated and controlled by the capitalist class, now especially by its monopoly fraction (see Chapter 4 for a detailed discussion on the origins and development of the U.S. state).

Given the greater strength and militancy of the organized working-class movement in Europe versus the United States, and given capital's thorough penetration and control of the state in the United States and its relative weakness in Europe because of the effective opposition of independent workers' parties and organizations and their role in politics and the state, it is not surprising that an instrumentalist view of the state has so easily become the predominant mode of state theorizing among Marxists in the United States, while structuralism has been better able to explain the prevailing complex realities of politics and the state in Europe, where power has been distributed among a multitude of political parties and coalition governments within the framework of the structural imperatives of capital accumulation and the prevalence of the capitalist mode of production.

Commenting on this variation in the nature of capitalist states across national boundaries, Szymanski concurs with the above analysis and explains:

> In France, for example, it is often argued that the state bureaucracy is not directly controlled by capitalist interests because the capitalist class in France is rather fractionated; whereas in Great Britain, where the capitalist class has a tradition of unity, the state machinery is directly controlled by the upper class. . . .

In the United States since World War II there has been no significant autonomy of the U.S. state. Throughout this period the capitalist class has maintained direct control of the state apparatus.[98]

Thus the role of direct and indirect mechanisms of capitalist-class rule, as well as the degree of autonomy of the state, varies considerably among formations dominated by the capitalist mode of production and becomes even more pronounced in other, less-developed capitalist states. This, in turn, points to the need for a concrete analysis of states across national boundaries and over extended historical periods.

In this vein, adopting the historical-materialist approach, the next two chapters examine the origins and development of the state in general and the capitalist state in particular; subsequent chapters take up the task of analyzing its nature and transformation in different comparative and historical settings.

Notes

1. Frederick Engels, *The Origin of the Family, Private Property and the State*, in Karl Marx and Frederick Engels, *Selected Works* (New York: International Publishers, 1972), pp. 587–88.

2. Karl Marx and Frederick Engels, *Manifesto of the Communist Party*, in Marx and Engels, *Selected Works*, p. 53.

3. V.I. Lenin, *The State*, in Karl Marx, Frederick Engels, and V.I. Lenin, *On Historical Materialism* (New York: International Publishers, 1974), p. 641.

4. V.I. Lenin, *Selected Works*, vol. 2 (Moscow: Progress Publishers, 1975), p. 374.

5. See Karl Marx and Frederick Engels, *The German Ideology* (New York: International Publishers, 1969); Karl Marx, *The Poverty of Philosophy* (New York: International Publishers, 1963); Karl Marx, *Preface to a Contribution to a Critique of Political Economy*, in Marx and Engels, *Selected Works*; Karl Marx, *Capital*, vol. 3 (New York: International Publishers, 1967); Frederick Engels, *Anti-Duhring* (New York: International Publishers, 1976), part 2; and other writings of Marx and Engels as well as their letters and correspondence.

6. Marx, *Preface to Critique of Political Economy*, p. 182.

7. Marx, *Capital*, vol. 3.

8. Martin Carnoy, *The State and Political Theory* (Princeton: Princeton University Press, 1984), p. 46.

9. Frederick Engels, *Ludwig Feuerbach and the End of Classical German Philosophy*, in Marx and Engels, *Selected Works*, p. 626.

10. Ibid.

11. Marx and Engels, *The German Ideology*, p. 59.

12. Marx and Engels, *Manifesto of the Communist Party*, p. 37.

13. Engels, *Ludwig Feuerbach*, p. 627.

14. Marx and Engels, *The German Ideology*, p. 39.

15. Marx is referring here to the uprising of the French workers in Paris in 1871.

16. Karl Marx, *The Civil War in France*, in Marx and Engels, *Selected Works*, p. 288.

17. Karl Marx, *Marx to L. Kugelmann in Hanover*, in Marx and Engels, *Selected Works*, p. 680; emphasis in original.

18. V.I. Lenin, *The State and Revolution*, in V.I. Lenin, *Selected Works* (New York: International Publishers, 1971), p. 268.

19. Ibid., p. 272.

20. By *hegemony*, Gramsci meant the ideological predominance of the dominant ruling class(es) over the subordinate. At the same time, and in response to this, he introduced the concept of counterhegemony, which occurs when the proletariat, with the aid of "organic" intellectuals, exerts hegemony and exercises its superiority over society through the establishment of a proletarian socialist state.

21. Antonio Gramsci, *Prison Notebooks* (New York: International Publishers, 1971), p. 244.

22. Carnoy, *The State and Political Theory*, p. 70.

23. Ibid., p. 66.

24. Ibid.; emphasis in original.

25. See Louis Althusser, *For Marx* (London: Penguin, 1969) and idem, *Lenin and Philosophy and Other Essays* (New York: Monthly Review Press, 1971). Also see Louis Althusser and Etienne Balibar, *Reading Capital* (London: New Left Books, 1970).

26. Louis Althusser, *Lenin and Philosophy and Other Essays* (New York: Monthly Review Press, 1971), p. 135.

27. Ibid., p. 137.

28. See David Gold, Clarence Y. H. Lo, and Erik Olin Wright, "Some Recent Developments in Marxist Theories of the Capitalist State," parts 1 and 2, *Monthly Review*, October and November 1975; Gosta Esping-Andersen, Roger Friedland, and Erik Olin Wright, "Modes of Class Struggle and the Capitalist State," *Kapitalistate*, nos. 4–5 (Summer 1976); Albert Szymanski, *The Capitalist State and the Politics of Class* (Cambridge, Mass.: Winthrop, 1978); Bob Jessop, *The Capitalist State* (New York: New York University Press, 1982); Carnoy, *The State and Political Theory*.

29. The debate began with a review of Ralph Miliband's *The State in Capitalist Society* (London: Basic Books, 1969) by Nicos Poulantzas, "The Problem of the Capitalist State," *New Left Review*, no. 58 (1969), to which Miliband responded in the next issue of the same journal. See Ralph Miliband, "The Capitalist State—Reply to Nicos Poulantzas," *New Left Review*, no. 59 (1970). After some lapse of time, the debate continued with the publication in English of Poulantzas's book *Political Power and Social Classes* (London: New Left Books, 1973; originally published in French in 1968), Miliband's subsequent article "Poulantzas and the Capitalist State," *New Left Review*, no. 82 (1973), and Poulantzas's response "The Capitalist State: A

Reply to Miliband and Laclau," *New Left Review*, no. 95 (1976). Later works by Poulantzas—*Fascism and Dictatorship* (London: New Left Books, 1974; originally published in French in 1970), *Classes in Contemporary Capitalism* (London: New Left Books, 1975), *The Crisis of the Dictatorships* (London: New Left Books, 1976), *State, Power, Socialism* (London: New Left Books, 1978)—and Miliband's "Political Forms and Historical Materialism," in *Socialist Register, 1975* ed. R. Miliband and J. Saville (London: Merlin Press, 1975); and idem, *Marxism and Politics* (London: Oxford University Press, 1977) concentrated on various aspects of this debate throughout the 1970s.

30. This line of reasoning, regarding the state's "relative autonomy," is also provided by Gold, Lo, and Wright, "Some Recent Developments in Marxist Theories of the Capitalist State," p. 38.

31. Miliband, *The State in Capitalist Society*, p. 23.

32. Gold, Lo, and Wright, "Some Recent Developments in Marxist Theories of the Capitalist State," p. 33.

33. Ibid., pp. 32–33.

34. Poulantzas, "Problem of the Capitalist State," p. 73.

35. Ibid.

36. Poulantzas, *Political Power and Social Classes*; and idem, *State, Power, Socialism*.

37. Miliband, "Poulantzas and the Capitalist State," p. 85.

38. Miliband, *Marxism and Politics*, p. 83.

39. Ibid., p. 87.

40. Ibid., p. 91.

41. Nicos Poulantzas, "The Political Crisis and the Crisis of the State," in *Critical Sociology: European Perspectives*, ed. J.W. Freiberg (New York: Irvington, 1979), pp. 374–81.

42. Ibid., p. 375.

43. Ibid., pp. 357–93.

44. Gold, Lo, and Wright, "Some Recent Developments in Marxist Theories of the Capitalist State," pp. 37–38.

45. Claus Offe, "Structural Problems of the Capitalist State," in *German Political Studies*, vol. 1 ed. K. Von Beyme (London: Sage, 1974), pp. 37–40, 46–54. Also see Claus Offe, "The Theory of the Capitalist State and the Problem of Policy Formation," in *Stress and Contradiction in Modern Capitalism*, ed. L. Lindberg et al. (Lexington: Heath, 1975), p. 127; Claus Offe, "Crisis of Crisis Management: Elements of a Political Crisis Theory," *International Journal of Politics*, Fall 1976, pp. 91–97.

46. Offe, "Crisis of Crisis Management."

47. Gold, Lo, and Wright, "Some Recent Developments in Marxist Theories of the Capitalist State," p. 39.

48. This is all the more evident in Offe's more recent work. See Claus Offe, "The Separation of Form and Content in Liberal Democratic Politics," *Studies in Political Economy* 3 (Spring 1980); Claus Offe, "Some Contradictions of the Modern Welfare State," *International Praxis* 1, no. 3 (1981).

49. Joachim Hirsh, "The State Apparatus and Social Reproduction: Elements of a Theory of the Bourgeois State," in *State and Capital: A Marxist Debate*, ed. John Holloway and Sol Picciotto (Austin: University of Texas Press, 1979), p. 97.

50. Ibid., p. 65.

51. Ibid.

52. Ibid., p. 97. It should be pointed out that Hirsh's crisis theory of the state ultimately rests on the balance of class forces in the class struggle. And it is developments in this sphere that define the nature of the economic crisis.

53. Ibid.

54. James O'Connor, *The Fiscal Crisis of the State* (New York: St. Martin's, 1973). Also see James O'Connor, *The Corporations and the State* (New York: Harper & Row, 1974). Although O'Connor's theorizing has its origins in Marxist political economy, his more recent works (e.g., *Accumulation Crisis*. New York: Basil Blackwell, 1984), indicate a strong influence by the Frankfurt School of critical theory. His inclusion here with Offe and Hirsh is more for his state-focused approach to the capitalist crisis than as one representing the theoretical viewpoint of the Frankfurt School, although the signs of such an affinity are clearly there, even in his earlier works.

Manuel Castells, also influenced by this tradition, provides a similar approach to the crisis of the capitalist state. See Manuel Castells, *The Economic Crisis and American Society* (Princeton: Princeton University Press, 1980).

Erik Olin Wright's analysis of the crisis and the state's response to it is grounded in a much more direct, structural approach that takes into account the class struggle and its political implications while locating the source of the contradictions within the problematic of the realization crisis. See Erik Olin Wright, *Class, Crisis and the State* (London: New Left Books, 1978).

At another level of analysis, Alan Wolfe focuses on ideological factors and explains the crisis of the capitalist state in terms of the contradiction between the state's role in promoting the legitimacy of the capitalist order and its popularly expected and officially proclaimed tasks of preserving democracy and expressing the popular will. As the state fails to resolve this contradiction (as it indeed cannot, given its class nature), it plunges further into crisis. Thus, according to Wolfe, "The late capitalist state is incapable of working its way out of the contradictions that both the conditions of production and the expectations of political life have imposed on it." See Alan Wolfe, *The Limits of Legitimacy: Political Contradictions of Late Capitalism* (New York: Free Press, 1977), p. 259.

55. O'Connor, *The Corporations and the State*, p. 142.

56. Ibid., p. 105.

57. See E.K. Trimberger, *Revolution from Above: Military Bureaucrats and Development in Japan, Turkey, and Peru* (New Brunswick, N.J.: Transaction Books, 1978); Theda Skocpol, *States and Revolutions: A Comparative Analysis of France, Russia and China* (Cambridge: Cambridge University Press, 1979); Fred Block, "The Ruling Class Does Not Rule: Notes on the Marxist Theory of the State," *Socialist Review*, no. 33 (May-June 1977).

58. Trimberger, *Revolution from Above*, p. 4.

59. Ibid., p. 5; emphasis added.

60. Ibid., pp. 4–5.

61. Ibid., p. 7.

62. See Block, "Ruling Class"; and Fred Block, "Class Consciousness and Capitalist Rationalization: A Reply to Critics," *Socialist Review*, nos. 40–41 (July-October 1978).

63. Block, "Class Consciousness," pp. 40–41.

64. Ibid., p. 219.

65. Fred Block, "Marxist Theories of the State in World System Analysis" (Paper presented at the First Annual Political Economy of the World System Conference, American University, Washington, D.C., March-April 1977), p. 8.

66. Ibid.

67. Ibid.

68. Ibid.

69. Skocpol, *States and Social Revolutions.* For acknowledgement of these and other influences on Skocpol's views, see Ibid., p. 301, notes 73 and 77.

In an entirely different context, Bob Jessop also argues against the base-superstructure problematic, claiming that "both economic and class reductionism take a one-sided approach and define the state only in relation to the mode of production or to the class struggle." See Bob Jessop, *The Capitalist State* (New York: New York University Press, 1982), p. 24. Moreover, insisting that "it is impossible to establish a unitary and coherent theory of the state in general on the basis of the methods and principles of the Marxian critique of political economy" (p. 28), Jessop opts for an empiricist alternative, arguing that "such abstract and restricted forms of analysis are not equivalent to a concrete analysis of specific forms of state or state power in determinate conjunctures" (p. 24). Far from an affirmation of the historical materialist approach, such conceptualization of the problem actually denies the possibility of constructing a general theory of the state in class society through the base-superstructure relation. Rejecting this in favor of a concrete analysis of specific states, in effect, amounts to a parallel rejection of the validity of an analysis of the laws of motion of the capitalist mode of production in favor of a concrete analysis of a specific capitalist formation—thus rendering useless a general theory of the capitalist mode (e.g., Marx's *Capital*), the capitalist state (e.g., Lenin's *The State and Revolution*), and other monumental works of classical Marxism. It is one thing to opt for such an approach from outside (or in opposition to) Marxism; but, indeed, quite another to do so while claiming an affinity to Marxism. In this sense, Jessop's approach, irrespective of his intentions or claims to the contrary, yields results similar to those of Skocpol and other bourgeois empiricists, in the name of "scientific objectivity" or historical specificity—whichever may be the case.

70. Skocpol, *States and Social Revolutions*, p. 31.

71. Ibid., p. 27. In developing this view of the state, Skocpol cites the works of Trimberger and Block, among others, and states: "I have been very greatly influenced by these writings, and by personal conversations with Trimberger and Block." Ibid., p. 301, note 73.

72. Theda Skocpol, "Political Response to Capitalist Crisis: Neo-Marxist Theories of the State and the Case of the New Deal," *Politics and Society* 10, no. 2 (1981), p. 199.

73. Skocpol, *States and Social Revolutions*, p. 31.

74. Ibid., p. 29.

75. Ibid.

76. Karl Marx, *The Eighteenth Brumaire of Louis Bonaparte*, in Marx and Engels, *Selected Works*, p. 178.

77. Ibid., p. 171.

78. Ibid.; emphasis added.

79. Ibid., pp. 177–78; emphasis added.

80. Ibid., p. 178.

81. Goran Therborn, "Neo-Marxist, Pluralist, Corporatist, Statist Theories and the Welfare State," in *The State in Global Perspective*, ed. A. Kazancigil (Aldershot, U.K.: Gower and UNESCO, 1986), pp. 205–6.

82. See Goran Therborn, *Science, Class and Society* (London: New Left Books, 1976), esp. pp. 317–429; idem, "The Role of Capital and the Rise of Democracy," *New Left Review*, no. 103 (1977); idem, *What Does the Ruling Class Do When It Rules?* (London: New Left Books, 1978); and idem, *The Ideology of Power and the Power of Ideology* (London: New Left Books, 1980).

83. Therborn, *What Does the Ruling Class Do When It Rules?* p. 34.

84. Ibid., p. 35.

85. Ibid., p. 132.

86. Ibid., p. 162.

87. Ibid., p. 165.

88. Ibid.

89. Ibid., pp. 169, 181.

90. Szymanski, *The Capitalist State and the Politics of Class*.

91. Ibid., pp. 20–21.

92. Ibid., pp. 21, 25.

93. Ibid., p. 24.

94. Ibid., p. 27.

95. Ibid.

96. Ibid., p. 273.

97. Gold, Lo, and Wright, "Some Recent Developments in Marxist Theories of the Capitalist State," p. 38. In their attempt to construct a general Marxist theory of the state, Gold, Lo, and Wright provide a number of general propositions that directly deal with this issue. The first, and central, proposition is as follows: "The capitalist state must be conceived both as a structure constrained by the logic of the society within which it functions and as an organization manipulated behind the scenes by the ruling class and its representatives. *The extent to which actual state policies can be explained through structural or instrumental processes is historically contingent.* There are periods in which the state can be reasonably understood as a self-reproducing structure which functions largely independently of any external manipulation, and other times when it is best viewed as a simple tool in the hands of the ruling class. Certain parts of the state apparatus may be highly manipulated by specific capitalist interests while other parts may have much more structural autonomy. But in no situation can state activity be completely reduced to either structural or instrumental causation. The state is always *relatively* autonomous: it is neither completely autonomous (i.e., free from active control by the capitalist class) nor simply manipulated by members of the ruling class (i.e., free from any structural constraints)." (p. 46).

98. Szymanski, *The Capitalist State and the Politics of Class*, p. 272.

CHAPTER 3

THE ORIGINS AND DEVELOPMENT OF THE STATE

For thousands of years after the formation of human societies, no state existed; there was no bureaucratic institution of organized force and violence, and no political rule over an entire people. In fact, the first known states did not arise until about the fourth millennium B.C. The institution of the state has thus been around for only 6000 years, a relatively short time considering the entire history of human societies. Moreover, most societies during this period were without states. The prevalence of the state among a large number of societies around the world became a fact only during the past several hundred years.

The Origins of the State

The emergence of the state coincided with the emergence of social classes and class struggles resulting from the transition from a primitive communal to more advanced modes of production when an economic surplus (i.e., a surplus beyond all that is necessary to feed and cloth a people at the subsistence level) was first generated. Ensuing struggles over control of this surplus led to the development of the state, and once captured by the dominant classes in society, it became an instrument of force to maintain the rule of wealth and privilege against the laboring masses, to maintain exploitation and domination by the few over the many. Without the development of such a powerful instrument of force, there could be no assurance of protection of the privileges of a ruling class, who clearly lived off the labor of the masses. The newly wealthy needed a mechanism that would not only safeguard the newly-acquired property of private individuals against the communistic traditions of the gentile order, would not only sanctify private property, formerly held in such light esteem, and pronounce this sanctification the highest purpose of human society, but would also stamp the gradually developing new forms of acquiring property, and consequently, of constantly accelerating increase in wealth, with the seal of general public recognition; an institution that would perpetuate, not only the newly-rising class division of society, but also the right of the possessing class to exploit the non-possessing classes and the rule of the former over the latter.

And this institution arrived. The *state* was invented.[1]

To trace the historical origins and development of the state, we must go back to the time when human social organization took the form of distinct societies. The first social organization was the commune. Under this mode of social relations, and it accounts for some 80 percent of human history, no state existed. In primitive hunting and gathering societies with communal social relations, political decisions were made on a collective basis; through tribal councils, all members took part in the decision-making process. Organized along kinship lines, primitive communal societies had no powerful chiefs or strong leaders. In the absence of an institution such as the state, no official authority structure could govern society through force. Instead, voluntary consent to assemblies of the whole tribe constituted the basis of social cooperation to maintain order and effect change. In the absence of class distinctions and private ownership of land, the wealth of society belonged to the whole tribe, and the protection of the tribe's possessions was considered the duty of all its members. In this sense, tribal property, held in common, assured the politics of the primitive commune without the need for a state.

Until about 10,000 years ago, all human societies were at the stage of primitive communism. In fact, until a few hundred years ago, most societies on earth were still of this type. Today, primitive hunting and gathering tribes are found only in a few remote areas of the world. But about 10,000 years ago, clan and tribal relations gradually began to change, largely as a result of the division of labor among communes and tribes. First, cattle-breeding communes and tribes split off; later, artisans followed suit. Labor productivity began to grow and gave rise to a surplus. The production of food and other necessities surpassed that required for subsistence, and the possibility of accumulation arose. With an increased and formalized division of labor, came a rise in inequality and an inequitable distribution of the surplus among clan members. As a result, political power began to be expressed, not in the interests of all members of the clan, but to enrich the chiefs and elders. It also began to be more profitable to make slaves out of prisoners of war than to kill them because they could produce more than they consumed and thus add to the wealth of their owners.

> In this way, a minority which amassed wealth was formed in the commune. Organs of self-government began to be changed into organs for the suppression of the majority by the minority. But custom, the moral authority enjoyed by chiefs and joint decision-making were not sufficient any more to turn these organs into regular organs of power. Special detachments (armies, first and foremost) were created to effect, by force of arms, or by the threat of using them, the will of the rich—those who owned the land, livestock and slaves. The appearance of organs of suppression and coercion ushered in the history of the state.[2]

Thus the state developed as a social institution as a result of the growth of wealth and social classes:

> Former society, moving in class antagonisms, had need of the state, that is, an organization of the exploiting class at each period for the maintenance of its external conditions of production; that is, therefore, for the forcible holding down of the exploited class in the conditions of oppression (slavery, villeinage or serf-dom, wage labor) determined by the existing mode of production. The state was the official representative of society as a whole, its embodiment in a visible corpora-

tion; but it was this only in so far as it was the state of that
class which itself, in its epoch, represented society as a
whole; in ancient times, the state of the slave-owning
citizens; in the Middle Ages, of the feudal nobility; in
our epoch, of the bourgeoisie.[3]

Table 3.1 illustrates the various kinds of states in relation to
different modes of production in the historical process and provides
a summary of their associated conditions, main contradictions, and
social transformation from the historical-materialist perspective.

We next turn to an analysis of the earliest form of the state
emerging out of the primitive commune: Oriental despotism.

The Oriental Despotic State

With the growth of accumulation and the subsequent disintegration of the tribal communal structure, the state emerged as the
supreme political institution in society. It first developed in large
river valleys, such as along the Nile, Tigris, Euphrates, Ganges,
Yellow, and Yangtze rivers, where despotic empires were set up
under the auspices of an Imperial Court. The consolidation of
absolute power by the bureaucratic ruling class and the creation of
the great empires of antiquity marked the beginning stage of the
history of the state.[4] Over time, highly centralized states began to
develop, with large numbers of full-time officials to collect taxes,
keep official records, supervise the waterworks, and maintain the
police and armies for enforcing the law.

Side by side with the masses thus occupied with one and
the same work, we find the "chief inhabitant," who is
judge, police, and tax-gatherer in one; the bookkeeper,
who keeps the accounts of the village and registers
everything relating thereto; another official, who pros-
ecutes criminals, protects strangers traveling through
and escorts them to the next village; the boundary man,
who guards the boundaries against neighboring communities; the water-overseer, who distributes the water
from the common tanks for irrigation [etc.]. . . . This

Table 3.1
Modes of Production and Types of States in Historical Development

Modes of Production	Relations of Production	Superstructure	Associated Conditions	Contradictions	Transformations
Primitive communist	No classes or division of labor, except by sex	No state; tribal council; primitive religion	Low population density; small-scale societies	Possibility of economic surplus and exchange	Commodity production; emergence of private property
Asiatic	Imperial court vs. communal villages	Centralized state; formalized religion; surplus for luxury	High population density; need for irrigation & flood control	Court vs. village interests; external invasion	Stable system; resists change but can develop into any of the advanced modes
Ancient/slave	Master vs. Slave	Centralized state and military organization; formalized religion	Centralized; city-based; division between town and country	Wars and expansion; constant increase in slaves	Undermining of social structure leads to breakdown of whole order

Table 3.1 (continued)

Modes of Production	Relations of Production	Superstructure	Associated Conditions	Contradictions	Transformations
Feudal	Lords vs. Serfs	Weak central state; formalized religion; manor based	Low population density; division between town and country	Expanded demand for commodities; expanded trade; increased population	Bourgeois revolution against feudalism
Capitalist	Capitalists vs. wage laborers	Strong central state; formalized rligion; individualistic ideology	Increasing population; city-based; division between town and country	Accumulation of capital class polarization; increasing proletarian class consciousness	Proletarian socialist revolution against capitalism
Socialist[a]	Worker-worker; no antagonistic classes	Proletarian socialist ideology; strong central state	Centralized; city-based; division between town and country	Factory system; division of labor; centralized state; division between town and country	Gradual withering away of these nonantagonistic contradictions

Table 3.1 (continued)

Modes of Production	Relations of Production	Superstructure	Associated Conditions	Contradictions	Transformations
Communist	No division of labor; no class struggle	No state; communal consciousness; collective rule	Decentralized; no division between town and country	None	None

Source: Adopted from Albert Szymanski, *The Capitalist State and the Politics of Class* (Cambridge, Mass.: Winthrop, 1978); and idem, *Class Structure: A Critical Perspective* (New York: Praeger, 1983).

[a.] Although Marx does not mention socialism as a mode of production, Marxists generally agree that between capitalism and communism there exists a transitional phase called socialism, which Lenin called "the first phase of communist society." During this stage, the state is controlled by the working class, or what Marx calls "the dictatorship of the proletariat," through its political organ the Communist party. The main characteristic of this period is the dismantling of the capitalist system and the building of communist society. A strong central state and factory-based industrial production exists; society is still city based, although the division between city and country is being gradually reduced. Many nonantagonistic contradictions begin gradually to wither away, as does the state and other major institutions of society, as the society evolves toward full communism.

dozen of individuals is maintained at the expense of the whole community.[5]

Moreover, in these societies, the ruler or the emperor had absolute power. All the major institutions—economic, religious, military, and political—were merged into one, centered in an absolute ruler. As Marx put it:

> The despot here appears as the father of all numerous lesser communities, thus realizing the common unity of all. It, therefore, follows that the surplus product (which, incidentally, is legally determined in terms of [infolge] the real appropriation through labour) belongs to this highest unity. Oriental despotism therefore appears to lead to a legal absence of property. In fact, however, its foundation is tribal or common property, in most cases created through a combination of manufacture and agriculture within the small community which thus becomes entirely self-sustaining and contains within itself all conditions of production and surplus production.
>
> Part of its surplus labor belongs to the higher community, which ultimately appears as a *person*. This surplus labor is rendered both as tribute and as common labor for the glory of the unity, in part that of the despot, in part that of the imagined tribal entity of the god.[6]

The main contradictions in these early class societies, then, were between the masses of people who lived in village units and the ruling class, consisting of the ruler and the state bureaucracy.

An important characteristic of Oriental despotic societies was their strong resistance to change. The Egyptian, Aztec, Inca, Indian, Chinese, and Ottoman empires were highly stable, lasting for several centuries. Because of their highly stable nature, change often had to come from external sources.

This was true, for example, in China and India. The despotic empires in these two regions were penetrated by British and, more generally, European capitalism during the later colonial phase of expansion, which broke down all internal barriers to development along the capitalist path. The contemporary capitalist (as well as the feudal) mode was "introduced" from outside the prevailing system of production. This was also true of the Aztec and Inca empires which underwent a similar process of change with the impact of European mercantile expansion to the Americas and the subsequent penetration of commercial and feudal interests in transforming local economic and sociopolitical structures.

With Ottoman despotism, a combination of external *and* internal developments brought change to this centuries-old social formation. Although the expansion of European mercantile capital to the East undermined the Ottoman monopoly on trade in the Mediterranean, an equally important internal process was at work. This was the allocation of parcels of land in rural areas to warriors engaged in the despotic bureaucracy's militaristic adventures in Europe, the Middle East, northern Africa, and elsewhere. This system of land allocation (*timar*) and the subsequent introduction of tax farming (*iltizam*) brought about a major transformation of the Ottoman agrarian structure.[7] The accumulation of large tracts of land, initially by these warriors and later by an emerging landed gentry (*ayan*), led to the development of a landowning class that came to subordinate local communal villagers to its dictates. Through this process, the majority of the local population was turned into an unpaid laboring class tied to local landed interests and in a position not unlike the serfs under European feudalism. At the same time, interaction with Europe facilitated the expansion of European commercial capital into the empire and led to the transformation of the local merchant class into an intermediary of European capital. In this way, the state came to represent the interests of the landed gentry, local merchants, and European capital, as well as the political bureaucracy on which it was based.[8]

In other despotic societies, an alternative path of development led to the emergence of slavery and feudalism as dominant modes of production. The transition from Oriental despotic state under the Asiatic mode of production to its varied forms under slavery and feudal landlordism was a slow process that took hundreds of years. But, in time, the development of new modes of production resulted in the transformation of the superstructure as well, in a way that directly corresponded to the prevailing relations of production and the ensuing class struggles. Thus the evolution of changing property relations in society ushered in a new form of the state—a state that served the interests of new ruling classes (of slaveowners, landlords, and subsequently, capitalists) for purposes of control, domination, and exploitation of the laboring masses.

The Ancient Slaveowning State

In some societies, the state possessed immense power and served to advance the interests of masters against slaves. Societies based on the slave mode of production, such as Athens, were located along major trade routes and at the mouths of important rivers. They became major trading centers with strong military power. "In the ancient world," writes Marx, "commerce and the development of commercial capital . . . resulted in a slave economy, or sometimes, depending on the point of departure, it resulted simply in the transformation of a patriarchal slave system devoted to the production of direct means of subsistence into a similar system devoted to the production of surplus value."[9] Ancient society, then, was based on slavery as the dominant mode of production and exchange. Surplus value was extracted from slaves and appropriated, in turn, by the citizen ruling class, or masters.

Slaveowning societies, such as Athens, conquered large numbers of people and made them slaves. This practice enabled Athens to maintain a democracy for Athenian citizens while enslaving virtually all the people in the surrounding environs: "In Athens," writes V. Gordon Childe, "democracy was made completely effective. . . . Every citizen was expected to attend assemblies and to sit on juries. . . . In the latter part of the fifth century, countrymen did in fact attend the assembly and vote on questions of general policy."[10] Childe goes on to add:

> Fifth-century Athens thus provides the first adequately documented example of a through-going popular government. Its popular character must not be exaggerated. In the first place women had no place in public life. . . . Secondly, citizenship was now a hereditary privilege from which resident aliens were rigorously excluded. . . . Finally, industry was based on slavery; even the small

farmer generally owned a slave or two, and the majority
of the employees in mines and factories . . . were slaves.
. . . [A]liens had no share in the government and slaves
had no rights whatever.[11]

The primary contradiction in the productive scheme of ancient
societies such as Athens and early Rome was between slaves and
masters. While the surplus product created by forced (slave) labor
was converted into unproductive expenditure—on public works,
religious monuments, and works of art, as well as the extravagant,
aristocratic way of life of the citizen ruling class—the condition of
the slave masses deteriorated, and their position of subsistence
became more precarious as their impoverishment grew.[12]

The decay of ancient social organization was the result of a
decline in trade, the money economy, and cities, all of which—
accompanied by war, expansion, and a constant increase in slavery
and, with it, widespread slave rebellions[13]—made slavery no longer
profitable and undermined the entire community structure. These
developments led to the slaves' conversion into proto-serfs, that is,
neither citizens nor slaves. Although this meant a certain level of
improvement in their position compared to earlier periods, the
slaves nonetheless remained tied to the land and were bought and
sold with it. Herein lay the preconditions for the transition to
feudalism.

The Feudal State

The origins of classical European feudalism go back to the
Germanic invasions of the Roman Empire and the fusion of the
essentially household-based Germanic mode with Roman proto-
feudalism, which occurred after the collapse of the slave system of
ancient Rome. The forced unity of the two societies, originally at
different stages of development, led to the eventual dissolution of
the old forms and gave rise to the development of a yet new (feudal)
mode of production. "The last centuries of the declining Roman
Empire and its conquest by the barbarians," writes Marx,

destroyed a number of productive forces; agriculture had declined, industry had decayed for lack of markets, trade had died out or had been violently interrupted, and the rural and urban population had diminished. These conditions and the mode of organization of the conquest determined by them gave rise, under the influence of the Teutonic military constitution, to feudal property.[14]

The essential social relation of production in feudal societies was between lord and serf. There was very little division of labor, minimal trade or commerce (as all goods were produced in self-sufficient communities), and constant warfare among feudal lords to expand land. The village was the basic unit of the agrarian feudal economy and consisted of a population ranging from about a dozen to several hundred peasant families living in a cluster. The manor, in contrast, was a unit of political jurisdiction and economic exploitation controlled by a single lord; it was often geographically identical with the village, although some manors embraced two or more villages. "The village community," writes Hollister, was

> a closed system, economically self-sufficient, capable of sustaining the material and spiritual needs of the villages without much contact with the outside world. . . . The economy of the Early Middle Ages, lacking a vigorous commercial life and a significant urban population, failed to provide villages with much incentive to produce beyond their immediate needs. There was only the most limited market for surplus grain. Accordingly, village life tended to be uneventful, tradition-bound, and circumscribed by the narrowest of horizons. . . .
>
> Superimposed on the economic structure of the village was the political-juridical structure of the manor. The average peasant was bound to a manorial lord. . . . They owed various dues to their manorial lord, chiefly in kind, and were normally expected to labor for a certain number of days per week—often three—on the lord's fields.[15]

The obligations placed on the peasants were immense, and their function within the manorial system was one of productive subordination to the lord. In addition to their obligation to work on the lord's fields, the peasants paid their lord a percentage of the produce of their fields, as well as paying various fees and taxes. The following key excerpt from Engels's *The Peasant War in Germany* captures the condition of life of the peasant in feudal Germany:

> At the bottom of all the classes, save the last one, was the huge exploited mass of the nation, the peasants. It was the peasant who carried the burden of all the other strata of society: princes, officialdom, nobility, clergy, patricians and middle-class. Whether the peasant was the subject of a prince, an imperial baron, a bishop, a monastery, or a city, he was everywhere treated as a beast of burden and worse. If he was a serf, he was entirely at the mercy of his master. If he was a bondsman, the legal deliveries stipulated by agreement were sufficient to crush him; even they were being daily increased. Most of his time, he had to work on his master's estate. Out of that which he earned in his few free hours, he had to pay tithes, dues, ground rents, war taxes, land taxes, imperial taxes and other payments. He could neither marry nor die without paying the master. Aside from his regular work for the master, he had to gather litter, pick strawberries, pick bilberries, collect snail shells, drive the game for the hunting, chop wood, and so on. Fishing and hunting belonged to the master. The peasant saw his crop destroyed by wild game. The community meadows and woods of the peasants had almost everywhere been forcibly taken away by the masters.[16]

Engels points out that the domination of the lord or master over the peasant extended not only over the peasants' property but also over his person:

> And in the same manner as the master reigned over the peasant's property, he extended his wilfulness over his person, his wife and daughters. He possessed the right of the first night. Whenever he pleased, he threw the

> peasant into the tower, where the rack waited for him just as surely as the investigating attorney waits for the criminal in our times. Whenever he pleased, he killed him or ordered him beheaded. None of the instructive chapters of the Carolina[17] which speaks of "cutting of ears," "cutting of noses," "blinding," "chopping of fingers," "beheading," "breaking on the wheel," "burning," "pinching with burned tongs," "quartering," etc., was left unpracticed by the gracious lord and master at his pleasure. Who could defend the peasant? The courts were manned by barons, clergymen, patricians, or jurists, who knew very well for what they were being paid. Not in vain did all the official estates of the empire lie on the exploitation of the peasants.[18]

Although state rule was highly decentralized, and there was little in the way of a state bureaucracy, the power of the feudal lords rested on their military strength: "The hierarchical system of landownership, and the armed bodies of retainers associated with it gave the nobility power over the serfs. This feudal structure was, just as much as the communal property of antiquity, an association against a subject producing class, but the form of association and the relation to the direct producers were different because of the different conditions of production."[19]

Historically, the feudal mode of production in Western Europe began to give way to mercantilism in the sixteenth century. The growth of trade and the rise of the merchant class strengthened the rule of the state, which obtained monopoly over trade and the economy in general during the mercantile era and set the groundwork for the subsequent emergence of capitalism and the capitalist state.[20]

The transition from feudalism to mercantilism was marked by a transformation of the state from a coordinating institution of dispersed landed interests over a large agrarian territory to a centralized power representing the new merchant class concentrated in urban trading centers and port cities. The shift in the center of political rule thus resulted from a shift in production relations, and relations of exploitation in general, in favor of the merchant class in league with the early capitalists in transition from crafts production to large-scale manufacturing and industry. The protection provided to the merchants by the mercantile state in the transitional period resulted from the increasing power and influence of the merchant class in economic life and consequently in politics. In time, the merchants constituted the new ruling class in Europe (and elsewhere).[21]

The reappearance of a strong central state coincided with the dissolution of the feudal mode of production and the rise to prominence of the merchant class. Through the powers of the state, they ushered in a period of mercantilism. At the height of mercantilism, and with a greatly expanded overseas trade during the sixteenth to eighteenth centuries in Europe, we begin to see the emergence of the original accumulation of capital that subsequently gave rise to capitalism in Western Europe. Thus, overseas trade, the basis of the original accumulation of capital, played a crucial role in weakening the position of the landlords, in laying the foundations of capitalism and thereby facilitating the process of transition.[22] As Marx and Engels observed:

> The discovery of America, the rounding of the Cape, opened up fresh ground for the rising bourgeoisie. The East-Indian and Chinese markets, the colonization of America, trade with the colonies, the increase in the means of exchange and in commodities generally, gave to commerce, to navigation, to industry, an impulse never before known, and thereby, to the revolutionary element in the tottering feudal society, a rapid development.[23]

As trade and merchants' capital set the stage for the shift toward manufacturing and industrial production for further accumulation, the balance of forces in the economy began to swing in favor of the rising bourgeoisie, whose growing wealth and economic strength brought changes in the nature and role of the state as well—in favor of the bourgeoisie.

> At the same pace at which the progress of modern industry developed, widened, intensified the class antagonism between capital and labor, the State power assumed more and more the character of the national

power of capital over labour, of a public force organized for social enslavement, of an engine of class despotism.[24]

The absolutist monarchies that ruled much of Europe in an earlier period and were strengthened during the mercantilist era through strong state intervention in the economy worked to the benefit of the bourgeoisie as its expanded economic position vis-à-vis the landlords and the merchants, and the subsequent political pressure it exerted upon the state, resulted in the state's increasing isolation from the control and influence of the former ruling classes in both the economy and the polity. In time, the bourgeoisie forced a dissolution of the absolutist state and established republics (in France and Switzerland) or constitutional monarchies (in England and Holland). Eventually, the bourgeoisie set up its own states throughout much of Europe and ushered in a new era of capitalist expansion promoted and safeguarded by the new capitalist state.

It is to the analysis of the capitalist state that we turn in the next chapter.

Notes

1. Frederick Engels, *The Origins of the Family, Private Property, and the State* (New York: International Publishers, 1972), p. 263.

2. Gennady Belov, *What Is the State?* (Moscow: Progress Publishers, 1986), p. 21.

3. Frederick Engels, *Anti-Duhring* (New York: International Publishers, 1976), p. 306.

4. For a discussion of the Oriental despotic state and the Asiatic mode of production, see Perry Anderson, *Lineages of the Absolutist State* (London: New Left Books, 1974), pp. 462–549; Hal Draper, *Karl Marx's Theory of Revolution* (New York: Monthly Review Press, 1977), pp. 515–71; D.R. Gandy, *Marx and History* (Austin and London: University of Texas Press, 1979), pp. 18–25; and Lawrence Krader, *The Asiatic Mode of Production* (Assem: Van Gorcum, 1975).

5. Karl Marx, *Capital*. vol. 1 (New York: International Publishers, 1967), pp. 357–58.

6. Karl Marx, *Pre-Capitalist Economic Formations* (New York: International Publishers, 1965), pp. 69–70.

7. Halil Inalcik, *The Ottoman Empire* (New York: Praeger, 1973); H. Islamoglu and S. Faroqhi, "Crop Patterns and Agricultural Production Trends in Sixteenth Century Anatolia," *Review* 2, no. 3 (Winter 1979), pp. 401–36. For a detailed

discussion of the land-tenure system and the emergence of a landed gentry in the Ottoman Empire, see "Class and State in the Middle East" in Chapter 6 of this volume.

8. For further discussion on the nature of the Ottoman Empire and the controversy surrounding the applicability of the Asiatic mode of production to the Ottoman social formation, see Sencer Divitcioglu, *Asya Uretim Tarzi ve Osmanli Toplumu* (The Asiatic Mode of Production and Ottoman Society) (Istanbul: Koz Yayinevi, 1971).

9. Karl Marx, *Selected Writings in Sociology and Social Philosophy* (New York: McGraw-Hill, 1964), p. 113.

10. V. Gordon Childe, *What Happened in History* (Baltimore: Penguin, 1971), p. 215.

11. Ibid., p. 216.

12. Engels, *Origins*, pp. 217–37.

13. As Childe points out: "slave revolts ... assumed serious proportions for the first time in history after 134 B.C. Attica, Macedonia, Delos, Sicily, Italy, and Pergamon. The rebels were often joined by small peasants and tenants and even by 'free' proletarians." Childe, *What Happened in History*, p. 267.

14. Marx, *Selected Writings in Sociology*, pp. 117–18.

15. C. Warren Hollister, *Medieval Europe*, 3rd ed. (New York: Wiley, 1974), pp. 131–32.

16. Frederick Engels, *The Peasant War in Germany* (New York: International Publishers, 1973), p. 47.

17. *Carolina*, a criminal code of the sixteenth century, published in 1532 under Emperor Charles V.

18. Engels, *The Peasant War in Germany*, pp. 47–48.

19. Marx, *Selected Writings in Sociology*, p. 118.

20. See Immanuel Wallerstein, *The Modern World System* (New York: Academic Press, 1974), idem, *The Capitalist World Economy* (Cambridge: Cambridge University Press, 1979), and idem, *The Politics of the World Economy* (Cambridge: Cambridge University Press, 1984).

21. Ibid.

22. For an analysis of the debate on the transition from feudalism to capitalism in Western Europe, see Berch Berberoglu, "The Transition From Feudalism to Capitalism: The Sweezy-Dobb Debate," *Revista Mexicana de Sociologia*, December 1977. The original debate between Sweezy and Dobb, which took place in the pages of the journal *Science and Society* in the early 1950s, is compiled, with additional commentaries and discussion, in *The Transition From Feudalism to Capitalism*, ed. Rodney Hilton (London: New Left Books, 1976).

23. Karl Marx and Frederick Engels, "Manifesto of the Communist Party," in Karl Marx and Frederick Engels, *Selected Works* (New York: International Publishers, 1972), p. 36.

24. Karl Marx, "The Civil War in France," in Marx and Engels, *Selected Works*, p. 289.

CHAPTER 4

THE CAPITALIST STATE:
ITS NATURE AND CONTRADICTIONS

The decline of feudalism and the rise of capitalism in Europe marked the beginning of a new chapter in world history. The transition from the feudal to the capitalist mode was accompanied by a number of preconditions that gave rise to capitalism and capitalist relations, and came to dominate the social formations of Western Europe by the early eighteenth century.

The Origins of the Capitalist State

In examining the decline of feudalism and the rise of capitalism in Western Europe, Marx conceived of two possible paths of development that could lead to the emergence of capitalism in formations previously dominated by the feudal mode: (1) merchant to capitalist, and (2) craftsman to capitalist. Of the two, Marx characterized the second as the "really revolutionary way," pointing to the centrality of the internal contradictions lodged in the productive process under feudalism, which contained the germs of the emergent capitalist mode in the form of petty commodity production based on crafts.[1]

This was clearly true in Britain and France, where the new forces of production came into the hands of small craftsmen, who set up workshops and factories employing wage labor, thus transforming themselves into capitalists. In Prussia and most of Eastern Europe, however, the big merchants and landlords became the owners of

82

industry. In the absence of a strong, independent capitalist class, and with power in the hands of the merchants and landlords, capitalism in this region developed gradually and over an extended time; monarchist and feudal forms of the state continued to dominate society well into the twentieth century.[2]

Marx's careful examination of the European experience convinced him that, on balance, a combination of the two paths, dominated more by the first, actually led to the emergence of capitalism and capitalist relations in much of Europe. This prompted him to emphasize the importance of trade (especially colonial trade) as a major contributing factor in the dissolution of feudalism and the original accumulation of capital. This was the case in addition to the fundamental internal contradictions of the feudal mode, where trade provided the added impetus in bringing about the collapse of feudalism:

> ... trade with the colonies, the increase in the means of exchange and in commodities generally, gave to commerce, to navigation, to industry, an impulse never before known, and thereby, to the revolutionary element in the tottering feudal society, a rapid development. . . .
>
> In proportion as industry, commerce, navigation, railways extended, in the same proportion the bourgeoisie developed, increased its capital, and pushed into the background every class handed down from the Middle Ages.[3]

Historically, a number of conditions set the stage and led to the emergence of capitalism and the capitalist state in Western Europe and elsewhere. These included the availability of free laborers, the generation of moneyed wealth, a sufficient level of skills and technology, markets, and the protection provided by the state. In general, these conditions were the foundations on which a precapitalist society transformed itself into a capitalist one until capitalism developed through its own dynamics.[4] Once capitalism was established, it began to produce and reproduce the conditions for expanded commodity production and capital accumulation. From this point on, capitalism developed in accordance with its inherent contradictions.

With the principal relations of production that between wage labor and the owners of the means of production, capitalism established itself as a mode of production based on the exploitation of wage labor by capitalists, whose power and authority in society derived from their ownership and control of the means of production. Lacking ownership of the means necessary to gain a living, producers were forced to sell their labor power to capitalists in order to survive. As a result, the surplus value produced by labor was appropriated by the capitalists in the form of profit. Thus, private profit, generated through the exploitation of labor, became the motive force of capitalism.

The contradictions imbedded in such antagonistic social relations in time led to the radicalization of workers and the formation of trade unions and other labor organizations that were to play important roles in the struggles between labor and capital. The history of the labor movement in Europe, the United States, and elsewhere in the world is replete with bloody confrontations between labor and capital and the latter's repressive arm, the capitalist state. From the early battles of workers in Britain and on the Continent in the late eighteenth and early nineteenth centuries to the decisive role played by French workers in the uprising of 1848-51 to the Paris Commune in 1871 to the Haymarket massacre and the heroic struggle of the "Wobblies" in the United States in the late nineteenth and early twentieth centuries, the working class put up a determined struggle in its fight against capital on both sides of the Atlantic—a struggle spanning over two centuries.

Established to protect and advance the interests of the capitalist class, the early capitalist state assumed a pivotal role that assured the class rule of capitalists over society and thus became an institution of legitimization and brute force to maintain law and order in favor of capitalism. Sanctioning and enforcing laws to protect the rights of the new property owners and disciplining labor to maintain a wage system that generated profits for the wealthy few, the capitalist state became the instrument of capital and its political rule over society.

Among the major functions of the early capitalist state (e.g., in Britain and the United States in the nineteenth century) were guaranteeing private property at home and abroad; collecting taxes;

recording births, deaths, and income for purposes of taxation and raising armies; guaranteeing contracts; providing the infrastructure (railroads, canals, communication) for the new industries; facilitating the growth of private industry; mediating among various wealthy interests; securing a cheap and disciplined labor force for private enterprise; and preserving law and order to keep the masses under control. Corresponding to conditions under early industrial capitalism, the state had only a small bureaucracy, spent little on social programs, and had a relatively small standing army; taxes were greatly reduced and were collected largely through tariffs on imports in order to protect home industry.[5]

The central task of the early capitalist state in Europe and the United States was that of disciplining the labor force. Union activity, strikes, or collective actions of any kind by workers against businesses were prohibited; demonstrations, agitation, and propaganda initiated by workers against the employers and the system were systematically repressed. Thus, while state intervention in the economy was kept to a minimum to permit the capitalists to enrich themselves without regulation, the capitalist-controlled state became heavily involved in the conflict between labor and capital on behalf of the capitalist class, bringing to bear its repressive apparatus on labor and its allies who threatened the capitalist order. Law and order enforced by the state in early capitalism (and right up to the present) served to protect and preserve the capitalist system and prevent its transformation. In this sense, the state came to see itself as a legitimizing agency of the new social order and identified its survival directly with the capitalists who controlled it. This mutual relationship between state and capital in time set the conditions for the structural environment in which the state functioned to promote capitalist interests, now without the necessity of direct control by individual capitalists through specific state agencies. Within this process of the state's development from early to mature capitalism, the structural imperatives of capital accumulation placed the state in the service of capital, thus transforming it into a *capitalist state*.

With the growth and development of capitalism and its contradictions, and, in response to this, the growth of the working class and the trade union movement, the state began to take a more active role in the economy in order to regulate business activity and cyclical crises (e.g., the business cycle, finance, trade, the stock market). At the same time, to control the demands of labor and secure the long-term stability of the capitalist system, it granted certain concessions to the masses. The limited social programs enacted by the state, and the extension of the franchise to the masses, came to serve a legitimizing role and rationalized the actions of the state as "representing the interests of the entire society" (i.e., it was a "democratic state"). "But this democracy," we are reminded,

> is always bound by the narrow framework of capitalist exploitation, and consequently always remains, in effect, a democracy for the minority, only for the propertied classes, only for the rich. Freedom in capitalist society always remains about the same as it was in the ancient Greek republics: freedom for the slave-owners. Owing to the conditions of capitalist exploitation, the modern wage slaves are so crushed by want and poverty that "they cannot be bothered with democracy," "cannot be bothered with politics"; in the ordinary, peaceful course of events, the majority of the population is debarred from participation in public and political life. . . .
>
> Democracy for an insignificant minority, democracy for the rich—that is the democracy of capitalist society. . . .
>
> Marx grasped this *essence* of capitalist democracy splendidly when, in analyzing the experience of the Commune, he said that the oppressed are allowed once every few years to decide which particular representatives of the oppressing class shall represent and repress them in parliament![6]

The increasing involvement of the state in social life in order to promote the capitalist system accomplished its desired ends, as the masses were in general unable clearly to distinguish the state's democratic-appearing concessions from its real *class agenda*, as an instrument of capitalist rule. On the other hand, class-conscious workers and their organizations that were aware of this fact and tried to expose it through mass political action were severely repressed.

The Development of the Capitalist State in the United States

The transformation of the state in the United States from a colonial appendage of the British Empire to an independent *capitalist* state with jurisdiction over the entire national territory did not occur until the late nineteenth century. The War of Independence did, to be sure, change the political relations between Britain and its former American colony, but this change was not accompanied by a social transformation transferring power from one class to another. In this sense, the American Revolution was not a social revolution; rather, it constituted the transfer of power from the metropole to its ex-colony, similar to that achieved by wars of national liberation, without effecting a change in internal class power and class relations. From 1776 to the end of the Civil War in 1865, the United States developed within the framework of a "neocolonial" relationship with Britain, when the state represented the interests of both the emerging capitalist class in the North and the dependent slaveowning class in the South, which was tied to the British-dominated world economy. Specializing in agroindustrial raw material production (e.g., cotton) geared to the needs of the textile industry in England, the slaveowning planter class in the South came to articulate the interests of its ex-colonial master poised against northern capital, from which it carved out for itself a portion of the profits guaranteed by the imperial crown. The contradictory class relationship between the two rival ruling classes in postcolonial America continued to evolve and develop within the framework of a truce that permitted the coexistence of two distinct modes of production through the sharing of state power, at least for a time.

The balance of class forces in the state apparatus from the postindependence period to the Civil War was maintained by the Constitution drawn up by the two rival propertied classes in 1787. Intent on replacing the Articles of Confederation (the law of the land at the time) with a Constitution that would give power to a central state, the delegates to the Constitutional Convention in Philadelphia pushed through a document designed to protect their class interests and prevent popular democratic control of the U.S. state. Fifty-three of the fifty-five delegates to the Convention were or represented the economic interests of the propertied classes of slaveowners, merchants, creditors, and manufacturers.[7] Forty of the delegates held the paper money issued by the Continental Congress to finance the Revolutionary War, fourteen held vast tracts of land, twenty-four were creditors and mortgage holders, eleven were merchants or manufacturers, and fifteen were slaveowners.[8] They included James Madison, plantation owner and lawyer; Edmund Randolph of Virginia, owner of 5000 acres and 200 slaves; Robert Morris, the Philadelphia banker; and Gouverneur Morris, land speculator of New York and Philadelphia.[9] Moreover, "according to James McHenry, a delegate from Maryland, at least twenty-one of the fifty-five delegates favored some form of monarchy. Yet few dared venture in that direction out of fear of popular opposition."[10] Aware of widespread opposition among the people to the new Constitution, the delegates passed a resolution at the beginning of the convention to keep what they were doing completely secret; they even passed a subsequent resolution that no one was to take notes.[11] This was done to prevent the public from finding out the true nature of the document being written and the motives of those responsible for it. Despite the fact that the delegates were instructed both by the Congress and their own states to consider only a revision of the Articles of Confederation, and to submit their recommendations to the Congress and the states for approval,[12] they ignored these instructions and came up with a new document to replace the Articles:

> They did not amend the Articles of Confederation; they cast that instrument aside and drafted a fresh plan of government. Nor did they merely send the new document to Congress and then to the state legislatures for approval; on the contrary they appealed over the heads of these authorities to the voters of the states for a ratification of their revolutionary work. Finally, declining to obey the clause of the Articles which required unanimous approval for every amendment, they frankly proposed that the new system of government should go into effect when sanctioned by nine of the thirteen states, leaving the others out in the cold under the wreck of the existing legal order, in case they refused to ratify.[13]

Despite these maneuvers, the convention was unable to meet even its own requirements and secure the nine states necessary for ratification: the people of New York, New Hampshire, Massachusetts, Rhode Island, and North Carolina voted against ratification. Keenly aware of the need to reverse the situation by securing the votes, the pro-Constitution forces persuaded some of the delegates to the state conventions who had been elected to vote *against* the Constitution to vote *for* it instead. This maneuver reversed the results in three crucial states—New York, New Hampshire, and Massachusetts:

> In New Hampshire, New York, and Massachusetts, where the election returned avowed majorities opposed to the Constitution, a great deal of clever engineering induced several delegates to depart from their apparent instructions and cast their ballots for ratification. But to the very end, two states, North Carolina and Rhode Island, refused to give their consent. . . . From the fragmentary figures that are available, it appears that no more than one-fourth of the adult white males in the country voted one way or the other in the elections at which delegates to the state ratifying conventions were chosen. According to a cautious reckoning, probably one-sixth of them—namely, one hundred thousand— favored the ratification of the new form of government.[14]

After the Constitution was finally ratified and became the basis of government, both the intent of the Framers and the content of the document became increasingly clear to people, especially small farmers, who constituted the majority of the population:

> . . . the people as a whole were opposed to the document. Particularly hostile were the small farmers of the country. . . . They were quick to point out the essentially undemocratic character of the new frame of government. . . . They resented the fact that the proposed instrument was more concerned with the protection of property rights than in the maintenance of human rights.

> They did not fail to note that what the constitution was
> trying to do was to establish the same centralized system
> of political, judicial, and economic controls that the
> British ruling classes had attempted to foist upon them
> in the days of Grenville, Townshend, and North.[15]

Under pressure from the small farmers and other democratic forces in society, the newly emerging U.S. state, controlled by the wealthy, had no choice but to come forward with a Bill of Rights—the first ten amendments to the Constitution, which were added to the document in 1791.[16]

That the Framers of the Constitution wanted to establish a state guided by laws and principles reflecting the interests of the propertied classes is no secret even to a casual observer of the events of the time. Their antidemocratic pronouncements were in line with their class interests as against those of the slaves, the workers, the artisans, and the farmers, as well as the Native American people—in effect, the vast majority of the population.[17] The critical linkage between class and state in postcolonial America, then, was established precisely by the class nature and role of the U.S. Constitution, which provided the basis of the rule of property over labor and gave the state its subsequent class character.[18] For this reason, the Constitution can be seen both as a product *and* an instrument of the class forces that came to dominate the U.S. state until the Civil War.

Nevertheless, it soon became clear that the state apparatus that came under the control of the ruling classes could not function properly unless some mechanisms of mediation of conflict were instituted to resolve differences between rival forces within the ruling-class coalition. Thus: "In order to regulate the conflict of interests between capitalists and landowners, a series of checks and balances between judiciary, congressional, and executive powers were introduced, as well as different methods of representation for the Senate and the House of Representatives." [19] This was also recognized and articulated in no uncertain terms by the Framers of the Constitution who established the foundations of the modern U.S. state, as the following passage from James Madison's *Federalist Papers* indicates:

> But the most common and durable source of factions
> has been the various and unequal distribution of prop-
> erty. Those who hold and those who are without prop-
> erty have ever formed distinct interests in society.... A
> landed interest, a manufacturing interest, a mercantile
> interest, a moneyed interest, with many lesser interests,
> grow up of necessity in civilized nations, and divide
> them into different classes, actuated by different senti-
> ments and views. The regulation of these various and
> interfering interests forms the principal task of modern
> legislation, and involves the spirit of party and faction
> in the necessary and ordinary operations of the govern-
> ment.[20]

During the first half of the nineteenth century, slaveowners were the dominant force within the ruling-class alliance. This is evidenced by the fact that key positions within the federal machinery were controlled by slaveowners, assisted by their financial and mercantile allies in the North. The executive and legislative branches of the state were pro-slaveowner, and seven of the nine Supreme Court justices were either slaveowners or supported slavery.

By the middle of the nineteenth century, capitalist development had reached new heights throughout the North, requiring new markets, access to raw materials, cheap and abundant labor, and further capital accumulation. The slaveowning class in the South held on to its source of wealth through the exploitation of slave labor and safeguarded its neocolonial role in the world economy. The contradictions that had been developing between the two systems since the formation of the Union could no longer be contained within the existing state. Thus the two exploiting classes finally clashed, to solve, once and for all, the question of state power.

The level of development reached by the different modes of production at the time of independence was such that it took nearly a century for these contradictions to burst open and culminate in a civil war that would finally decide the answer to the decisive question: Which class alone shall rule the state? The northern, capitalist victory against the slaveowning South resulted in the transfer of state power to the capitalist class and thereby ushered in the rule of the capitalist state. In this sense, the northern victory in the Civil War marked a turning point in the social transformation of postcolonial America, when capitalism became the dominant mode of production and the capitalist state the dominant political authority in the land.

As capitalism came to dominate the national economy and the state following the Civil War, the primary struggle became that between industrial capital (and its associated moneyed interests) and the small farmers and a growing class of industrial workers. During this period of "reconstruction" (i.e., the period of transition to and establishment of capitalist dominance),

> The capitalist class turned the state completely into its instrument. The state heavily subsidized the building of the railways and internal improvements. High protective tariffs were established. Immigration of laborers was encouraged. Free land was given to the farmers and the railroads. The working class was kept in line and prevented from organizing. In every way the state facilitated the rapid and unimpeded advance of industrial capital.[21]

As a result, a tremendous expansion of capital took place, leading to the concentration and centralization of wealth in the hands of the capitalists, whose base of exploitation expanded through the accumulation of surplus value from both local and immigrant labor. As industry grew, production expanded, and capitalism spread throughout the nation, the ex-slaves (now paid labor), together with the established industrial proletariat of the northern cities, generated ever-higher rates of surplus value for the capitalists, yielding huge profits and fueling the fortunes of the super-rich, who set up immense financial empires that generated the first capitalist monopolies, cartels, and trusts. Through this process of expansion, capital, now in its monopoly stage, came to dominate the U.S. economy and the state by the late nineteenth and early twentieth centuries. As a result, the state's role in regulating the economy on behalf of capital began to increase, as did its role in repressing an increasingly militant working class.

The fierce conflicts of Chicago and Colorado, the strikes of steel workers, metal miners, and railroad men, the jailing of literally thousands of labor's rank and file . . . were cruel and bloody years that stretched between 1890 and 1900. . . .

It was the time in which American finance underwent a qualitative change, beginning to export its money and Marines into the Caribbean and the Pacific, grabbing Puerto Rico and the Philippines by force of arms, controlling Cuba as a protectorate, and annexing Hawaii outright.

And it was the decade which saw one more gallant effort by the common people, the workers and farmers, to wrest the country from the control of Wall Street through independent political action. It was the time of labor's tall Gene Debs and the miners' Big Bill Haywood, of Sockless Jerry Simpson and Mary Elizabeth Lease, who advised the nation's farmers to "raise less corn and more hell." It was a decade in which monopoly, steadily growing since the Civil War, pyramided into new heights of power . . . [while] the Knights of Labor . . . called for the abolition of the wage system and the establishment of an order whose factories, mines, mills, railroads, and utilities were owned and operated by the people. . . .

Despite these political struggles, monopoly steadily grew . . . ever increasing their grip on every aspect of American life. . . . And the great age of financial concentration, of the narrowing control of the few who reaped fabulous profits from the work of the many, had just begun.[22]

Beginning in the first two decades of this century and continuing throughout the Great Depression and World War II, the state played a key role in safeguarding and promoting the capitalist economy. With the entry of the United States into World War II, the U.S. embarked on the road to full recovery and thereby became a powerful force on the world scene, its economy rivaling that of Britain, France, Germany, and other mature capitalist states. In fact, with the devastation of Europe during World War II and the de facto defeat of the major European states at the conclusion of the war, the United States emerged as the leading imperial state among the rival powers dominating the world economy. The growth and expansion of U.S. transnational monopolies in the postwar period thus corresponds to the rise to power and prominence of the United States on the world scene.

The Postwar Expansion of the U.S. State

The transfer of political and economic control from Britain to the United States in the British spheres of influence (Latin America, Asia, Africa, and the Middle East) in the aftermath of World War II gave the United States access to oil and other raw materials and investment outlets in manufacturing to tap sources of cheap and abundant labor. With the postwar expansion of U.S. capital on a world scale came the political expansion of the U.S. state; together they came to articulate the interests of U.S. monopoly capital throughout the world.

The turning point for the rise to world prominence of the United States is the end of World War II. While Europe was devastated and in ruins, the United States emerged as the leading center of the capitalist world, practically unaffected by the war. In fact, the collapse of the infrastructure of the major European economies by war's end worked to the advantage of U.S. capital and permitted its penetration into Western Europe through the Marshall Plan.

From 1945 to the early 1970s, U.S. capital maintained its dominance of the world economy, supported by the political and military might of the U.S. state. The expanded role of the state in overseas political/military ventures during this period led both to the projection of U.S. power on a world scale and a tremendous expansion of overseas investments by large U.S. corporations throughout the world.

The ascendancy of the United States in the world economy thus dates mainly from the end of World War II, when weakened European economies coincided with a tremendous growth and expansion of U.S. monopoly corporations on the world scene. The internationalization of production began to take root on a world scale under the auspices of U.S. transnational corporations. From this point on, therefore, we begin to see a rapid increase in the volume of U.S. direct investment abroad.

In the early part of the twentieth century, U.S. foreign direct investment amounted to less than $1 billion, reaching a mere $1.6 billion in 1908.[23] Even by 1920, the total came to less than $4 billion. But by 1950, it had climbed to $11.8 billion, by 1970 to $76 billion, by 1990 to $431 billion, and by 1998 to a record $981 billion! [24] Together with all other forms of investments, the market value of total U.S. private assets abroad reached $5.7 trillion in 1998.[25]

The massive nature of U.S. corporate expansion abroad and the billions of investment dollars tied up in distant lands during the past several decades have led the U.S. state to take a more aggressive role in foreign policy in order to protect U.S. transnational interests abroad. This has become an enormous burden on the U.S. state, greatly affecting both the U.S. economy and the working people of the United States who have come to shoulder through increasing taxation the colossal cost of maintaining a global empire whose vast military machine now encompasses the world.[26]

Parallel to this expansion, the state's growing role in domestic spending, especially military spending, has served to protect and advance the interests of U.S. corporations through the public purse. Total U.S. government spending increased from $61 billion in 1950 to $120 billion in 1960 to $287 billion in 1970 to $812 billion in 1980 to $1.8 trillion in 1990; by 1998 it had reached $2.5 trillion.[27] Much of this spending was on the military, as military contracts to private capital became the decisive factor in the postwar expansion of the U.S. economy. Military expenditures, as a percentage of all governmental budgets, rose from 6 percent in the 1930s to around 30 percent during the 1950s and 1960s, increasing from about 1 percent of the GNP to about 10 percent during this period.[28]

Together with increased government intervention in the economy, the state played a key role in facilitating political stability of the system through the regulation of national politics via the two party monopoly. The electoral arena thus became the centerpiece of party politics and the mechanism of control and domination of the state by capital in the postwar period. However, continued state expenditures in favor of capital led, by the early 1970s, to the state's budgetary crisis and exacerbated related economic problems confronting the state, such as rising public debt; together with other factors (discussed in the next chapter), this has contributed to the political crisis of the U.S. state.

Notes

1. Karl Marx, *Capital*, vol. 1 (New York: International Publishers, 1967).

2. See Perry Anderson, *Passages from Antiquity to Feudalism* (London: New Left Books, 1974).

3. Karl Marx and Frederick Engels, "Manifesto of the Communist Party," in Karl Marx and Frederick Engels, *Selected Works* (New York: International Publishers, 1972), pp. 36–37.

4. Karl Marx, *Pre-Capitalist Economic Formations* (New York: International Publishers, 1965).

5. In other parts of the world (e.g., Germany and Japan), the state took a more active role in production and industrial expansion as it came to manage major sectors of the economy directly. See Barrington Moore, Jr., *The Social Origins of Democracy and Dictatorship* (London: Penguin, 1968); and John Clapham, *The Economic Development of France and Germany* (Cambridge: Cambridge University Press, 1948).

6. V.I. Lenin, *The State and Revolution*, in V.I. Lenin, *Selected Works in One Volume* (New York: International Publishers, 1971), pp. 326–27.

7. The only exceptions were Benjamin Franklin (Pennsylvania) and Luther Martin (Maryland). Martin refused to sign the Constitution, and both Martin and Franklin campaigned against the ratification of the Constitution in their respective states.

8. Charles Beard, *An Economic Interpretation of the Constitution of the United States* (New York: Macmillan, 1962).

9. Kenneth Neill Cameron, *Humanity and Society: A World History* (New York: Monthly Review Press, 1977), p. 421.

10. Michael Parenti, *Democracy for the Few*, 6th ed. (New York: St. Martin's, 1994), p.62.

11. One of the delegates, James Madison, did not abide by the group's decision, and his notes were later published as *The Federalist Papers*, which contain revealing statements by some of the delegates during the convention. See James Madison, *The Federalist Papers*, esp. No. 10.

12. Herbert M. Morais, *The Struggle for American Freedom* (New York: International Publishers, 1944), pp. 248–49.

13. Charles Beard and Mary Beard, *The Rise of American Civilization* (New York: Macmillan, 1930), pp. 313–14.

14. Ibid., p. 332. Of course, women, who constituted half the adult population; slaves, who made up one-fourth of the population; Native Americans; and poor, propertyless whites were not allowed to vote. This, many have argued, is another testimony to the racist, sexist, elitist, and class-biased nature of the early U.S. state and the Constitution, both of which reflected the class interests of the forces that came to dominate the state after independence.

15. Morais, *The Struggle for American Freedom*, pp. 253–54.

16. Colonel Mason recommended at the Constitutional Convention that a committee be formed to draft "a Bill of Rights," but his motion was voted down unanimously.

17. Herbert Aptheker, *The American Revolution, 1763–1783* (New York: International Publishers, 1976).

18. Ibid.

19. Cameron, *Humanity and Society*, p. 421.

20. Madison, *Federalist Papers*, No. 10.

21. Albert Szymanski, *The Capitalist State and the Politics of Class* (Cambridge, Mass.: Winthrop, 1978), p. 160.

22. Richard O. Boyer and Herbert M. Morais, *Labor's Untold Story* 3rd ed. (New York: United Electrical, Radio and Machine Workers of America, 1980), pp. 105–7.

23. Cleona Lewis, *America's Stake in International Investments* (Washington, D.C.: Brookings Institution, 1938), pp. 605–6.

24. U.S. Department of Commerce, *Selected Data on U.S. Direct Investment Abroad*; U.S. Department of Commerce, *Statistical Abstract of the United States, 1999*, p. 797, *1981*, p. 833.

25. U.S. Department of Commerce, *Survey of Current Business* (July 1999); U.S. Department of Commerce, *Statistical Abstract of the United States, 1999*, p. 793; U.S. Council of Economic Advisers, *Economic Report of the President, 2000*, p. 427.

26. For an extended discussion and data on the cost of maintaining the U.S. empire and its impact on the U.S. working class, see Berch Berberoglu, *The Legacy of Empire: Economic Decline and Class Polarization in the United States* (New York: Praeger Publishers, 1992), Chap. 4–6.

27. U.S. Council of Economic Advisers, *Economic Report of the President, 2000*, p. 401.

28. U.S. Department of Commerce, *Statistical Abstract of the United States* (various issues). For detailed discussion and data on the role of military spending in the postwar expansion of the U.S. economy, see Paul Baran and Paul M. Sweezy, *Monopoly Capital* (New York: Monthly Review Press, 1966). See also Szymanski, *The Capitalist State and the Politics of Class*, Chap. 9.

CHAPTER 5

THE CRISIS OF THE ADVANCED CAPITALIST STATE

While the changes at work in the U.S. economy and society have their roots in earlier decades when the consolidation of U.S. monopoly power began to take hold on a world scale, the increased internationalization of U.S. capital under the auspices of U.S. transnational monopolies in recent decades has affected various classes and segments of U.S. society unevenly. The diverse impact of economic changes during this period on different classes and fractions of classes are precipitating causes of the unfolding political crisis of the capitalist state in the United States. In this context, the intensified internationalization of U.S. capital and the decline of the U.S. domestic economy since the early 1970s constitute the material basis of the crisis of the advanced capitalist state in the United States during the past three decades.

The Crisis of the U.S. State

The period from 1945 to the present saw an unparalleled growth of U.S. transnational capital throughout the world, but the postwar boom that reached its peak during the Vietnam war came to an abrupt end when the U.S. defeat in Southeast Asia (which brought to a halt major war contracts to U.S. corporations) plunged the economy into a severe recession by the mid 1970s. So powerful was the impact of the defeat in Vietnam that the United States has been unable to alter the situation. As a result, the decline of U.S. hegemony on the world scene has become irreversible.

Given the logic of capital accumulation on a world scale in late capitalist society, it is no accident that the decline of the U.S.

domestic economy since the early 1970s corresponds to the accelerated export of U.S. capital abroad in search of cheap labor, access to raw materials, new markets, and higher rates of profit. The resulting deindustrialization of the U.S. economy has had a serious impact on workers and other affected segments of the laboring population and has brought about a major dislocation of the domestic economy. This has necessitated further state intervention on behalf of the monopolies and has heightened the contradictions that led to the crisis of the U.S. state. The crisis of the advanced capitalist state in the United States manifests itself at different levels, ranging from international conflicts (interimperialist rivalry, disintegration of regional political and military alliances, inability to suppress national liberation struggles and revolution in the Third World) to domestic economic problems (trade and budget deficits, monetary and fiscal crisis, inflation, unemployment, recession, etc.) to national political crisis (factional struggles within the capitalist class, problems of legitimacy, repression of the working class and mass movements, militarization of the polity and society, and so on).[1]

The most critical problem facing the advanced capitalist state, however, is the crisis emanating from the restructuring of the international division of labor involving plant closings in the center states and the transfer of the production process to overseas territories, in line with the internationalization of capital.[2] The consequent deindustrialization of advanced capitalist centers, especially the United States,[3] has led to higher unemployment and underemployment, pressing down wages to minimum levels, while imperial-installed puppet regimes have intensified the repression of workers and peasants in the Third World and forced on them starvation wages in order to generate superprofits for the U.S. monopolies.

The contradictions of this process of global expansion and accumulation have brought to the fore new realities of capitalist economics, now characterized by industrial decline and decay in the center states, accompanied by renewed repression at home and abroad to control an increasingly frustrated and angry working class.

The Crisis of the U.S. Economy

A number of factors have brought about the crisis of the advanced capitalist state in the United States, all of which are based on crises afflicting the U.S. economy during the past three decades—the ending of the war in Vietnam, the oil crisis, the rise to world prominence of European and Japanese economies (i.e., interimperialist rivalry), the effects of the internationalization of U.S. capital on the U.S. economy, and problems associated with the capitalist business cycle. These, combined with the structural transformation of the U.S. economy in line with its role in the new international division of labor, brought forth in 1974-75 the most severe recession since the 1930s.[4] The gravity of the situation in the mid 1970s was such that the post-1975 recovery could not sustain itself for more than a few years, then sank the economy into another recession in 1979-80 and a much deeper one in 1982.[5] While short-term government policies since 1983 have managed to regulate symptoms of the underlying structural defects in the economy and postponed the crisis, the expected big crash in the coming period may prove to be much worse than any crash previously, for the cumulative impact of the developing capitalist crisis is destined to bring the world economy to a head, especially in its nucleus, the United States.[6]

The highly speculative nature of the stock market in the 1990s (a situation similar to that of the 1920s) points to such an outcome as a likely development in the early years of the twenty-first century. Decline in capacity utilization in manufacturing industry, record trade deficits, growing unemployment, decline in real wages and purchasing power, small business bankruptcies and farm foreclosures, bank failures, a shaky international financial system, record government deficits, as well as a highly speculative stock market, are grave symptoms of a declining national economy at a time of a decade-long bull market, record corporate profits, megamergers, and wholesale acquisitions and takeovers affecting favorably the biggest U.S. corporations.[7]

In examining the data for the period from the mid 1960s to the early 1980s, we see that capacity utilization in manufacturing fell from 89.5 percent in 1965 to 77 percent in 1971, to 72 percent in 1975, to 70 percent in 1982 — during the three consecutive recessions. The decline in durable goods production was even more pronounced as it fell from 87 percent in 1967 to 73 percent in 1971 to 70 percent in 1975 to 67 percent in 1982.[8] Similarly, there was a sharp decline in net private domestic investment during the 1975 and

1982 recessions, falling from $257 billion in 1973 to $96 billion in 1975, and from $253 billion in 1978 to $64 billion in 1982.[9] The ups and downs of the business cycle over this period show that the general trend in business activity is in a downward direction, with each peak lower than the one that preceded it and each trough deeper and worse than what came before.

This is also indicated by the data on unemployment rates: The rate was 6 percent at the height of the 1971 recession, 8.3 percent during the 1975 recession, and 9.5 percent during the 1982 recession; similarly, the rate was higher at the peak of each of the three succeeding recoveries: 4.8 percent in 1973; 5.8 percent in 1979; and 6.9 percent in 1986.[10] Black unemployment has followed an identical pattern at a much higher level; it increased from 10.4 percent in 1972 to 14.8 percent in 1975 to 19.5 percent in 1983, at the height of the three succeeding recessions; it was 9.4 percent in 1973, 12.3 percent in 1979 and 14.5 percent in 1986 during the three succeeding recoveries.[11] While in 1998 the overall unemployment rate stood at 4.5 percent, the rate for blacks was 8.9 percent (more than double the white unemployment rate of 3.9 percent).[12]

With increasing unemployment and spiraling inflation during the 1970s and early 1980s,[13] real wages of workers continued to decline, registering a drop of 7.2 percent during 1974-75 and nearly 12 percent during 1979-82, covering the last two recessions; during the two decades 1974-95 U.S. workers showed a net loss of 20 percent in their real income, although the situation has improved a bit during the second half of the 1990s, when workers were able to gain 6.3 percent in real wages (see Table 5.1). The general decline in real wages since the mid 1970s, however, has led to a decline in purchasing power and living standard for U.S. workers, such that in 1998, the purchasing power of the dollar, as measured by consumer prices in 1982-84 dollars, declined to its lowest level in 30 years (60 cents).[14]

A key factor in the decline in purchasing power and living standard for workers in the United States has been a rise in the rate of surplus value (or exploitation) and a consequent drop in labor's share over the years. Thus the rate of surplus value in U.S. manufacturing industry doubled in the period 1950 to 1984, from 150 percent in 1950 to 302 percent in 1984.[15] At the same time, labor's share drastically fell during this period, from 40 percent in 1950 to 25

Table 5.1
Inflation and Wages: Consumer Price Index and Average Weekly Earnings for Private Nonagricultural Workers, 1970-99

| | C.P.I. | | Money Wages | Real Wages | |
Year	(1982-84 = 100)	(% incr.)	(current $)	(constant 1982 $)	(% chg. /yr.)
1970	38.8	5.7	120	298	-.9
1971	40.5	4.4	127	303	1.7
1972	41.8	3.2	137	315	4.1
1973	44.4	6.2	145	315	-.0
1974	49.3	11.0	155	302	-4.2
1975	53.8	9.1	164	293	-3.0
1976	56.9	5.8	175	297	1.5
1977	60.6	6.5	189	301	1.2
1978	65.2	7.6	204	301	-.0
1979	72.6	11.3	220	292	-3.1
1980	82.4	13.5	235	275	-5.8
1981	90.9	10.3	255	271	-1.5
1982	96.5	6.2	267	267	-1.2
1983	99.6	3.2	281	273	2.0
1984	103.9	4.3	293	275	.8
1985	107.6	3.6	299	271	-1.3
1986	109.6	1.9	305	272	.3
1987	113.6	3.6	313	269	-1.0
1988	118.3	4.1	322	267	-.9
1989	124.0	4.8	334	264	-1.0
1990	130.7	5.4	345	259	-1.8
1991	136.2	4.2	354	255	-1.6
1992	140.3	3.0	364	255	-.2
1993	144.5	3.0	374	255	-.0
1994	148.2	2.6	385	257	.7
1995	152.4	2.8	394	255	-.6
1996	156.9	3.0	407	256	.3
1997	160.5	2.3	425	261	2.2
1998	163.0	1.6	442	268	2.7
1999	166.6	2.2	457	271	1.1

Source: Economic Report of the President, 2000, pp. 360, 376, 378.

Table 5.2
Corporate Profits: Financial and Nonfinancial Industries,
1970-99 (in billions of current $)

Year	Total Corporate Profits[a]	Domestic Industries[b]		
		Total	Financial	Nonfinancial
1970	74.0	66.9	15.0	52.0
1971	87.9	80.0	17.3	62.7
1972	100.7	91.2	18.8	72.4
1973	114.6	99.7	20.3	79.4
1974	108.5	91.1	19.7	71.4
1975	134.3	119.6	19.7	100.0
1976	164.5	148.0	24.2	123.8
1977	193.3	174.2	30.7	143.5
1978	221.2	198.4	37.7	160.7
1979	229.9	195.3	38.4	156.9
1980	209.3	173.8	32.3	141.5
1981	216.3	186.6	27.1	159.6
1982	188.0	155.2	25.8	129.4
1983	223.9	188.5	35.2	153.3
1984	262.0	225.1	33.8	191.3
1985	255.2	216.8	44.5	172.3
1986	250.5	210.7	55.8	154.9
1987	298.4	250.4	57.1	193.3
1988	359.8	303.1	67.9	235.2
1989	360.4	296.1	76.8	219.3
1990	388.6	315.9	91.6	224.3
1991	421.1	346.7	120.2	226.5
1992	448.8	380.1	124.8	255.2
1993	506.4	429.6	127.9	301.7
1994	561.0	483.7	114.7	369.0
1995	650.2	558.2	154.3	403.8
1996	729.4	628.6	165.3	463.3
1997	803.2	695.1	184.2	510.9
1998	802.8	702.8	191.3	511.5
1999*	826.0	721.0	202.0	519.0

Notes:
a. Includes domestic and foreign profits, with inventory valuation
adjustment and without capital consumption adjustment.
b. Domestic profits, with inventory valuation adjustment and without
capital consumption adjustment.
* Estimates based on data for the first, second, and third quarters of
1999.
Source: Economic Report of the President, 2000, p. 410.

Table 5.3
U.S. Merchandise Exports and Imports, 1970-99
(in billions of current $)

Year	Total			Manufactured Goods		
	Exports	Imports	Balance	Exports	Imports	Balance
1970	42.5	-39.9	2.6	35.1	-36.9	-1.8
1971	43.3	-45.6	-2.3	35.5	-41.9	-6.4
1972	49.4	-55.8	-6.4	39.9	-51.1	-11.2
1973	71.4	-70.5	.9	53.4	-62.1	-8.7
1974	98.3	-103.8	-5.5	75.9	-77.2	-1.3
1975	107.1	-98.2	8.9	84.8	-71.2	13.6
1976	114.7	-124.2	-9.5	91.4	- 89.7	1.7
1977	120.8	-151.9	-31.1	96.5	-106.9	-10.4
1978	142.1	-176.0	-33.9	112.2	-133.4	-21.2
1979	184.4	-212.0	-27.6	149.0	-151.6	-2.6
1980	224.3	-249.8	-25.5	182.2	-170.2	12.0
1981	237.0	-265.1	-28.1	193.0	-186.7	6.3
1982	211.2	-247.6	-36.4	173.9	-185.7	-11.8
1983	201.8	-268.9	-67.1	164.7	-213.8	-49.1
1984	219.9	-332.4	-112.5	181.5	-274.4	-92.9
1985	215.9	-338.1	-122.2	186.3	-286.7	-100.4
1986	223.3	-368.4	-145.1	196.2	-334.1	-137.9
1987	250.2	-409.8	-159.6	220.4	-366.8	-146.4
1988	320.2	-447.2	-127.0	281.4	-407.6	-126.2
1989	362.1	-477.4	-115.2	319.9	-426.5	-106.6
1990	389.3	-498.3	-109.0	349.1	-436.1	-87.0
1991	416.9	-491.0	-74.1	376.8	-439.2	-62.4
1992	440.4	-536.5	-96.1	396.3	-484.9	-88.6
1993	456.8	-589.4	-132.6	413.1	-538.0	-124.9
1994	502.4	-668.6	-166.2	455.3	-617.3	-162.0
1995	575.8	-749.6	-173.8	518.6	-693.4	-174.8
1996	612.1	-803.3	-191.2	550.6	-730.6	-180.0
1997	679.7	-876.4	-196.7	621.3	-804.6	-183.3
1998	670.2	-917.2	-247.0	617.1	-866.3	-249.2
1999*	670.0	-976.0	-306.0	610.0	-922.0	-312.0

Note: * Estimates based on data for the first and second quarters of 1999.
Source: Economic Report of the President, 2000, p. 424.

percent in 1984.[16] This, together with favorable government policies toward big business (e.g., capital gains tax cuts), has resulted in record corporate profits. Thus, we find that total *net* corporate profits increased more than eleven times in the period 1970 to 1999, from $74 billion in 1970 to $209 billion in 1980 to $389 billion in 1990 to $826 billion in 1999 (see Table 5.2). Paralleling this, profits of domestic industries likewise increased several-fold during this period, mostly accounted for by nonfinancial industries. Even taking inflation into account—it has been quite low in the 1990s— net corporate profits have surged during this period, more than doubling in real terms.[17]

To obtain a more accurate picture of the situation and be able to calculate the rate of surplus value, however, we need to look at *gross* profits, for net profits hide the amount of total value created by workers that has already been distributed to other segments of the nonlaboring population, such as, in the case of corporate executive salaries, to federal, state, and local governments in the form of taxes and to numerous other industries and commercial enterprises, such as advertising firms. All these deducted business expenses are paid for from the total amount of value created by workers. Thus, after a detailed analysis of corporate and government data through the mid 1980s, Perlo concluded that both at the aggregate level and at the level of specific corporations, "The ratio of gross profits to net income after taxes was about 5 to 1 or 6 to 1."[18] For example: "The IRS report for all corporations for 1979 shows gross profits (total receipts less cost of sales and other operations) at $1426 billion— almost one and a half *trillion* dollars—compared with net income of $279 billion before taxes and $213 billion after taxes."[19]

Turning to the economy in general, we observe that while record bankruptcies among small businesses, especially family farms, led to further centralization of the U.S. economy during the recessions of the 1970s and early 1980s, the intensified overseas expansion of U.S. transnational monopolies had a serious impact on the U.S. export-import structure, resulting in large trade deficits. This came about as a result of a continuous drop in U.S. exports due to plant closings, and a sharp increase in imports from overseas subsidiaries of U.S. transnational monopolies.[20]

As the data in Table 5.3 show, the U.S. trade deficit has greatly increased since the mid 1970s, reaching $25 billion in 1980, $109 billion in 1990, and $306 billion in 1999. While U.S. transnational expansion abroad continued with exceptional speed during the 1970s, it took on a new significance by the early 1980s, as imports into the United States of manufactured goods produced by U.S. transnational subsidiaries overseas began to affect the U.S. trade balance in a consistently negative direction beginning in 1982. Thus, as imports of manufactured goods increased from $186 billion in 1982 to $922 billion in 1999, the trade deficit for manufactured goods increased from $12 billion in 1982 to $312 billion in 1999 (see Table 5.3). Although foreign imports are partly responsible for the shift in the balance of U.S. merchandise trade in manufactured goods, increasing penetration of the Japanese and European economies by U.S. transnationals has led to the acquisition of a growing percentage of the stocks of foreign competitors in their home territories.[21] For example, General Motors has substantial control of Isuzu, Chrysler owns a large share of Mitsubishi, and Ford has a controlling interest in Mazda. There is a similar move by these and other U.S. corporations to take over some of the largest firms in South Korea, such as Samsung. This new development, coupled with the transfer of productive facilities of U.S.-based transnational monopolies to cheap labor areas overseas, not "unfair competition" by foreign companies, explains in large part the record U.S. trade deficit in recent years.[22]

Another major problem endemic to the present U.S. political economy is the budget deficit. As an extension of postwar Keynesian "remedies" to recessions and depressions brought about by the capitalist business cycle, government spending has led to an enormous growth in the national debt over the past three decades. The situation worsened during the 1980s when a huge increase in military spending combined with a large tax cut for business resulted in record annual budget deficits, vastly increasing the total government debt and the interest paid on the debt.[23] As military spending more than doubled since 1980 and more than tripled since the mid 1970s (reaching nearly $300 billion in the 1990s), the gross federal debt increased immensely, from $909 billion in 1980 to $2.9 trillion in 1989 to $5.6 trillion in 1999, while the net interest paid on the debt rose from $53 billion in 1980 to $169 billion in 1989 to $230 billion in 1999 (see Table 5.4).

Table 5.4
Military Spending, Federal Deficit, and Interest Paid on Debt,
1970- 2001 (in billions of current $)

Year	Military Spending	Gross Federal Debt	Annual Budget Deficits	Net Interest Paid
1970	81.7	380.9	-2.8	14.4
1971	78.9	408.2	-23.0	14.8
1972	79.2	435.9	-23.4	15.5
1973	76.7	466.3	-14.9	17.3
1974	79.3	483.9	-6.1	21.4
1975	86.5	541.9	-53.2	23.2
1976	89.6	629.0	-73.7	26.7
1977	97.2	706.4	-53.7	29.9
1978	104.5	776.6	-59.2	35.5
1979	116.3	829.5	-40.7	42.6
1980	134.0	909.1	-73.8	52.5
1981	157.5	994.8	-79.0	68.8
1982	185.3	1,137.3	-128.0	85.0
1983	209.9	1,371.7	-207.8	89.8
1984	227.4	1,564.7	-185.4	111.1
1985	252.7	1,817.5	-212.3	129.5
1986	273.4	2,120.6	-221.2	136.0
1987	282.0	2,346.1	-149.8	138.7
1988	290.4	2,601.3	-155.2	151.8
1989	303.6	2,868.0	-152.5	169.3
1990	299.3	3,206.6	-221.2	184.4
1991	273.3	3,598.5	-269.4	194.5
1992	298.4	4,002.1	-290.4	199.4
1993	291.1	4,351.4	-255.1	198.7
1994	281.6	4,643.7	-203.3	203.0
1995	272.1	4,921.0	-164.0	232.2
1996	265.8	5,181.9	-107.5	241.1
1997	270.5	5,369.7	-22.0	244.0
1998	268.5	5,478.7	69.2	241.2
1999	274.9	5,606.1	124.4	229.7
2000*	290.6	5,686.3	166.7	220.3
2001*	291.2	5,769.0	184.0	208.3

Note: * Estimates.

Sources: Economic Report of the President, 2000, pp. 397, 399.

This vast amount of government spending, especially on the military and the interest paid on the debt, together with an expanded consumer credit system now over $10 trillion, has thus far averted the collapse of the U.S. economy. The widening gap between the accumulated wealth of the capitalist class and the declining incomes of workers and the self-employed (within a deteriorating national economy and the state's budgetary crisis) has led to the ensuing political crisis within the state apparatus and has sharpened the class struggle.

Class Struggle in the United States

The persistent crisis of the U.S. economy in the 1970s and 1980s has had a contradictory effect on state and class politics in the United States. On the one hand, there has been a sharp turn to the right, as manifested in the rise of the New Right and right-wing religious fundamentalism, an all out assault on labor, reversals of civil rights gains, attacks on women's rights, a repressive immigration policy, renewed militarization, an increase in FBI domestic surveillance, and covert CIA operations to accompany an interventionist policy in Central America, the Middle East, and elsewhere. On the other hand, there has been a rise in the militancy of workers and other progressive forces in society in response to this assault.

As the crisis of the capitalist economy has brought the advanced capitalist state to the center stage of economic life and revealed its direct ties to the monopolies,[24] thus exacerbating the state's legitimation crisis, the struggles of the working class and the masses in general have become more political than ever and are directed not merely against capital, but against the state itself. This transformation of the workers' struggle from the economic to the political sphere will set the stage for protracted struggles in the years ahead.

While capital's answer to the growing ills of the U.S. economy has been further repression of the working class and people's movements, working people across the country have taken the initiative to struggle against capital and the state by strikes, protests, demonstrations, and other forms of defiance. These actions are clear examples of a growing class consciousness within the U.S. working class; they are taking place in the context of an intensifying worldwide capitalist crisis and in the midst of a much more politicized international labor movement, from the Philippines and South Korea to Central and South America, South Africa, the Middle East, and Western Europe.

The internationalization of U.S. capital is bound to accelerate the politicization of the U.S. working class and lead to the building of a solid foundation for international solidarity of workers on a world scale, directed against transnational capital and the advanced capitalist state in labor's long-term struggle for state power.

Notes

1. For a discussion of various aspects of the crisis at different levels, see James O'Connor, *The Fiscal Crisis of the State* (New York: St. Martin's, 1973) and idem, *Accumulation Crisis* (New York: Basil Blackwell, 1984); Ernest Mandel, *Late Capitalism* (London: New Left Books, 1975) and idem, *The Second Slump* (London: Verso, 1980); and Albert Szymanski, *The Capitalist State and the Politics of Class* (Cambridge, Mass.: Winthrop, 1978).

2. See Berch Berberoglu, *The Internationalization of Capital* (New York: Praeger, 1987).

3. Barry Bluestone and Bennett Harrison, *The Deindustrialization of America* (New York: Basic Books, 1982); and idem, *The Great U-Turn: Corporate Restructuring and the Polarizing of America* (New York: Basic Books, 1988).

4. See Mandel, *The Second Slump*; Howard Sherman, *Stagflation* (New York: Harper & Row, 1976).

5. See Jim Devine, "The Structural Crisis of U.S. Capitalism," *Southwest Economy and Society* 6, no. 1 (Fall 1982).

6. I would argue that, while the massive 508–point drop in the stock market on "Black Monday" in October 1987 was a reflection of long-term structural defects in the financial system and the economy in general, it may actually prove to be a sign of a much worse decline to come during the early years of the 21st century.

7. Harry Magdoff and Paul Sweezy, *Stagnation and the Financial Explosion* (New York: Monthly Review Press, 1987). See also Berch Berberoglu, *The Legacy of Empire: Economic Decline and Class Polarization in the United States* (New York: Praeger Publishers, 1992). In 1998 there were 9,634 mergers totaling $2.5 trillion, up from $206 billion in 1990. See U.S. Department of Commerce, *Statistical Abstract of the United States, 1999* (Washington, D.C.: Government Printing Office, 1999), p. 563.

8. Council of Economic Advisers, *Economic Report of the President, 1989*, p. 365.

9. Ibid., p. 327.

10. U.S. Department of Commerce, *Statistical Abstract of the United States, 1988*, p. 382; Council of Economic Advisers, *Economic Report of the President, 1989*, p. 352.

11. Ibid.

12. U.S. Department of Commerce, *Statistical Abstract of the United States, 1999*, p. 412.

13. During the first half of the 1970s, the rate of inflation averaged 7 percent per year; during the second half of the 1970s, it averaged 9 percent per year, reaching a high of 13.5 percent in 1980. In comparison, it was about 1 percent per year in the early 1960s and 3 percent per year in the late 1960s. U.S. Department of Commerce, *Statistical Abstract of the United States, 1987*, p. 455.

14. U.S. Department of Commerce, *Statistical Abstract of the United States, 1999*, p. 493.

15. Victor Perlo, *Super Profits and Crises: Modern U.S. Capitalism* (New York: International Publishers, 1988), p. 512.

16. Ibid.

17. Except for 1981, when the rate was 10.3 percent, and 1982, when the rate was 6.2 percent, annual increases in the inflation rate have averaged between 3 to 5 percent during the rest of the 1980s and between 2 to 3 percent during much of the 1990s (see Table 5.1).

18. Perlo, *Super Profits and Crises*, pp. 116–17. It should also be noted that actual gross profits of corporations are often understated, through such practices as intrafirm trade and transfer pricing, in order to reduce tax liabilities across national boundaries. Thus the ratio of gross profits to net profits for many of the largest U.S. transnational corporations may well be higher than can be calculated from the reported IRS statistics.

19. Perlo, *Super Profits and Crises* p. 117.

20. It is now estimated that nearly 40 percent of all imports entering the United States are goods produced by overseas subsidiaries of U.S. transnational corporations. In addition, a substantial part of the remainder are produced through subcontracting arrangements between U.S. transnationals and local firms—goods produced in accordance with U.S. corporate specifications for sale at major U.S. retail outlets, such as Sears and J.C. Penney's.

21. Bluestone and Harrison, *The Deindustrialization of America*.

22. See Berberoglu, *The Internationalization of Capital*, pp. 47–48.

23. See Magdoff and Sweezy, *Stagnation and the Financial Explosion*.

24. For a detailed discussion on the relationship of the state to capital and the mechanisms of direct and indirect domination of the state by capital, see Szymanski, *The Capitalist State and the Politics of Class*, pp. 163–273. See also Michael Parenti, *Democracy for the Few*, 6th ed. (New York: St. Martin's Press, 1994) and G. William Domhoff, *Who Rules America? Power and Politics in the Year 2000* (Mountain View, Calif.: Mayfield Publishing Company, 1998).

CHAPTER 6

THE STATE IN THE THIRD WORLD

This chapter examines the class nature of the state in the Third World on the basis of the dominant mode(s) of production and balance of class forces within both society and the state apparatus. In adopting this approach, I examine the origins and development of the state in different regions of the Third World and show the historical roots of the contemporary capitalist states that dominate social formations throughout these regions.[1]

In general, the class forces that have been active in control of the capitalist state in the Third World are the local bourgeoisie (consisting of national and comprador segments), the large landowners, and the transnational corporations and their imperial states. The bureaucratic political-military apparatuses of the peripheral capitalist states have always operated within the framework of control of the state by one or a combination of these class forces, whose class interests are implemented by the state's juridical and repressive bureaucratic machine.

In societies dominated by large landowners and the comprador bourgeoisie dependent on imperialism, the state has taken on a neocolonial character; its survival is based on its role as an appendage of the transnational monopolies and the imperial state. In these societies, the state has become increasingly repressive and authoritarian in order to crush any popular opposition to its role in promoting the interests of local and transnational ruling classes.[2] As the states in these settings have found it necessary to legitimize their increasingly unpopular rule to maintain law and order, protect private property, and prevent a revolution against the prevailing social order, they have attempted to convey a "technocratic" image

111

with a focus on capital accumulation and economic growth, combined with severe repression of labor and other popular sectors of society. Characterized by some as "corporatist" and by others as "bureaucratic authoritarian," or even "neofascist," these states have played a key role in the internationalization of capital and its predominance in much of the Third World, promoting further penetration of their economies and societies by the transnational monopolies.[3] This process of integration of neocolonial dependent states into the world economy, seeking the protection of the imperial state, has been to a large degree a reaction to a perceived threat to the survival of capitalism in the Third World—one that is becoming dangerous for both imperialism and the local bureaucratic authoritarian state.

In other formations of the periphery, popular uprisings, based on different alliances of class forces struggling against imperialism and the dependent state, have led to state capitalism or socialism. Class forces mobilized by the petty bourgeoisie and other intermediate sectors of society in state capitalist formations have seized power by rallying the people around a nationalist ideology directed against imperialism and its internal reactionary allies, the landlords and compradors.[4] Contrary to the role of its bureaucratic authoritarian counterpart, the state in state capitalist formations promotes the interests of the national and petty bourgeoisies against imperialism and the transnationals. Nevertheless, the class agenda of these anti-imperialist states yields similar results with regard to the exploitation and repression of labor, as capital accumulation, however nationalistically defined, accrues profits and wealth to local capitalists and the state while subjecting the working class to the dictates of state-directed capitalism, the central priority of which is the extraction of value from wage labor.

Going beyond the state capitalist alternative to neocolonial dependency, revolutions led by worker-peasant coalitions against imperialism and local reaction have resulted in the establishment of socialist states. Unlike neocolonial bureaucratic authoritarianism or national state capitalism, the socialist state has taken as its priority the redistribution of land, property, and income to elevate the living standard of the masses, without the exploitation of labor for private profit.[5]

These three variants of the peripheral state have developed out of the complex relations within and between societies in the Third World and between them and the imperial centers ever since the advent of colonialism and imperialism. We discuss these states in this and the next chapter, by region and type, focusing first on the origin and development of the capitalist state in different areas of the periphery.

The development of capitalism and the capitalist state in the Third World has been uneven chiefly because of variations in local precapitalist modes of production but also as a result of the nature and duration of contact with outside capitalist formations. This process took place during the period of Western colonialism and imperialism on a world scale, which began in the sixteenth century. The changes effected by this interaction yielded different results in different regions and led to alternative paths of development in Latin America, Asia, Africa, and the Middle East. This, in turn, gave way to the emergence and development of variants of the capitalist state throughout the Third World.

The State in Latin America

Prior to European expansion to the New World in the sixteenth century, the dominant mode of production in the Americas was tributary (i.e., the Asiatic mode of production) in some areas and tribal (i.e., the primitive communal mode) in others. In Mexico, much of Central America, and vast areas of South America, the Asiatic mode predominated in the Inca, Aztec, and Mayan empires. The central state, which had ultimate property rights, was the dominant force in society; peasants lived in villages and were obliged to pay tribute to the state. In North America, parts of the Caribbean, and some areas of South America, the primitive communal mode of production predominated among indigenous tribes. These societies were classless and stateless; they relied on hunting, fishing, gathering, and some early forms of horticulture for their subsistence. Lack of a substantial surplus and relative distance from aggressive empires prevented them from evolving toward a tributary mode through the emergence or imposition of a parasitic state. These formations remained intact until the arrival of the European colonizers in the early sixteenth century, which brought about major transformations in tributary and tribal societies throughout the New World.

The colonization of the Americas began at a time when Spain was in transition from feudalism to capitalism, with feudalism still dominant. Spanish expansion into the New world was characterized by plunder of the newly acquired colonies. The Spanish military leaders who conquered the Indian territories were granted the right to collect tribute or obtain labor services from the local populations. This system of labor relations throughout most of Spanish America came to be known as the *encomienda* system.[6] Essentially it meant that the conquering state (Spain) replaced the empires previously dominant over the native territories, although it upheld the tributary mode that served the feudal (and increasingly capitalist) Spanish state in its worldwide mission to secure precious metals and luxury goods for the ruling classes of Europe. During the initial stage of plunder, the colonies became an appendage of Spain without undergoing a major transformation in their mode of production or social relations.

As the Indian population declined as a result of the plunder, and Spain accelerated its acquisition of new land, it became necessary to secure Indian labor to work the land. The system of *repartimiento* (corvée labor), which allocated Indian workers to Spanish estates (*haciendas*), came to supplanted the *encomienda.* Under the new system, Indians were required to work on the *haciendas* on a rotational basis for specific periods of time. Gradually, European forms of feudal relations were introduced as Indians became permanently bound serfs on the *haciendas*. This was facilitated by the destruction of native irrigation systems, the incorporation of native land into Spanish estates, and the forced evacuation of Indians from their land.[7] The subservience of the natives to the new landowning class ushered in a period of lord-serf relations similar to those practiced in Spain. Feudal relations of production were dominant throughout much of Spanish America until the early nineteenth century.[8]

Elsewhere, in Brazil, an insufficient number of Indians necessitated the importation of slaves from Africa. Thus feudal Portugal set up slavery as the dominant mode of production in its Brazilian colony in order to facilitate the extraction of precious metals and other raw materials for sale on the world market. Slaves were used first in sugarcane fields and later in mining gold and diamonds. This continued until the late eighteenth century when slavery was abolished and the ex-slaves were turned into "semiserfs"—they still worked their masters' land but had some rights granted to them. Sharecropping developed alongside these feudal relations and, with the expansion of an export sector and later capitalist agriculture, wage labor as well.

In the Caribbean and along the Atlantic coast of North America, a similar pattern was established. Black slaves from Africa worked the sugar and cotton plantations, while the Native Americans of these areas were displaced or physically eliminated, thus transforming local social structures.[9] In these regions, the British colonialists became the dominant force.

The colonial expansion of Europe not only transformed the mode of production in the New World through the introduction of slavery and feudalism, but also facilitated the development of capitalism in Europe and led to its later spread to the colonies. With the development of European capitalism in the eighteenth century, trade with the colonies increasingly took on a capitalist character. As a result, alongside the feudal landowning class in the colonies, a class of merchants developed, tied to the world market controlled by European commercial interests. In time, some of these merchants expanded into industrial pursuits and set the basis for capitalist development. Small-scale manufacturing, based on wage labor, began to take root in the colonies and provided an outlet for capital accumulation among a section of the propertied elite. Nevertheless, the feudal landowning class and its political ally, the commercial bourgeoisie, remained the dominant economic and political forces in the colonies even after independence.

In the early nineteenth century, while the main sources of wealth in Latin America were controlled by the local propertied classes, political power was monopolized by the Spanish crown. This division of economic and political control of Latin colonies served as the principal source of conflict between the Creole[10] bourgeoisie and Spain.

The independence movement of the nineteenth century was an attempt to obtain political autonomy from Spain. From 1830 to 1880, most of the newly formed nations of Latin America underwent a series of brutal civil wars. Federalists, provincialists, nationalists (both economic and political) and manufacturers stood on one side; unitarists, Latin American free traders, exporters and importers, landowners, and British or French imperialism were on the other side.[11] These groups opposed one another in a seemingly perpetual battle that lasted for decades. In the end, the latter group emerged victorious. The victory, first a political and military one and subsequently an economic one, subjugated the industrial and internally oriented national bourgeoisie. It was the beginning of an intimate relationship between British imperialism and the externally oriented Latin American commercial bourgeoisie, which implemented policies that would promote its interests. The end result of these policies was the concentration of income in the hands of compradors tied to the world economy, dominated by British imperialism.

During the period of British imperialism, Latin American economies, especially those of Brazil and Argentina, were thoroughly penetrated by British finance capital. Such penetration manifested itself in the direct control of raw materials by British interests. The investment of foreign capital in the Latin economy consequently integrated the Latin bourgeoisie into the global system in such a way that most Latin American countries became semicolonies of the expanding British Empire.

The outbreak of major global crises during the first half of the twentieth century brought about important changes in the external relations and internal structures of the majority of Latin American countries. The disruption of world trade during World War I was to be intensified by the Great Depression of the 1930s and by World War II. The decline in foreign trade and foreign capital substantially weakened Latin America's economic ties with Britain. These changes in the structure of the world economy created economic conditions and allowed political changes in Latin America that were to begin the region's strongest nationalist policy and largest independent industrialization drive since the 1830s. The drive subsequently opened for the Latin American industrial bourgeoisie the period of import-substituting industrialization directed toward the diversification of the production structure in manufactures. International crises thus freed Latin America from outright subordination to imperial centers and accelerated its growth toward independent capitalist development. During this period, the state came under the control of the national bourgeoisie, whose interests dictated the development of a strong capitalist state.

The ascendancy of the United States in the Western hemisphere after World War II, a result of Britain's declining economic power and near defeat during the war, effected the interimperialist transfer of control over Latin America from Britain to the United States. U.S. economic expansion into Latin America accelerated during the 1950s, as the United States began to rely increasingly on strategic raw materials from abroad. The need for metals and minerals brought about a rapid expansion of U.S. investment in Latin America in subsequent decades. While extractive industries (e.g., petroleum and mining) continued throughout the 1950s and 1960s to constitute an important part of U.S. investment in Latin America, by the mid 1960s the pattern of U.S. economic penetration in the hemisphere had taken on new forms. From this point onward, U.S.-based transnational corporations began to penetrate the national industries of Latin America and to control the manufacturing sector developed by the local industrial bourgeoisie.[12] As a result, the independent industrialization process initiated by the national bourgeoisie in the more advanced countries of the region in the 1930s was gradually transformed, and their economies became an appendage of the world capitalist economy dominated by U.S. monopolies. Moving them in the direction of export-oriented satellites as they fulfilled their role in the new international division of labor, the economic changes effected by this new relationship required the introduction of political changes as well. Repressive military rule was needed to stabilize the dependent social order.[13] The "democratic" capitalist state of an earlier period—in Brazil, Argentina, Chile, Peru, and elsewhere—gave way to the authoritarian and repressive neocolonial state, followed by a transition to civilian rule orchestrated by the military. Capitalist development in Latin America in the postwar period has thus brought about a transformation in the balance of class forces and transferred state power into the hands of comprador elements tied to the transnationals and the U.S. imperial state.[14] And in the post-Cold War unipolar world of globalization, this linkage to the current center of world imperialism has been further strengthened through renewed integration of the Latin economies into the structure of the new global political economy.[15]

The State in Asia

Vast areas of Asia were colonized by Western powers until the middle of the twentieth century. British and European imperialism mercilessly plundered these regions at the height of their empires. Through their presence in the area, they effected major changes in the social and economic structures of the societies of Asia they came to dominate.

As in Latin America, feudal relations of production were introduced in Spain's Asian colony, the Philippines; the slave mode was introduced and despotic rule was reinforced in Java and other parts of colonial Indonesia by the Dutch; and capitalism made headway in British India and British-controlled parts of Southeast Asia. Although not formally colonized, China too came under the influence and control of the Western powers, as traditional forms of exploitation were reinforced through the link to Europe and other centers of Western imperialism.

Before the arrival of colonial and imperial powers, many Asian societies evolved within the framework of an Oriental despotic system where the Asiatic mode of production was dominant. With the expansion of Europe to remote corners of Asia, these societies came into contact with and were transformed by different colonizers. Thus the results were different in British colonies from those in colonies held by Spain, Holland, France, or other colonial powers. While today the remnants of semifeudal relations are the product of an earlier phase of colonial transformation, capitalism and capitalist relations were introduced in later periods of imperial expansion.

Before the arrival of the British in India, the dominant mode of production there was the Asiatic mode. Unlike European feudalism, land in India did not belong to any private landlord; the state was the supreme owner of the soil. The central authority, the king, delegated to some persons the right of *zamin*, or the right to collect revenues for the state. The *zamindars* were intermediaries between the communal villages and the state, and had no rights over the land. In return for their function as tax collectors, the *zamindars* were given a share of the taxes they collected. The absence of proprietary rights in land thus hindered the accumulation of wealth and the development of social classes on the basis of ownership of the means of production.[16] From the late sixteenth century onward, however, the *zamindars* had the right to sell their *zamindari* with the approval of the state, but were unable to acquire proprietary rights over the land.[17] Such prescriptions for the mode of surplus extraction made the nobility in pre-British India a class dependent on the state.[18]

Britain assumed political sovereignty in India late in the eighteenth century, and the *zamindars* emerged as an independent class with full rights in the ownership of land. In some parts of India, such as Bengal, the British decreed that the *zamindars* were to be considered landlords, thus creating a class of large landowners with inheritable ownership rights in the land. Elsewhere in India (e.g., in the south), the British considered the peasants to have ownership rights in the land and collected taxes from them directly. As a result, this section of the country saw the development of the small landholding. During the course of the nineteenth century, market forces led to an increasing concentration of wealth and gave rise to a large landowning class on the one hand, and renters, sharecroppers, rural laborers, or urban proletarians on the other. British entry into India accelerated the activities of merchants as well; they were to become the intermediaries through whom the British would control the local economy. Engaged in import-export trade and incorporated into the world capitalist system, these merchants became the equivalent of the comprador bourgeoisie. Through both the landlords and the compradors, who together constituted the local upper classes (tied to a weakened central state), the British were able to preserve the existing order and protect and advance their interests.[19]

Thus, while the domination of a class of landlords in the countryside ensured the development of feudal or semifeudal relations of production in agriculture in some parts of the country (and the emergence of capitalist relations through wage labor in other parts), the growth of merchants' capital led to the development of an urban commercial economy tied to Britain through international trade.[20] As trade with Britain increased, and the demand for Indian goods grew, local capital expanded into crafts, textiles, and industrial production. This gave rise to a renewed expansion of local manufacturing industry and with it the development of a national industrial bourgeoisie that came to be seen as a competitor of British imperialism. This prompted Britain to take steps to crush Indian industry and turn India into an appendage of Britain's colonial economy.[21] Antagonism between the British and local industrial capital led to the national bourgeois alliance with the peasantry to throw off the British yoke through the independence movement.[22] Much as in North America, but unlike the situation in Latin America, the national bourgeois forces were able to consolidate power and capture the leadership of the movement in a victory over the British. By the late 1940s, they installed a state committed to the development of local capitalism in India following independence. Given the relatively weak position of the national bourgeoisie, the victorious national forces were able to utilize the powers of the state and establish a state capitalist regime to assist the accumulation of capital by the Indian bourgeoisie.[23]

In the period following independence in 1947, the state played an important role in accelerating the development of capitalism in India. Industrial production grew at a rapid rate, as did total productive capital in large-scale industries. The most significant growth took place in capital goods industries. This growth in the first two decades following independence led to a steady increase in the share of industry in the gross domestic product (GDP). The development of private industry in the postindependence period, together with the expansion of state enterprises since the 1950s, accelerated the development of capitalism and the capitalist state, thus securing the domination of capitalism and capitalist relations of production. This process in turn gave rise to a large working class. The number of wage earners in India doubled between 1951 and 1971—reaching more than 23 million—and grew further during the 1970s and 1980s, to a total of 28 million in 1996.[24]

With the growth of the working class, conflict between labor and capital intensified. The capitalist assault on workers' wages and democratic rights met stiff resistance from organized labor and the trade union movement and led to the radicalization of large segments of the working class, whose demands became increasingly political. Threatened with these developments and fearful of a general social explosion based on a revolutionary alliance of workers and peasants, the bourgeois state became more repressive; it also opened its doors to transnational monopolies, thus seeking refuge in imperialism.

Over the years, the United States gradually replaced British control over India and emerged as a powerful force with the promotion of the "Green Revolution" in the 1960s. Thus, while the British share in total foreign investment in the private sector was roughly 80 percent in 1948, it fell to 48 percent by the mid 1960s; in contrast, the U.S. share in total private foreign investment increased from 4 percent in 1949 to 25 percent by the mid 1960s.[25] This trend continued during the 1970s and 1980s, and accelerated during the 1990s. Today, at the turn of the 21st century, U.S. transnationals, along with the Indian bourgeoisie, have a dominant position and control the "commanding heights" of the Indian economy.

A move from a state capitalist to a noncolonial comprador capitalist path tied to foreign capital is the typical outcome of a state capitalist formation developing within the parameters of the world capitalist system. India, as with many other state capitalist regimes in the Third World, has not been able to escape from this general rule of capitalist development in the age of imperialism. Its development within the context of the world economy has resulted in massive economic dislocations and crises over the past two decades and has led to further consolidation of the reactionary forces' grip over the state in more fully integrating India into the world capitalist system. This, in turn, has galvanized popular opposition forces in their struggle against the capitalist state and has given new impetus to their efforts to transform Indian society.

China's experience in state formation has been somewhat different than that of India. Until the nineteenth century, China was ruled by a series of despotic states under successive dynasties, but the imperial state was relatively weak and depended on private landlords who owned vast tracts of land.[26] The widespread presence of private property in the means of production in Imperial China meant that it was not dominated by the Asiatic mode of production (it is precisely the *absence* of private property that defines this mode). But the private landlords did not have such control of the state that they could turn it into an instrument of feudal rule; a fairly strong state bureaucracy maintained relative autonomy from the landlord class and exercised its rule over society as a whole. Thus it would be erroneous to characterize Chinese society at this time as feudal. During the imperial epoch, China possessed a despotic state, within the boundaries of which existed a landed nobility, a merchant class, petty commodity producers (consisting of peasants and artisans), and hired laborers. The economic strength of an already developed landed gentry, by way of its access to and control over a significant portion of the means of production, compelled the state to share power with the landlords over the peasants and landless laborers from whom they extracted a share of the surplus in the form of taxes, produce, and/or rent. Within this framework of domination under a semi-Asiatic/semifeudal mode, a merchant class tied to overseas trade flourished. The capital accumulated from trade was gradually invested in crafts and manufacturing production and, together with a merger with expanding artisan elements in basic home industries, led to the development of a national bourgeoisie. At the same time, some peasants were able to improve their lot and accumulate sufficient wealth to constitute a rich peasant class (similar to *kulaks*). Others lost their land to large landowners, ending up either working for them as rural laborers or migrating to the cities and becoming wage workers. These parallel developments in city and countryside strengthened the development of feudalism and capitalism through-out China and laid the basis for the transformation of Chinese society following the disintegration of the central state. With the landlords allied with commercial interests in firm control of the state, China entered a period of feudal rule and later evolved toward capitalism.

By the end of the eighteenth and beginning of the nineteenth centuries, Western powers had begun to intervene in China and attempted to incorporate it into the world capitalist orbit.[27] A protracted struggle against Western imperialism followed, and ushered in a period of intense nationalism that paved the way for the national bourgeois forces that captured state power by the early twentieth century. Remaining within the world capitalist system and unable to suppress internal reaction, the nationalist government of Sun Yat-Sen was considerably weakened. Taking advantage of the situation, the reactionary anticommunist forces within the Kuomintang, under the leadership of Chiang Kai-shek, captured power and imposed an iron rule over China that led to a long and bloody civil war during which thousands of communists and revolutionaries were executed. The betrayal of the national-democratic, anti-imperialist revolution by the rightists in the Kuomintang, who embraced imperialism to crush the growing working-class and communist movements, led to the reemergence of an independent communist movement based on a worker-peasant alliance under the leadership of the Chinese Communist Party (CCP) headed by Mao Zedong. After a long struggle against Japanese and U.S. imperialism, and internal reaction and the mobilization of millions of workers and peasants during the 1930s and 1940s, the Chinese masses triumphed in a communist-led revolution in 1949 that brought to an end feudalist-capitalist exploitation and imperialist plunder and launched a new, people's democracy through the institution of a socialist state. Thus was born the People's Republic of China. (The development of socialism and the socialist state in China following the 1949 revolution is discussed in the next chapter.)

Elsewhere in East and Southeast Asia, a number of states emerged as appendages of the world capitalist system following World War II. Evolving as neocolonies of the expanding U.S. empire in the postwar period, these states came to serve the economic and strategic interests of U.S. monopolies and the state in providing cheap labor, raw materials, new markets, new investment outlets, and a military foothold throughout the area to protect transnational interests and encircle and contain socialist states in the region. South Korea, Taiwan, the Philippines, Indonesia, Thailand, Malaysia, Hong Kong, Singapore, Cambodia, and South Vietnam (until 1975) served one or more of the above functions and provided the material base for U.S. transnational expansion in the area after the fall of Japan. By the early 1950s, South Korea, Taiwan, and the Philippines, together with defeated Japan, came under the U.S. military umbrella in the Pacific Basin and provided a foundation for the expansion of U.S. transnational corporations in these countries. A similar stance was taken toward South Vietnam, Cambodia, Laos, and Thailand in the aftermath of the British and French defeat in the region, which brought the United States into the conflict there during the late 1950s and early 1960s. The U.S. military escalation in Southeast Asia expanded the conflict into one of the biggest wars in the region's recent history—one that lasted over three decades. By the mid 1970s, U.S. efforts at domination over the region collapsed, as the Indochinese drove the U.S. forces out of their territories. With Vietnam, Cambodia, and Laos out of the U.S. grip, Thailand, Indonesia, and especially the Philippines took on the role of regional policemen to protect U.S. interests in southeast Asia and provide security for regional operations of U.S. transnationals. Thus, while U.S. military presence in or economic aid to these countries turned them into de facto neocolonial states, their subsequent economic integration into the world capitalist system transformed their social and economic structures to suit the needs of U.S. and other transnational monopolies. They advanced along the capitalist path—with high growth rates and profits for foreign and local capitalists on the one hand, and the exploitation of workers and peasants on the other.[28]

With the expansion of U.S. capital in East and Southeast Asia in the 1960s and 1970s, these regions became more fully integrated into the world economy. Through such investments, and other economic arrangements, these states were to fulfill their special role in the international division of labor controlled by the United States.[29] This prompted a rapid expansion of capitalism in these countries through increased foreign investment and subcontracting with local firms to fill transnational orders destined for markets in advanced capitalist countries.[30]

But this transnational-directed industrialization process exacerbated larger social and economic problems confronting these countries while creating employment at very low wages, maintaining control over the technology transferred to the recipient country, and draining the profits made from the sale of exported goods. Additionally, it resulted in (1) the destruction of an integrated national economy and the installation of enclave export zones controlled by transnational firms; (2) the bankruptcy of small and medium-size businesses and the monopolization of the local economy by foreign capital; (3) income inequalities based on an internal market dependent on no more than 5 percent of the population; (4) low wages leading to a decline in the standard of living of the majority of the population with its it attendant consequences on diet, housing, health care, education, and other needs; (5) rising unemployment, poverty, malnutrition, and related ills; (6) social and political repression through the installation of brutal (often military) dictatorships that violated basic human rights. These effects of export-oriented industrialization in states under the grip of foreign capital are the outcome of a system of relations imposed on the working people by imperialism, which is based on the exploitation of the working class and the peasantry.[31] The social significance of international capitalist expansion in these regions lies in the transformation of local relations of production in a capitalist direction and the consolidation of a capitalist state that is subservient to imperialism, with all its inherent class contradictions.

The increase in number of workers in the manufacturing sector and, more broadly, in all major branches of industry, accompanied by below-subsistence wages and antilabor legislation enacted by repressive neocolonial states, have led to the intensification of the class struggle in these countries, with some of them (e.g., South Korea, the Philippines, and Indonesia) reaching a near-revolutionary stage, as the masses challenge the rule of the neocolonial capitalist state.

The State in Africa

Prior to European intervention, Africa had a diverse social structure based on various modes of production in different regions of the continent. The primitive communal mode was dominant in some areas, and the Asiatic and feudal modes were paramount in others. Although slavery was practiced in various parts of the continent before the European-initiated slave trade, it never became a dominant mode of production in precolonial Africa. Primitive communal relations of production were prevalent in central and parts of southern Africa, while the Asiatic mode dominated much of North Africa until the end of the nineteenth century. Feudalism in various forms was practiced in parts of East and West Africa.[32]

Despite the prevalence of these diverse modes in various parts of the continent, precolonial Africa consisted in large part of self-sufficient village communities engaged in subsistence agriculture. Where feudalism or a despotic state existed, villagers provided a surplus to the ruling classes in the form of tribute or a part of their produce. With the widespread introduction of the slave trade by European imperialism, greater stratification was induced in the continent, and many newly created tribal chiefs were corrupted by European conquerors and turned into tyrants serving the interests of Western imperialism. The artificial creation of "district chiefs" in the French colonies and of "headmen" in the English colonies was done for this purpose.[33] After the sixteenth century, when the world economy facilitated the spread of the slave trade in Africa, slaves become Africa's major export. They were bought and sold to masters in various parts of the world, especially in the Americas.

The slave trade inhibited indigenous capital accumulation and thus the development of local capitalism, as it deprived Africa of able-bodied workers, undermined local artisan production because of the cheap European goods received for the slaves, and reinforced slavery as a mode of production. The economic development that did take place during this period was highly dependent on the European colonial economy tied to the slave trade.[34] With the end of the slave trade in the first half of the nineteenth century, African economies shifted to commercial export crops. Commodities such as cocoa, peanuts, palm oil, coffee, and rubber became the principle exports. As a result, the previously dominant ruling classes, whose wealth and power were based on the slave trade, transformed themselves into planters who imposed semifeudal production relations on their ex-slaves, who now labored on vast plantations in serflike conditions. The wealth and power of the local ruling class declined during the course of the nineteenth century as European colonialism gained a more direct foothold in the continent and became involved in production and trade throughout the area. By the end of the nineteenth century, the European powers had moved in with full force against local states and chiefdoms and set up colonial regimes. Labor migration became the main mechanism to secure a labor force in the mining sector, as well as in commercial crop production. Africans engaged in subsistence production on communal lands were manipulated into providing labor to the Europeans, who introduced taxes payable in money. In this way they were able to force Africans to work in European-owned enterprises to secure the means to pay their taxes. At the same time, labor services (corvée) were introduced, although they could often be avoided in exchange for a cash payment. To avoid corvée, one had to prove gainful employment. Either way, the European colonialists were the only ones to gain from these practices.

In time, the notion of private property was introduced, which undermined traditional subsistence agriculture and led to increased demands for commercial goods. This provided sufficient incentive to get Africans to sell their labor power for a wage. Over time, the African economies became increasingly commercial, wage labor became more prevalent, raw material exports grew, and the demand for European industrial imports increased. As a result, Africa evolved along the capitalist path tied to the European-dominated world economy, which at the end of the nineteenth and beginning of the twentieth centuries had transformed Africa by introducing capitalist relations of production into the continent through colonial rule.

The different forms of exploitation and the different class structures that developed during the colonial era in Latin America, Asia, and Africa can thus be explained in terms of the different modes of production prevailing in Europe and in the colonies, as well as the interaction between the two at different points in history. In this sense, the precapitalist imperialism of Spain in Latin America and elsewhere produced a legacy of feudalism that lingers today, while the capitalist imperialism of a more developed industrial Europe in transition to monopoly capital at a later period produced a qualitatively different result in Africa, as well as in parts of Asia, where capitalist relations of production began to take root.[35]

Until the middle of the twentieth century, when most African countries won their formal independence, the local economies were a direct appendage of the colonial center, which directed development in the colonies. The pattern was based on the logic of the capitalist mode of production that dominated the economies of the center states and evolved according to its needs of accumulation, resulting in uneven development between the imperial center and the colonies, and within the colonies. In general, most African colonies specialized in one or a few raw materials for export and depended on the importation of finished manufactured goods from the imperial center.

This classic colonial relationship prevailed in a number of African countries after the granting of formal independence, and led to the restructuring of social-economic relations on a neocolonial basis—that is, the continuation of colonial relations through the intermediary of a local ruling class dependent on and nourished by imperialism. This has been the case in various parts of the continent, from Kenya in the east to Nigeria and the Ivory Coast in the west, to Zaire, Uganda, and other countries elsewhere in Africa.[36] As in the colonial period, the main characteristic of these neocolonial states is their heavy reliance on the export of raw materials to the advanced capitalist countries and the importation of finished manufactured goods from them — a condition that has become an impediment to industrialization and held back the development of the industrial sector in these countries.[37]

Within this broader framework of the neocolonial structure, there has nevertheless occurred a parallel development of transnational corporate expansion into the manufacturing sector of some of these countries in order to utilize cheap labor in a variety of manufacturing and industrial undertakings. This has contributed to the growth of the industrial sector and effected changes in the sectoral distribution of the gross domestic product (GDP) in favor of industry. As a result, the share of industry relative to agriculture has increased over time. This is most evident in western and northern Africa, notably in Nigeria, Liberia, Ivory Coast, Tunisia, and Egypt.

Despite the fact that the pace of industrialization in these countries is considerably slower than in Latin America and East and Southeast Asia, the move in the direction of investments in industry has brought about a significant change in the economic and labor force structure of these countries and placed them on the road to further capitalist development within the bounds of the world economy. Thus, while neocolonial African states continue to remain primarily agricultural or raw-material-exporting countries, the relative growth of manufacturing and other industry vis-à-vis agriculture indicates an overall trend toward industrialization within a neocolonial framework tied to imperialism.[38]

In other neocolonial countries, such as the Sudan, Uganda, and Zaire, semifeudal relations based on raw material production continue with little progress on the industrial front. This shows the dual nature of imperialist penetration in different regions and countries of the continent where traditional colonial relations are reinforced in some areas, while comprador-capitalist neocolonial relations are developed and strengthened in others.

Elsewhere in Africa, nationalist forces have taken the initiative to lead the newly independent states along a less dependent path. Utilizing the military and state bureaucracy as supportive institutions to carry out their development programs, the petty-bourgeois leaders in these countries have opted for a state capitalist path that has corresponded well with their class vision of society and social-economic development. Nasser in Egypt, Boumedienne in Algeria, Kaunda in Zambia, and Nyerere in Tanzania could be cited as prime examples of petty-bourgeois nationalist leaders in charge of postcolonial states developing along the state-capitalist path. Unlike neocolonial dependent states, such as Zaire under Mobutu, Ethiopia under Haile Selassie, or Morocco under Hassan II, the national state capitalist formations of Africa became the leading progressive force on the continent in the first decades of the postcolonial period. On the economic front, these regimes made significant progress in industrialization, as the share of industry in the GDP of these countries reached impressive levels relative to agriculture and other sectors of the economy. This was reflected in the labor force structure as well, with a general trend of decline in the proportion of the labor force in agriculture and steady increase in the labor force in industry.

To focus on some countries more closely, Algeria and Tanzania represent the clearest examples of state capitalist regimes in Africa in recent decades. Following its independence from France in the late 1950s, Algeria became a leading exponent of national liberation throughout the continent and helped accelerate the decolonization process in the early 1960s. The war of national liberation in Algeria brought the masses to the forefront of the struggle for independence. Following independence, the state played an active role in the establishment of cooperatives, state-owned enterprises, and public works projects.[39] But because state power remained in the hands of petty-bourgeois technocrats and intellectuals without a base in the working class, imperialist pressures from the outside eventually derailed the state-directed nationalist project and led to the gradual adoption of neocolonial policies in conformity with the world economy. The limited internal social transformations initiated earlier were eroded within a decade in order to meet international commercial and financial obligations resulting from ties with imperialism.

This was also true in Tanzania. Tanzania won its independence by the withdrawal of Britain from the region through negotiations. As the pre-colonial bureaucratic structure was kept intact, it was easier for the imperial center to exercise control over the economy and society through indirect means. Thus while the newly created state agencies provided the basis for a state capitalist economy, the pragmatic outlook of an otherwise progressive petty-bourgeois leadership functioning within the parameters of the world economy led Tanzania, too, in a neocolonial direction.[40]

The experience of other countries on the state capitalist path (e.g., Ghana, Zambia, and Somalia) has shown similar results: Independent capitalist development through state aid, under the leadership of a petty-bourgeois technocratic elite, cannot succeed as long as it remains firmly within the boundaries of the world capitalist system.

On the other hand, in countries in which workers and peasants have played an active role in the struggle for liberation against colonialism and imperialism (such as in Angola, Mozambique, and Zimbabwe), strides have been made toward genuine economic and political independence, accompanied by deep social transformations. With political power in the hands of workers, peasants, and intellectuals committed to advancing the interests of the masses, these countries have progressed in all facets of social-economic life, despite the enormous international (imperialist) and regional South African (colonial/racist) encroachments into their territories.

Historically, the presence of a racist apartheid regime in South Africa has been a great impediment to the development of revolutionary forces in the southern cone of Africa and has had a major impact on the scope and pace of development on the continent in a progressive direction. With the abolition of the apartheid regime in South Africa in the 1990s, however, the last vestiges of racist colonial and neocolonial oppression has been removed, so that an open political struggle could be waged by the masses to take control of their destiny and build a new society free of oppression and exploitation that they have suffered for so long.

The State in the Middle East

Until the beginning of the twentieth century, the Ottoman Empire was the major political force in the Middle East. For seven centuries, the predominant mode of production in the Ottoman formation had been the Asiatic mode. Although it came in contact with many different modes of production and exchange, the Ottoman formation retained its powerful despotic state.

Interaction between Ottoman and Byzantine society developed after the invasion of Constantinople by Ottoman forces in 1453. This, along with other European formations following the Ottoman expansion into Europe in the fifteenth and sixteenth centuries, plus the state's land-allocation system (*timar*),[41] eventually led to feudal forms in Ottoman agriculture (*iltizam*, or tax farming) where, over time, large-scale private property in land (*çiftlik*) acquired increasing importance, transferring a higher proportion of the land to a few owners.[42] This transformation of the agrarian structure took place during the seventeenth and eighteenth centuries; as a result, a landed gentry (*ayan*) developed, displacing the *sipahis* as intermediaries between the state and producers. By the end of the eighteenth and beginning of the nineteenth centuries, the *ayan* was a fully developed feudal landowning class that began to challenge the authority of the central state by equipping its own armies. But the *ayan* never became powerful enough to overthrow the central state.[43]

While the position of landlords was strengthened as a result of the introduction of tax farming initiated by the state, interaction with Europe also facilitated the expansion of European commercial capital into the empire, leading to the development of a comprador class tied to European imperialism. Nevertheless, the development of feudalism in agriculture and, later, capitalism in commerce and industry, took place within the confines of a society dominated by the Asiatic state, which permitted the coexistence of these diverse modes.

The collapse of the Ottoman Empire came gradually. After centuries of expansion and conquest, the Ottoman state began to lose ground to rival forces in Europe during the eighteenth and nineteenth centuries and became vulnerable to pressures from the West. European powers, taking advantage of the endless wars in the empire's various provinces, found their way in through direct economic controls and military occupation of large parts of Ottoman territory at the end of the nineteenth and beginning of the twentieth centuries, which culminated in the occupation of virtually every corner of the empire during World War I. Following the collapse of the empire at the end of the war, Britain, France, Italy, Greece, and other European countries colonized its territories and remained in control of its various provinces for several decades. From Persian Gulf to Palestine, to the Suez Canal, down to the Arabian peninsula, and across

North Africa came under the jurisdiction primarily of Britain and France, who divided up these territories to secure trade routes, raw materials, and new markets for the expanding European-controlled world economy.

In time, local populations resented foreign domination and attempted to oust the Europeans from their lands. After long struggles for national liberation, some colonized regions of the empire gained political independence and set up a series of nation-states. Turkey, Egypt, Syria, Lebanon, Iraq, and Algeria are examples of these struggles.

The independence movement in Turkey and the origins of the modern Turkish state go back to the Young Turk Revolution of 1908. The Committee of Union and Progress, which led the 1908 revolution, was mainly composed of Turkish intellectuals greatly influenced by European nationalist thought.[44] Their ideology brought them in line with their main allies, the *esnaf* (artisans) and *tüccar* (merchants) of the towns—the class out of which they sought to forge a Turkish bourgeoisie.[45] In this context, and after massive territorial losses following the two Balkan wars (1912-13) and the failure of the ruling Young Turk government to safeguard Turkey from imperialist occupation forces during World War I, the stage was set for Mustafa Kemal and the Kemalists to assume the leadership of the liberation forces and secure a nationalist victory. With the coming to power of the bourgeois nationalist forces, Turkey embarked on a path of national capitalist development under the guidance and control of the state and a military-civilian bureaucracy.

The state's role in the economy expanded into local industry in the 1920s to develop the infrastructure, establish banks, and regulate commerce. Among the most notable activities of the state were the development and expansion of state-owned and controlled enterprises and the establishment of several major industrial and commercial banks. In addition, the state acquired full ownership and control of major sectors of the economy, including raw materials and petroleum, railways, major seaport facilities, and a number of enterprises in mining and extractive industries.

Parallel to these developments, important steps were taken by the state to accelerate capital accumulation in the countryside.

Among them were the abolition of the *ösür* (tithe tax) in 1925 and the distribution of land to landless peasants in 1927 and 1929.

The industrialization drive of the 1930s, coupled with increased agricultural production during the same period, had a significant impact on national trade. In 1930, Turkey began to register a trade surplus, which continued throughout the decade and into the 1940s.

While the state-induced capitalist development of the 1930s significantly improved Turkey's overall economic position and placed the country on a favorable footing with respect to industrialization, it sharpened the contradictions inherent in the system. The accumulation of capital under the state capitalist regime in Turkey during the 1930s and early 1940s was mainly achieved through an intensified exploitation of wage labor in public private industries. In this sense, the contradiction between state or private capital and wage labor constituted the primary contradiction in Turkey. At the same time, other internal and external problems contributed to increased conflict between the state and various classes within the country: between the state and the landlords on the question of land reform; between the state and the comprador bourgeoisie on trade and industrial policy; between the landlords and the peasantry on feudal-like bondage and exploitation, and the uneven distribution of land; between the state and national bourgeoisie and wage labor on the exploitation of labor through the appropriation of surplus value; and between the state and foreign capital on imperialist control of the economy and society.[46] All these contradictions played major roles in shaping the direction of the state capitalist regime in Turkey, but the most decisive proved to be that between the state and the landlords and compradors allied with imperialism.

The landlords blocked attempts to redistribute land to smallholders and landless peasants, attempted to prevent the development of cooperatives, manipulated programs intended to serve peasants by diverting public funds for local development projects into their private accounts, and resisted capitalist development to preserve their oligarchic position in the countryside over the impoverished peasantry. The Turkish compradors resisted all attempts by the state to transform them into industrial capitalists. Accustomed to their position as middlemen between landlords and foreign capital in import-export trade and other commercial ventures, they viewed the policies of the state as a threat to their cozy relationships and boycotted all efforts at independent national capitalist industrialization initiated by the state.[47]

This "natural" alliance of compradors and large landowners coincided with the interests of U.S. imperialism in the region. Taking advantage of the opening provided by the postwar crisis of state capitalism in the latter half of the 1940s, they moved in to prop up the landlord-comprador forces and help bring them to state power.

The late 1940s marked a new stage in Turkey's political economy. This period witnessed the final and decisive phase of the struggle between the Kemalist state and the landlord-comprador interests. With increased financial and political support from the United States, they formed a new political party (Demokrat Parti, DP) and captured state power in 1950. The coming to power of the DP placed the feudalist-comprador forces in control of the state and secured the U.S. hold on Turkey. This marked the beginning of the era of Turkish dependence and satellization under the aegis of U.S. imperialism and its reactionary internal class allies.

The DP rule during the 1950s brought a full-scale transformation of the regime into a neocolonial state dependent on imperialism. Discontent felt by the masses against DP actions in domestic and foreign policy led to protests and uprisings at the end of the 1950s that were brutally suppressed by the Menderes regime, leading to the military coup of May 1960. Superficial reforms to calm an angry populace did not stop the masses from pressing forward with more radical demands during the 1960s, resulting in more repression and a turn toward fascism through the military police intervention of March 1971 and again in September 1980. During this period, tens of thousands of workers, trade unionists, students, progressive intellectuals, lawyers, and journalists were put in prisons and concentration camps of the military regime, many of them dying of torture and executions.

With the rise of religious fundamentalism in the Middle East following the Islamic Revolution in Iran in 1979, Turkey was governed in the 1980s and 1990s by a series of conservative, right-wing governments that were openly welcomed by both the Turkish military and the United States in an effort to thwart the leftist opposition and prevent a popular uprising. The right-wing reign of terror, under the cover of promoting Islamic values, moved Turkey in a fascist direction when all popular opposition to its rule was crushed, including the Kurdish movement for autonomy and national self-determination.[48]

Thus, by the late 1990s, Turkey had turned into a hotbed of fascists and Islamic reactionaries who had succeeded in tearing down the fabric of Turkish society and eliminated even the appearance of a pseudo-democratic neocolonial capitalist order. This was, of course, too much even for the military to accept, which had earlier brought these forces to power to crush the progressive working class movement. Thus, a series of changes in government by century's end brought the military to center stage to play its role as power broker to maintain the facade of a Western-style bourgeois-democratic regime to continue along its neocolonial path acceptable to both the United States and the European Union to which Turkey has been trying to join for more than quarter of a century.

As we enter the new millennium, the prospects for progress and change in Turkey remains uncertain. The extent to which the working class and the left forces will once again become active and challenge the prevailing neocolonial order remains to be seen. But a combination of an economic collapse (effected by a serious economic downturn in the West) and renewed labor activism, together with continued ethnic (Kurdish) resistance that frustrates the state and the military in the early years of the 21st century, could trigger another round of fascist repression through a military coup, or it may indeed lead to its opposite that ignites the sparks of a developing revolutionary situation that may erupt to topple the state and transform the prevailing social order.

Elsewhere in the Middle East, in the various provinces of the Ottoman Empire, the state played an important role in directing the course of events in relation to the Ottoman central state. In Egypt, a distant and semiautonomous province of the empire, the governor maintained his title as long as the province met its tributary obligations to the Ottoman central state. This relationship continued until 1893 when Governor Mehmet Ali Pasa and his provincial army rebelled and marched on Kutahya, defeating the imperial army not far from the Ottoman capital, Istanbul. One of the strongest *ayans* of the time, Mehmet Ali attempted to free Egypt from ties to the Ottoman state and acquire direct control over the region. But

Mehmet Ali's forces were soon driven back by Britain and France, which intervened on behalf of the Ottoman throne.

After the collapse of the Ottoman Empire at the end of World War I, Britain occupied Egypt, as it did other parts of the empire, and remained in the Middle East through the first half of the twentieth century. It was during this period that Britain, France, and lesser imperial powers set up a series of colonial states—Egypt, Jordan, Iraq, Syria, Lebanon, Palestine (later Israel), Kuwait, Saudi Arabia, Libya, Tunisia, Algeria, Morocco, Cyprus—and a chain of dependencies in the Gulf region. Local rulers stayed on as figureheads, but the occupied territories served the economic and strategic interests of the imperialist forces by securing access to oil and other raw materials; a passage to India, China, and the rest of the Far East; and military domination of a region joining three continents. Egypt played an important role in this regard by allowing imperialism to use the Suez Canal, linking the Mediterranean with the Indian Ocean.

As in Turkey, however, nationalist sentiment ran deep in Egypt. The Egyptian intelligentsia, youth, and junior army officers resented the foreign occupation and the dictates of European powers over the social, economic, and political life of the nation. Supported by a series of revolts of poor peasants and agricultural workers, and by industrial strikes in Shubra El Khaima, Kafr El Dawwar, and Elmahalla Elkubra in the late 1940s and early 1950s, the petty-bourgeois nationalist forces within the army led a coup in 1952, under the leadership of Gamal Abdel Nasser, and overthrew the monarchy.

Nasser's victory ushered in a period of anti-imperialism and state centered capitalist development.[49] As in Turkey, the Nasser regime rallied the support of broad segments of the propertyless masses and used the state as an instrument of national development under petty-bourgeois technocratic bureaucratic rule. Although a desire to elevate the masses to a higher standard of living led them to improve education, work conditions, health care, and other social programs, as well as to improve the national economy, the petty-bourgeois perspective of the officers prevented them from having a clear understanding of Egyptian society and its class divisions. Without a class analysis of the prevailing social structure, the new rulers ended up supporting and enhancing capitalist relations of production in a new state-sanctioned setting.[50] Thus, along with the nationalization of foreign firms and the development of cooperatives, state-owned banks, production facilities, credit, and social projects, this period witnessed the expansion of private capital through state aid.

In time, this led to conflict between the public and private sectors, and by the mid 1960s the state capitalist economy entered a period of crisis. The private capitalist sector challenged the economics of Nasserism from which it had itself emerged in an earlier period.[51] The gradual integration of Egypt into the world capitalist economy during the 1960s also contributed to this development and paved the way for the disintegration of state capitalism and the emergence of Anwar Sadat and a new capitalist class allied with the largest interests in the private sector, as a ruling coalition of class forces dependent on imperialism.[52]

The transition to a neocolonial capitalist economy further enhanced the penetration of foreign capital into Egypt during the 1970s and 1980s and reversed the trends set in motion in the two previous decades. With the shift in the balance of forces in the postwar world economy in favor of the United States, U.S. investment and interest in Egypt became more pronounced. By the late 1990s, foreign and joint-venture investments totaled over \$12 billion, the overwhelming majority of them from the United States. Foreign investment in Egypt is concentrated most heavily in petroleum, banking, chemicals, pharmaceuticals, and other branches of manufacturing industry, notably electronics and transportation equipment.[53]

The trend away from state capitalism and toward a neocolonial "open door" policy evolved during the Sadat regime. This development was the logical outcome of the evolution of state capitalism that became subordinated to foreign interests. Thus, state capitalism in Egypt facilitated the transition to a neocolonial capitalism dependent on imperialism. Class conflict and struggles between contending class forces in Egyptian society contributed to the unfolding crisis of the Egyptian state and led to the assassination of Anwar Sadat in 1981. Despite these developments, the government of Husni Mubarak has throughout the 1990s represented a further evolution along Sadat's path toward neocolonial integration into the world economy with greater ties with U.S. imperialism.

In Iraq, a similar colonial history under British rule yielded comparable results in the formation and transformation of the state. Prior to World War I, Basra, Baghdad, and Mosul were provinces of the Ottoman Empire. After the war, Britain took control of this territory. The motive forces behind British colonization were oil and access to the Persian Gulf. The British installed a monarchy including pro-British local officers from the Ottoman army, large merchants, and local bureaucrats with ties to the shaikhs and landlords in the countryside. The colonial regime in Iraq shored up the large shaikh and comprador elements and turned the state into an instrument of imperial rule designed to fulfill the dictates of the British-controlled world economy. The monarchy installed by Britain carried out the British mandate over the colony and safeguarded British interests in the region.

The onset of the Great Depression and the sharp fall in world prices for Iraq's chief exports (barley and wheat) brought about an economic and political crisis that led to limited independence in 1932. The expansion of industrial and commercial activity during the 1930s and 1940s brought into being newer social forces, including a small proletariat and a more numerous petty bourgeoisie. Excluded from centers of political and economic power, and subordinated to a monarchy propped up by British imperialism, these sectors came to articulate widespread resentment of foreign control and local ruling-class collaboration with imperialism. This led to numerous clashes between the state and popular sectors of Iraqi society, including a series of tribal rebellions from 1936 to 1941.[54]

The outbreak of World War II gave Britain an opportunity to intervene in the simmering political climate, but doing so only intensified anti-British sentiment and sparked a series of strikes, demonstrations, and clashes. By 1948, the political situation in Iraq had reached crisis proportions. Mass repression quelled efforts to overthrow the colonial puppet regime, but the oil boom in the 1950s began to transform the economic structure of the country through increased trade, construction, and manufacturing, thus moving the economy in a capitalist direction. Such expansion led to the emergence and growth of a capitalist class whose interests were distinct from those of the old power block of comprador merchants and landlords that formed the power base of the monarchy.

At the same time, industrial activity expanded the number of workers in industry and led to further labor organizing by trade unions and other workers' organizations, such as the Iraqi Communist party (ICP). The ICP became an influential political force, organizing strategic concentrations of workers, those working on the state railway and at the port of Basra and the oil fields.[55]

The growth of national capital and the aspiration of middle layers of society to nationhood and independence on the one hand, and the growth and development of an increasingly organized and class-conscious working class on the other, coupled with the massive dislocation of peasants forced to migrate to large cities, led to unrest in the army and resulted in a coup by the Free Officers, led by Colonel Abdul-Karim Qasim, in 1958. Representing the interests of the rising national bourgeoisie and the disaffected petty bourgeoisie, the Qasim regime set out to restructure the economy on a state capitalist basis that protected and advanced the interests of these two classes while providing social services, government programs, and benefits directed at workers and poorer sectors of society in order to maintain a mass support base for the regime. The revenues accrued from oil provided the funds to achieve these goals without disturbing the prevailing urban class structure.

The transformation of the class structure in Iraq involved the dismantling of the power of both the landowning class and foreign capital, and the transfer of this power to the national and petty bourgeoisies. In line with this development, the 1960s saw an agrarian reform program and the nationalization of oil. Soon, the largest manufacturing, trading, and financial firms were transferred to the public sector.[56] Despite a crisis in the mid 1960s—largely the result of a drop in oil revenues, which precipitated the coup of 1968 by right-wing military officers allied with the Ba'th party, bringing to power Sadam Hussein—Iraq continued to develop along the state capitalist road, further strengthening the power of the state.

The industrial and commercial expansion of the 1960s and 1970s led to the development of a local bourgeoisie tied to state-directed national industry. As in Turkey and Egypt, the maturing local industrial bourgeoisie asserted itself in Iraq by the late 1970s and opened up ventures with foreign capital in both the Arab world and the West, integrating itself even more into the world economy, thus undermining the state capitalist project. The repression of popular forces, the attack on the communists, and the exercise of authoritarian rule over the people in Iraq have coincided with the crisis of state capitalism and the gradual transition to a neocolonial state allied with imperialism.

The Gulf War of 1991, directed at Iraq to settle the question of which imperialist power would rule over the region, was a serious blow to Iraq's own designs as an emerging sub-imperialist power in alliance with one or another of the leading imperialist forces engaged in rivalry for control over sources of oil in the Middle East.[57] The showdown between the United States and Iraq, which culminated in a major catastrophe for the latter, derailed Iraq's efforts in this direction and led to the reexertion of U.S. power over the entire region to the end of the 20th century and beyond.

Syria and Lebanon were also colonized by the West; France received the League of Nations mandate over this territory. The French mandate turned the area into a colonial outpost until the middle of the twentieth century.

During the mandate, peasants and small-scale commodity producers of the region increasingly came under the control of large landowners, merchants, and capitalists supported by the colonial state. Semifeudal relations of production flourished in the countryside, while capitalist relations, dependent on imperialism, were promoted in commerce and industry in urban areas (e.g., Damascus, Aleppo, and Beirut). Given its strategic location, Beirut became a regional commercial center, facilitating the penetration of French capital into the Middle East. During the two decades of the French mandate, there was constant struggle by Syrian nationalists to wrest political power from France. Weakened by World War II and faced with protests and demonstrations in Damascus, France was no longer able to maintain its hold over the area by the mid 1940s. Syria and Lebanon gained their independence in 1946.[58]

From this point onward, Syria and Lebanon developed along divergent paths. By the mid 1950s, Syria was on a state capitalist path modeled after the Nasser regime in Egypt. In 1958 the two countries became part of the United Arab Republic (UAR), which lasted for three years.[59] The temporary reversal of state capitalist policies following the UAR episode was halted by the reemergence of the petty-bourgeois forces which wrested power from the traditional Syrian elite in the coup of 1963, bringing the Syrian Ba'th party back into power. This assured the continuation of development along a state capitalist path parallel to that in Egypt. A subsequent coup in 1966 further consolidated petty-bourgeois nationalist rule in Syria by bringing to power the Ba'th's left wing. A factional split within the Ba'th on the question of how far to move on the state capitalist road led to the coup of 1970, when the right wing of the Ba'th overthrew the leftist regime. General Hafez el Assad, who has since presided over the country's fate, had the whole of the Ba'thist left wing arrested, including President Atassi and Ibrahim Makhos.[60] In this way, the Assad regime effectively halted any further development along the state capitalist path.

Despite the factional power struggles within the Ba'th, Syria has managed to maintain an independent economy and foreign policy. The continued protection of the national bourgeoisie by the petty-bourgeois state in Syria allows the former the possibility of establishing an independent capitalist state[61] and at the same time prepare the material conditions for the development of an organized and disciplined working class that would in time lead a popular revolution against it.

Developments in Lebanon since independence have led that country on an entirely different path. The bourgeois forces that came to power in the wake of independence, especially the Maronite Christian community, were firmly tied to French and other European interests and wanted Lebanon to remain a French client-state.[62] This was achieved through economic means, as Lebanon adopted an "open door" policy toward foreign capital, especially in trade and finance, so that the local bourgeoisie involved in trade, commerce, and banking could prosper through links with European imperialism.[63]

The late 1940s and early 1950s saw major economic expansion in Lebanon, especially in finance, as the country experienced a massive inflow of foreign private capital in the form of investments and bank deposits. At the same time, the establishment of the State of Israel in 1948 closed to the Arab world the main ports of Palestine. Thus, Arab trade, which formerly had moved through the port of Haifa, was rerouted through Beirut, turning that city into the largest entrepot of transit trade in the entire Middle East. The combination of trade and investment in Lebanon soon led to the expansion of the financial sector; the number of Lebanese banks increased from ten in the mid 1950s to fifty-five in the mid 1960s, with an additional thirty foreign banks and a dozen or so joint Lebanese-foreign financial institutions. By the mid 1970s, the total volume of bank deposits in Lebanon had multiplied thirty-eight times since 1950, and the proportion of total deposits in the national income had risen from 20 percent in 1950 to 122 percent in 1974, the highest in the world.[64] Lebanon became a regional trade and banking center, and a reliable commercial and financial outpost of Europe in the Middle East.

With the postwar expansion of the United States in the world economy, U.S. capital began to penetrate the region and increasingly became associated with local capitalist interests, gradually replacing Britain and France as the dominant outside force in the region.[65] Thus, when the conflict between right-wing Maronite (Christian) forces tied to imperialism and the Lebanese national movement consisting of less affluent sectors of society (including Shiites, Druze, Palestinians, and others—mostly Moslem) resulted in a full-scale civil war in the late 1950s, the United States readily intervened and landed thousands of marines in Lebanon to keep the Maronite government in power.[66] This, coupled with U.S. financial and military backing of Israel and the plight of the Palestinians— who had been turned into refugees in their homelands—increased resentment against the United States and led to further polarization of Lebanon, where the U.S./Christian-Phalange/Israeli tripartite hold over the country had turned it into a U.S. client-state. This volatile situation led to another civil war in the mid 1970s and to a much wider and deeper conflict in the early 1980s when Israel invaded in 1982.[67] The recent tragedy in this beleaguered country can be traced directly to the United States and its client state client-state Israel and the Lebanese fascist forces (the Christian Phalange), keeping the rightists in power and Lebanon in the Western imperialist orbit. Given the persistence of the Lebanese anti-imperialist national forces, however, the United States has not been able to succeed in achieving its aims in Lebanon and has left this part of the Middle East to its Israeli junior-partner to keep in check.

Iran, unlike most Middle Eastern states, was never formally colonized. Its economic and strategic importance to the West was apparent by the turn of the century and became paramount during and following World War II. The transfer of power in the region from Britain to the United States at the conclusion of the war set the stage for the restructuring of the Iranian state along lines complementary to the interests of U.S. oil monopolies and the Pentagon's geopolitical involvement in the region. This transformation of the Iranian state into an appendage of U.S. imperialism came following the CIA-engineered overthrow of the Mossadeq regime in the early 1950s, which brought to a halt a brief experiment in state capitalism and reinstalled the discredited Pahlavi dynasty. The regime of Shah Reza Pahlavi was thus set up as an arm of the U.S. state, as a strategic outpost of the United States in the Middle East.[68]

During the shah's reign, from 1953 until his overthrow in 1979, the Iranian state began to bear the classic characteristics of a neocolonial state dependent on imperialism. From the so-called White Revolution of the early 1960s, which implemented a U.S.-initiated capitalist transformation of the agrarian sector, to the agro-mineral enclave of the transnationals in the 1970s, Iran became a well-financed subimperialist power with a 300,000-man army and U.S. military purchases in excess of $20 billion.[69] Iran's close economic, political, and military relationship with the United States, combined with its bureaucratic corruption, the economic disaster faced by small farmers and *bazaari* merchants, and the repression of the working class and other progressive sectors of society (which included torture, imprisonment, and executions), gave the necessary opening to the clerics to launch an attack on the shah's regime. Joined by workers, students, and the masses in general (through prolonged strikes and mass demonstrations), the clerics overthrew the shah in February 1979, bringing to an end twenty-five years of U.S.-sponsored authoritarian rule.[70]

Although a popular uprising ushered in the 1979 Iranian revolution, ended the shah's rule, and expelled the United States from the country, bringing with it hopes of a democratic transition to popular rule and social justice for the laboring masses, what actually resulted from the revolutionary turmoil was an organized political takeover by clerical elements.[71] The *mullahs* and *imams*, allied with reactionary landed interests able to mobilize a critical mass of the dispossessed peasantry and marginalized sectors of the urban population, gained a mass base with which to take the seats of power.[72] Strikes in the oil fields, in public services and utilities, in communication, and in related sectors of the economy thus provided the necessary political momentum to topple the shah and place power in the hands of the Islamic clergy and their reactionary allies. In this sense, and to the extent that no major social transformation took place following the uprising, the Iranian revolution *cannot* be seen as a social revolution; it was in fact a political rebellion that consolidated power in the hands of a reactionary coalition of class forces—landlords, merchants, and an assortment of small and medium-sized propertied interests—led by Islamic fundamentalist clerics. Thus the February revolution transferred power from one propertied ruling class to another, in the name of the people, with Islam as the organizing ideology directed at the dispossessed.[73] Islam, in essence, was used as a mobilizing force by traditional class forces that wanted to prevent a socialist revolution in the wake of the shah's downfall. What they succeeded in installing was a reactionary landlord/clerical dictatorship.[74]

Today, after more than two decades of Islamic rule and continued exploitation and repression (including the torture and execution of thousands of progressives and revolutionaries),[75] after a decade-long war with Iraq that cost thousands of Iranians their lives, and after continuing crises in the Iranian economy have so deteriorated living standards as to force the masses into desperation, the Islamic Republic faces an imminent social explosion. How soon the crisis-ridden conditions will reach a revolutionary stage and trigger an uprising against the regime, only time will tell. What is certain is that signs of such an outcome are becoming increasingly clear. Now, as ever, how well organized the popular forces are, and will become in the months and years ahead, in order to topple the regime, remains largely a *political* question.

Class, State, and Social Transformation in the Third World

The historical development of states in different regions of the Third World illustrate the varied nature and dynamics of the capitalist state that has evolved out of the interaction between local, precapitalist modes of production and capitalism originating in Europe and other colonial and imperial centers of the world economy.

In some regions, such as Latin America and parts of Asia, Africa, and the Middle East, the Oriental despotic state was overrun by

European colonialism. Feudal land-tenure practices were introduced, together with merchant's capital tied to the colonial center. Despite revolts against the European colonial empires, the introduction of feudal and commercial modes of production had a profound effect on the later development of capitalism and the capitalist state in these areas. Despite formal independence from the center states, they developed as appendages of them. This relationship continued despite shifts in power in the colonial centers, so that the transition from colonial status did not alter the underlying relationship between the ruling classes in the ex-colonies and the center states. Remnants of feudal landed and commercial moneyed interests lingered on in the context of an emerging local capitalist class in a changing world economy that accommodated all three segments. Within this framework of the colonial and neocolonial states in these regions, there resulted the development of two variants of the neocolonial capitalist state: the semifeudal/semicapitalist, and the more developed comprador-capitalist. While they have a similar political relationship with the imperialist centers, these two variants of the capitalist state are nevertheless ruled by classes that occupy different positions in the social and economic structure.

Prevailing in much of the less-developed capitalist world, the comprador-capitalist states are the main variant of the capitalist state in the Third World today. The dominant mode of production in comprador-capitalist formations, such as Brazil, Mexico, Argentina, South Korea, Taiwan, the Philippines, Iran under the shah, and Turkey, is capitalist, with precapitalist (i.e., feudal and/or transitional petty commodity) modes surviving in the countryside and sometimes exercising considerable influence within their domain. The expansion of foreign investment in manufacturing, agriculture, and raw materials in these countries since the early 1960s has accelerated the process of capitalist development so that previously precapitalist production relations have been transformed into capitalist ones. With the spread of capitalism and capitalist relations in these formations, state power has increasingly come under the influence and later control of the comprador capitalists, as the traditional alliance of landlords and compradors has proven to be an obstacle to the further expansion of the economic interests of the local bourgeoisie collaborating with imperialism. The change in relations between imperialism and the local ruling classes came in the 1960s in many parts of the Third World: In Latin America, it coincided with and was reinforced by the so-called Alliance for Progress; in Asia, it came with the "Green Revolution" in India; in the Middle East, it was facilitated by the "White Revolution" in Iran and by the Menderes regime in Turkey; and in Africa, it came with the transition from colonial rule to independence.

In these and other comprador-capitalist formations, state power is no longer shared equally between landlords and compradors, but it is in the hands of comprador capitalists tied to imperialism. At the current stage of development of these neocolonial states, the comprador-imperialist alliance is directed against the precapitalist landowning class for the transformation of the countryside into capitalist agriculture. Mechanization and wage labor, introduced and expanded by transnational agricultural monopolies, are part of the ongoing consolidation of these states into the world capitalist economy, dominated and controlled by the bourgeoisie of the advanced capitalist formations, particularly the United States.

The transformation of the internal social structure of comprador-capitalist states has been most visible in formations receiving the greatest amount of foreign (primarily U.S.) manufacturing investments since the early 1960s. Largely as a result of these investments, there has occurred a high rate of growth in the manufacturing sector, signifying the new relationship between local comprador capitalists and imperialism as these countries have come to serve the special needs of the transnational monopolies, especially the need for cheap labor.

Nevertheless, the expansion of foreign capital into the local economy through the intermediary of the comprador bourgeoisie has increasingly become a threat to national and petty-bourgeois sectors, giving rise to nationalist sentiments among them. More fundamentally, the unfolding process of dependent development, which has accelerated the spread of capitalist production relations in these formations, has given rise to the growth of an increasingly militant working class that is beginning to challenge the prevailing comprador-capitalist power structure.

Unlike the current neocolonial comprador-capitalist states, but similar to their earlier stage of development, state power in semifeudal/ semicapitalist formations (e.g., Guatemala, El Salvador, Paraguay, Zaire, Bangladesh, Oman, and Saudi Arabia) is shared by comprador capitalists and precapitalist landowners tied to imperialism, although the landowners constitute the dominant force within the alliance. Clearly, landowners in these formations are not capitalists, but have a feudal, semifeudal, or despotic character, depending on the formation. The labor force in the countryside remains outside wage relations, as payment in kind and the accompanying lord-serf production relationship persist.

Although feudal or semifeudal relations continue in the villages, this does not mean that large landowners function in isolation from the capitalist mode of production and exchange. In fact, they are an integral part of the larger semifeudal/semicapitalist formation and are actively engaged in a variety of capitalist activities, including import-export trade, banking, shipping and transport, marketing, raw material extraction, and even manufacturing. Indeed, the expanded capitalist economic activities of an otherwise precapitalist landowning class explains well the convergence of the interests of landlords and compradors as the dominant ruling classes in these formations, hence the sharing of state power between them. While a tendency exists for commercially involved landowners to become part of a single ruling comprador-capitalist class, a countertendency also exists. Comprador elements allied with transnational monopolies expand to the countryside to transform the landowning class along capitalist lines, followed by an erosion of the power of landlords in the state apparatus. This signals the transition of the semifeudal/semicapitalist state to its later comprador-capitalist form.

Given the low level of development of the productive forces and the importance of agriculture and raw material production in these states, foreign penetration and domination of the local economy is carried out through the intermediary of the landowning class—the dominant class within the landlord-comprador state. Thus while the domination of compradors in neocolonial comprador-capitalist states has opened the way for capitalist industrialization from the outside, the domination of the landlord class in semifeudal/semicapitalist states, together with the latter's traditional role as suppliers of raw materials and/or agricultural products, has stifled capitalist expansion in these formations. As a result, these states have been locked into a position of specialization in line with the raw material needs of the transnational monopolies.

The variation in the economies of these different sets of neocolonial formations tells us something about the effects generated by the relations between imperialism and dominant class forces. These relations reinforce a development pattern that either perpetuates *or* restructures social-economic forms, thus affecting the class structure and the form of the state in different ways. It is in terms of the significance of this latter effect that a differentiation of comprador-capitalist and semifeudal/semicapitalist states becomes so important.

In other parts of Asia, Africa, and the Middle East, successful national liberation movements against imperialism and the neocolonial state, led by the national and/or petty bourgeoisie, have generally resulted in the establishment of a nationalist state capitalist state. With the petty bourgeoisie in control of the state machine, these states have adopted various measures to advance the class interests of the petty bourgeoisie as well as its closest ally, the national bourgeoisie.

The main objective of the petty-bourgeois states, such as Turkey and Mexico in the 1930s, India in the 1950s, Egypt in the 1950s and 1960s, Algeria in the 1960s, and Iraq and Syria in the 1960s and 1970s, has been to provide the necessary capital to develop and expand the national economy where a national bourgeoisie has not developed sufficiently to assume ownership in the major sectors of the economy. Hence, the state in these formations has played a major role in the realization of the long-term interests of the developmental agency of capitalist accumulation in the Third World (i.e., the national bourgeoisie). In addition to its active role in the development of the productive forces, the state in these formations has attempted to eliminate the remnants of precapitalist relations of production in the countryside through a series of agrarian reforms that include expropriation of large tracts of land controlled by feudal landlords. It has also nationalized the major means of production and restricted or expelled foreign capital. Parallel to these developments has been the planning and implementation of a broad-based industrialization program with high levels of state investment in heavy industry, the regulation of commerce by the state, and the creation of special organs such as state banks and development corporations.

The historical experience of peripheral social formations following a state capitalist path shows that the struggle between the national/petty-bourgeois state and various antagonistic classes (land-lords and compradors on the one hand, workers and peasants on the other) significantly weakens these nationalist regimes and makes them politically vulnerable. Moreover, because of the highly un-stable nature of this form of capitalist accumulation in the Third World, state capitalist regimes ultimately are either overpowered by imperialism and local reaction and transformed into neocolonial states or are overthrown by the working class and transformed into socialist states.

There has been a growing number of socialist transformations in the Third World during this century. Some of the most important of them are examined in the next chapter.

Notes

1. This chapter draws heavily from my earlier study of class-state relations in the Third World. See Berch Berberoglu, *The Internationalization of Capital* (New York: Praeger, 1987), part 2. See also Berch Berberoglu, *The Political Economy of Development: Development Theory and the Prospects for Change in the Third World* (Albany: State University of New York Press, 1992), part 3.

2. Leo Panitch and Colin Leys (eds.), *Global Capitalism Versus Democracy* (New York: Monthly Review Press, 1999).

3. On corporatist interpretations of the peripheral state, see Alfred Stepan, *The State and Society: Peru in Comparative Perspective* (Princeton: Princeton University Press, 1978). On bureaucratic authoritarianism, see Guillermo O'Donnell, *Modernization and Bureaucratic Authoritarianism: Studies in South American Politics* (Berkeley: Institute of International Studies, University of California at Berkeley, 1973) and idem, "Tensions in the Bureaucratic Authoritarian State and the Question of Democracy." In *The New Authoritarianism in Latin America*, edited by David Collier (Princeton: Princeton University Press, 1979). On the neo-fascist character of dependent states ruled by military dictatorships, see James Petras, *Class, State and Power in the Third World* (Montclair, NJ: Allanheld, Osmun, 1981), Chap. 7, p. 10. For a discussion on the nature of the bureaucratic authoritarian and other forms of the dependent state, see Berch Berberoglu, *The Internationalization of Capital*, Chap. 7, and idem, "The Contradictions of Export-Oriented Development in the Third World," *Social and Economic Studies* 36, no. 4 (December 1987). Also see Martin Carnoy, *The State and Political Theory* (Princeton: Princeton University Press, 1984), Chap. 7.

4. On state capitalism in the Third World, see Berch Berberoglu, "The Nature and Contradictions of State Capitalism in the Third World," *Social and Economic Studies* 28, no. 2 (1980).

5. The nature of the socialist state is discussed at length in the next chapter which, following a general analysis of its principal features, focuses on the development of

the Soviet and Chinese state. Also see Berch Berberoglu, *The Internationalization of Capital*, Chap. 7.

6. Stanley J. Stein and Barbara H. Stein, *The Colonial Heritage of Latin America* (New York: Oxford University Press, 1970).

7. Ibid.

8. Ernesto Laclau, "Feudalism and Capitalism in Latin America," *New Left Review* 67 (May–June 1971).

9. Eric Williams, *Capitalism and Slavery* (New York: Capricorn, 1966).

10. This term refers to native-born Latin Americans of Spanish descent.

11. Andre Gunder Frank, *Capitalism and Underdevelopment in Latin America* (New York: Monthly Review Press, 1967).

12. Analysis of the evolution of U.S. direct investment in Latin American manufacturing industries reveals that capital held by parent companies rose from $780 million in 1950 to $4.2 billion in 1970 to $17.9 billion in 1988 to $46.1 billion in 1997. U.S. Department of Commerce, *Survey of Current Business*, (August 1989), p. 62 and (July 1999), p. 56.

13. Atilio Boron, *State, Capitalism, and Democracy in Latin America* (Boulder, Colo.: Lynne Rienner Publishers, 1995).

14. See Sander Halebsky and Richard L. Harris (eds.), *Capital, Power, and Inequality in Latin America* (Boulder, Colo.: Westview Press, 1995).

15. Ash Narain Roy, *The Third World in the Age of Globalization* (London: Zed Books, 1999).

16. See Anupam Sen, *The State, Industrialization, and Class Formations in India* (London: Routledge & Kegan Paul, 1982).

17. See Irfan Habib, *The Agrarian System of Mughal India* (London: Asia Publishing House, 1963), p. 115.

18. Sen, *The State, Industrialization, and Class Formation in India*, p. 28.

19. Berch Berberoglu, ed., *India: National Liberation and Class Struggles* (Meerut: Sarup & Sons, 1985). See also, Berch Berberoglu (ed.), *Class, State, and Development in India* (Delhi: Sage Publications, 1992).

20. Sen, *The State, Industrialization, and Class Formation in India*.

21. Hamza Alavi, "India and the Colonial Mode of Production," *Economic and Political Weekly*, August 1975.

22. See Bipan Chandra, "The Indian Capitalist Class and Imperialism Before 1947," *Journal of Contemporary Asia* 5, no. 3 (1975).

23. A.I. Levkovsky, *Capitalism in India* (Delhi: People's Publishing House, 1966). See also, Berberoglu, *Class, State, and Development in India*.

24. International Labour Office, *Yearbook of Labour Statistics, 1998* (Geneva: ILO, 1998), Table 2E, p. 311.

25. Paresh Chattopadhyay, "Some Trends in India's Capitalist Industrialization," in *Class, State and Development in India* ed. Berch Berberoglu (New Delhi: Sage Publications, 1992).

26. Frances V. Moulder, *Japan, China and the Modern World Economy* (Cambridge: Cambridge University Press, 1977), pp. 60–62.

27. Ibid., pp. 98–127.

28. See Sam Wynn, "The Taiwanese 'Economic Miracle,'" *Monthly Review* 33, no. 11 (April 1982); Clive Hamilton, "Capitalist Industrialization in East Asia's Four

Little Tigers," *Journal of Contemporary Asia* 13, no. 1 (1983); Charles W. Lindsey, "The Philippine Economy," *Monthly Review* 36, no. 11 (April 1985).

29. Thus, while large investments were made in the Indonesian oil industry, countries such as South Korea, Taiwan, Hong Kong, Singapore, and the Philippines came to serve as cheap labor reserves, and Hong Kong and Singapore took on additional roles as important financial and trade centers for the Western monopolies. Moreover, South Korea, the Philippines, and Thailand took up the further strategic role of providing a military shield in the area for the expansion of the newly established export-oriented economies.

30. See Martin Landsberg, "Export-Led Industrialization in the Third World: Manufacturing Imperialism," *Review of Radical Political Economics* 11, no. 4 (Winter 1979). Also see Bill Warren, *Imperialism, Pioneer of Capitalism* (London: Verso, 1980). Warren argues that imperialism, in the form of overseas investments, promotes the development of capitalism and capitalist relations, regardless of its point of origin and deformed character.

31. Berch Berberoglu, "The Contradictions of Export-Oriented Development in the Third World," *Social and Economic Studies* 36, no. 4 (December 1987).

32. Feudalism practiced in these regions, especially in the East, however, was based mainly on control of cattle, rather than of land, as in Europe.

33. See Richard Harris, ed., *The Political Economy of Africa* (Cambridge, Mass.: Schenkman, 1975).

34. Basil Davidson, *The African Slave Trade* (Boston: Little, Brown, 1961).

35. See Berch Berberoglu, "Pre-Capitalist Modes of Production: Their Origins, Contradictions, and Transformation," *Quarterly Review of Historical Studies* 19, nos. 1–2 (1980).

36. Colin Leys, *Underdevelopment in Kenya* (Berkeley: University of California Press, 1975); Mahmood Mamdani, *Politics and Class Formation in Uganda* (New York: Monthly Review Press, 1976).

37. For a fuller discussion on this, see Berberoglu, "The Contradictions of Export-Oriented Development in the Third World," pp. 106–10.

38. Berberoglu, *The Internationalization of Capital.* Chap. 5.

39. See Karen Farsoun, "State Capitalism in Algeria," *MERIP Reports*, no. 35 (1975).

40. Issa G. Shivji, *Class Struggles in Tanzania* (New York: Monthly Review Press, 1976).

41. This was the allocation of parcels of conquered lands to *sipahis* (rural cavalry with military and administrative functions in the provinces) and to the civilian sector of the *devsirmes* (top officials of the central bureaucracy) in the form of fiefs (*timar*). The *sipahis* and the civilian *devsirmes* were given these lands for the purpose of administering them in the name of the state. This system of land allocation was put into effect during the reign of Suleyman I and continued for quite some time.

42. As the central state began gradually to lose its authority in the countryside, however, the *sipahis* and other fief holders increasingly evaded their obligations to the state and attempted to take over the ownership of state lands. In reaction to these developments, realizing that the old rural military-administrative system had out-lived its usefulness, the state moved against the *sipahis* and displaced them. This was done, above all, by the introduction of tax farming (*iltizam*).

43. Although private property in land and feudal relations of production began to develop in the Ottoman formation in the seventeenth century and rapidly expanded and surpassed that owned by the state in many parts of the empire by the eighteenth century, the feudal lords were never able to overthrow the central state and exert political domination over the empire's affairs. Nevertheless, in one instance at least, a rebellion by the landlords led by Mehmet Ali Pasa, the governor of Egypt, in the late nineteenth century nearly succeeded, but the rebellion was put down with the aid of the French and British armies. The *ayans* nevertheless continued to exercise economic control over vast areas of the empire.

44. Bernard Lewis, *The Emergence of Modern Turkey*, 2nd ed. (New York: Oxford University Press, 1969).

45. Niyazi Berkes, *The Development of Secularism in Turkey* (Montreal: McGill University Press, 1964), p. 329.

46. See Berch Berberoglu, *Turkey in Crisis: From State Capitalism to Neo-Colonialism* (London: Zed Press, 1982).

47. Dogu Ergil, "From Empire to Dependence: The Evolution of Turkish Underdevelopment," Ph.D. dissertation, State University of New York at Binghamton, 1975. See also, Caglar Keyder, *State and Class in Turkey: A Study in Capitalist Development* (London: Verso, 1987).

48. See Ferhad Ibrahim, "The Kurdish National Movement and the Struggle for National Autonomy," in Berch Berberoglu (ed.), *The National Question: Nationalism, Ethnic Conflict, and Self-Determination* (Philadelphia: Temple University Press, 1995). See also, Robert Olson (ed.), *The Kurdish Nationalist Movement in the 1990s* (Lexington: University Press of Kentucky, 1996).

49. Samir Amin, *The Arab Nation: Nationalism and Class Struggles* (London: Zed Press, 1978).

50. Mahmoud Hussain, *Class Conflict in Egypt, 1945–1970* (New York: Monthly Review Press, 1973).

51. See Mark Cooper, "Egyptian State Capitalism in Crisis," in *The Middle East*, ed. Talal Asad and Roger Owen (New York: Monthly Review Press, 1983).

52. Joel Beinin, "Egypt's Transition under Nasser," *MERIP Reports*, no. 107 (July–August 1982).

53. Jim Paul, "Foreign Investment in Egypt," *MERIP Reports*, no. 107 (July–August 1982); U.S. Department of Commerce, StatUSA, *Country Commerce Guide: Egypt*, FY 2000 (available online).

54. See Joe Stork, "Iraq and the War in the Gulf," *MERIP Reports*, no. 97 (June 1981), p. 5.

55. Ibid.; Hanna Batatu, *The Old Social Classes and the Revolutionary Movements of Iraq* (Princeton: Princeton University Press, 1978).

56. Majid Khadduri, *Republican Iraq* (London, 1969); Patrick Clawson, "The Internationalization of Capital and Capital Accumulation in Iran and Iraq," *Insurgent Sociologist* 7, no. 2 (Spring 1977).

57. Berch Berberoglu, *Turmoil in the Middle East: Imperialism, War, and Political Instability* (Albany: State University of New York Press, 1999), Chap. 7.

58. Youssef M. Choueiri (ed.), *State and Society in Syria and Lebanon* (New York: St. Martin's Press, 1994).

59. Tabitha Petran, *Syria* (New York: Praeger, 1972).

60. Amin, *The Arab Nation*.

61. Elizabeth Longuenesse, "The Class Nature of the State in Syria," *MERIP Reports* 9, no. 4 (May 1979).

62. Maronite Christian hegemony was secured through the portioning of the official governmental structure (i.e., the selection of president, prime minister, etc.) on a 1933 census that favors Christians, who are now the minority.

63. B.J. Odeh, *Lebanon: Dynamics of Conflict* (London: Zed Press, 1985).

64. Salim Nasr, "The Crisis of Lebanese Capitalism," *MERIP Reports* 8, no. 10 (December 1978).

65. Samih Farsoun, "Student Protests and the Coming Crisis in Lebanon," *MERIP Reports*, no. 19 (August 1973).

66. Charles Winslow, *Lebanon: War and Politics in a Fragmented Society* (London: Routledge, 1996).

67. James A. Reilly, "Israel in Lebanon, 1975–82," *MERIP Reports* 12, nos. 6–7 (September–October 1982).

68. See Fred Halliday, *Iran: Dictatorship and Development* (New York: Penguin, 1979).

69. Ervand Abrahamian, *Iran: Between Two Revolutions* (Princeton: Princeton University Press, 1982). Also see Eric Hooglund, *Land and Revolution in Iran, 1960–1980* (Austin: University of Texas Press, 1982).

70. Farideh Farhi, "Class Struggles, the State, and Revolution in Iran," in *Power and Stability in the Middle East*, ed. Berch Berberoglu (London: Zed Books, Ltd., 1989), pp. 90–113. See also John Foran (ed.), *A Century of Revolution: Social Movements in Iran* (Minneapolis: University of Minnesota Press, 1994).

71. See Mansoor Moaddel, *Class, Politics, and Ideology in the Iranian Revolution* (New York: Columbia University Press, 1993).

72. See *MERIP Reports*, no. 98 (July–August 1981).

73. See Saeed Rahnema and Sohrab Behdad (eds.), *Iran After the Revolution: Crisis of an Islamic State* (London: I.B. Tauris, 1995).

74. Ahmad Ashraf, "Bazaar and Mosque in Iran's Revolution," *MERIP Reports*, no. 113 (March–April, 1983), pp. 16–18.

75. Ervand Abrahamian, *Tortured Confessions: Prisons and Public Recantations in Modern Iran* (Berkeley: University of California, 1999).

CHAPTER 7

THE SOCIALIST STATE

Born in revolution against an exploitive system propped up by capitalists and landlords, the socialist state constitutes a new kind of state ruled by the working class and the laboring masses. The cornerstone of a workers' state, emerging out of capitalism and the remnants of feudalism, is the abolition of private property in the major means of production and an end to the exploitation of labor for private profit. The establishment of a revolutionary democratic government of the proletariat (as against the dictatorship of capital) is what distinguishes the socialist state from its capitalist counterpart. As the class essence of the state lies at the heart of an analysis of the nature and role of the state in different epochs throughout history, the class nature of the socialist state gives us clues to the nature and role of the state in a socialist society developing toward communism. For, as Marx has pointed out in *Critique of the Gotha Program*, the dictatorship of the proletariat (i.e., the class rule of the working class) is a transitional phase between capitalism and communism: "Between capitalist and communist society lies the period of the revolutionary transformation of the one into the other. Corresponding to this is also a political transition period in which the state can be nothing but *the revolutionary dictatorship of the proletariat*."[1] During this period, the state represents and defends the interests of the working class against capital and all other vestiges of reactionary exploitive classes, which, overthrown and dislodged from power, attempt in a multitude of ways to recapture the state through a counterrevolution. "The theory of the class struggle, applied by Marx to the question of the state and the socialist revolution," writes Lenin,

154

leads as a matter of course to the recognition of the *political rule* of the proletariat, of its dictatorship, i.e., of undivided power directly backed by the armed force of the people. The overthrow of the bourgeoisie can be achieved only by the proletariat becoming the *ruling class*, capable of crushing the inevitable and desperate resistance of the bourgeoisie, and of organizing *all* the working and exploited people for the new economic system.[2]

In this context, then, the proletarian state has a dual role to play: (1) to break the resistance of its class enemies (the exploiting classes); and (2) to protect the revolution and begin the process of socialist construction. The class character of the new state under the dictatorship of the proletariat takes on a new form and content: "During this period the state must inevitably be a state that is democratic *in a new way* (for the proletariat and the propertyless in general) and dictatorial *in a new way* (against the bourgeoisie)."[3] Thus,

> *Simultaneously* with an immense expansion of democracy, which *for the first time* becomes democracy for the poor, democracy for the people, and not democracy for the money-bags, the dictatorship of the proletariat imposes a series of restrictions on the freedom of the oppressors, the exploiters, the capitalists. . . .[4]

Used primarily to suppress these forces and to build the material base of a classless, egalitarian society, the socialist state begins to wither away once there is no longer any need for it. As Engels points out:

> The first act in which the state really comes forward as the representative of society as a whole—the taking possession of the means of production in the name of society—is at the same time its last independent act as a state. The interference of the state power in social relations becomes superfluous in one sphere after another, and then ceases of itself. The government of persons is replaced by the administration of things and

the direction of the processes of production. The state is not "abolished," *it withers away.*[5]

In this sense, the state no longer exists in the fully matured communist stage, for there is no longer the need in a classless society for an institution that is, by definition, an instrument of class rule through force and violence. Lenin writes:

> Only in communist society, when the resistance of the capitalists has been completely crushed, when the capitalists have disappeared, when there are no classes (i.e., when there is no distinctions between the members of society as regards their relation to the social means of production), *only* then "the state . . . ceases to exist," and "*it becomes possible to speak of freedom.*" Only then will a truly complete democracy become possible and be realized, a democracy without any exceptions whatever.[6]

It is thus in this broader, transitional context that the class nature and tasks of the state in socialist society must be understood and evaluated.

The extent to which today's socialist states approximate the theoretical formulations of Marx, Engels, and Lenin on this question is hotly debated among the Left. Whether the former Soviet Union, China, Cuba, and other postcapitalist states are to be classified as socialist states (i.e., ruled by the working class) has often been influenced by political ideology and affiliation, rather than by a concrete Marxist scientific analysis of the nature of these societies.[7] For as China's characterization of the Soviet state during the past several decades illustrates, factional struggles within a party (or a movement) may dictate the characterization of a state as socialist at one point in time, "state monopoly capitalist of the fascist type" at another point, and "postcapitalist" or "state socialist" at yet a later point, depending on the party line.[8] Aside from their limited propaganda value for internal consumption, such unscientific pronouncements on the nature of a state and society are worthless at best and in fact *distort* our understanding of these states in the long run. The question thus arises, How then to examine the existing, self-proclaimed socialist states in order to arrive at an independent assessment of their real nature (i.e., their class character)? To answer this question, one can do no better than examine their actual historical experience in social and economic development and sort out the net results of their long-term policies in different spheres of life in class terms. That is, to provide answers to the broader question: Which class(es) gained and which class(es) lost from the long-term policies of these states in the process of their social transformation? An answer in favor of the working class and other laboring sections of society would confirm these states as socialist states.

Historically, the October Revolution in Russia marked the first successful proletarian revolution of the twentieth century that brought workers to state power. Thus the new Soviet state soon became the prime example of a revolutionary proletarian socialist state. In the years since 1917, workers and peasants have risen up in many lands to throw off the imperialist yoke and free themselves from feudal-capitalist exploitation. In China, Vietnam, Korea, Cuba, and many other countries, the victorious laboring masses have, through working-class leadership, set out to build a socialist society.

This chapter examines two of the most prominent socialist states that came to power during the first half of the twentieth century, the Soviet Union and the People's Republic of China.

The Development of the Soviet State

Following the October Socialist Revolution in 1917, which brought to power the proletariat led by the Bolshevik party, and ended the domination of foreign capital and local feudal and capitalist elements tied to it, the Soviet Union went through several important stages in its political economic development. First came War Communism (mid 1918 to 1921), followed by the New Economic Policy (1921 to 1928), and finally the Five-Year Development Plans and the consolidation of socialism after 1928. Moreover, Soviet policy since the mid 1950s has been a controversial one, alternating between liberalization and consolidation of the gains of socialism achieved during the past several decades.

October 1917 to June 1918

In the months immediately following the revolution, no sweeping measures of confiscation or nationalization were proposed. This initial, transitional period, which Lenin called "state capitalism," was "characterized by control over private trade and industry rather than by extensive socialization . . . [and] an immediate transition to a socialist economy was not on the agenda in the early months of the new Soviet regime."[9] Lenin, in his *The Principal Tasks of Our Day*, spoke of state capitalism as a "gigantic step forward," and emphasized that the "period of transition between Capitalism and Socialism" would be mixed.[10] State Capitalism was thus seen as a mechanism utilized by the proletarian state that would generate rapid economic growth and at the same time prepare the conditions for the transition to a socialist economy. In such circumstances, writes Maurice Dobb, "It was urgently necessary both to study and copy the State Capitalism of the war-time countries of Central and Western Europe."[11]

By the summer of 1918, two decisive factors brought the policies of the initial period to a close. The first was directly tied to the workplace; the revolution had matured, and the consciousness of the workers had elevated to a level where the workers challenged the underlying relations of production of the mixed economy. They pressed the state to transfer the administrative process of the factories into their hands and completely nationalize the means of production. The second decisive factor was the outbreak of civil war, supported by the armed intervention of foreign powers, led by German imperialism.

War Communism (June 1918 to 1921)

Under these conditions, the Soviet state made a move to introduce a decree for the wide-based nationalization of major industries that were still in private hands.

> At the end of June (1918) a governmental measure was precipitately adopted which closed one chapter of policy and opened another. This was the Decree of General

Nationalization of June 28th, which applied nationalization by a stroke of the pen to practically all large-
scale enterprises without distinction. It applied to all
companies with more than a million roubles of capital
... in mining, metal, textiles, glass, leather, cement, and
the timber and electrical trades. .... And in the next six
or nine months a series of particular decrees followed,
nationalizing whole groups of enterprises or sections of
an industry. By the end of the year the nationalized
concerns reached the figure of 1000, and by the autumn
of 1919 some 3000 or 4000.[12]

The decree on nationalization of June 28, 1918, was the prelude
to War Communism. For the next two years, the Soviet state was
fighting a war for survival against both domestic and foreign
enemies.[13]

The drift toward nationalized control of industry, centralized allocation of supplies and centralized collection
and distribution of products was to be rapid. What came
to be known as the period of "War Communism" had
been launched: a product of the forcing house of a
mortal struggle of the new regime against extinction,
when military necessity ruled all and problems of industry were virtually identified with the problem of military
supplies.[14]

War Communism, as most Soviet leaders—including Lenin—
agreed, was a temporary measure, not a normal economic policy. It
was historically and economically inevitable under the conditions in
which the state found itself. There was the civil war on the one hand,
and external invasion on the other. Hence the measures adopted by
the Soviet state were precisely to deal with concrete, historically
created conditions over which the state had little or no control. In his
pamphlet *The Tax in Kind* (April 1921), Lenin said quite explicitly
that "War Communism was forced on us by war and ruin. It was not,
and could not be, a policy that corresponded to the economic tasks
of the proletariat."[15] Indeed, the measures adopted during this period
(1918-21) were emergency measures under stress of war.

In the midst of the continuing crisis faced by the Soviet state there was no choice but to abandon War Communism. "The switch of trains we made in the spring of 1921," wrote Lenin, "was dictated by circumstances which were so overpowering and convincing that there were no debates and no differences of opinions among us."[16] The new policy, which Lenin introduced to the Tenth Congress and which was subsequently adopted to replace War Communism, was the New Economic Policy (NEP).

New Economic Policy (1921 to 1928)

The adoption of the NEP meant a return to the "state capitalism" experimented with during the period immediately following the October Revolution. The central measure of the NEP

> was the granting to the peasantry of the right to trade in the open market in whatever produce they had left, after a certain specified amount had been turned over to the government. This decision meant the return of the profit motive and exchange relationships to an important sector of the economy. In the field of industry the government retreated to the "commanding heights" of control over banking, transportation, and certain large industries, permitting private enterprise to take over the rest.[17]

For Lenin, the key for rapid progress toward socialism was not in the state control of the entire economy and the overall socialization of the means of production, all at once, as the state was forced into in 1918; rather, it was the political control of the state machinery by proletarian leadership, through which the state, coupled with its control of large-scale industry, would direct the national economy as a whole toward the realization of socialist goals. Hence, during the period of the New Economic Policy most retail and wholesale trade and small business firms were returned to private hands. This not only was to accelerate trade and exchange between industry and agriculture but to serve a political purpose as well—the consolidation of the peasant masses, as Lenin put it, "in such a way that the entire mass will actually move forward with us."[18]

One question of private capital under the NEP, Bukharin, in agreement with Lenin, stated:

> By using the economic initiative of peasants, small producers, and even bourgeois, by tolerating subsequently private accumulation, we are putting them objectively to the service of the socialist state industry and of the economy as a whole: this is what the meaning of NEP consists in.[19]

Although Lenin's economic program under the NEP meant a retreat from the policies adopted under War Communism, the success of the NEP was so overwhelming that it carried the Soviet economy beyond the range in which its immediate survival was at stake.

> The output of large-scale industry which had plummeted to 14 percent of its pre-war level by 1920 rose to 46 percent in 1924 and to 75 percent in the following year. The marketable output of agriculture climbed by 64 percent from 1922 to 1925. Last but not least, the year 1924 saw the sum total of gross investment for the first time since 1917 exceed annual depreciation.[20]

And by 1927, the overall performance of the economy had reached the 1913 level.[21] This pronounced progress in all the major areas of economic activity set the stage and provided the impetus for the emergence of new ideas for accelerated growth and for the expansion of the economic base to a point where it would elevate the Soviet Union to the rank of a major industrial power in the world.

Five-Year Development Plans (1928 and Beyond)

With the introduction of the First Five-Year Plan in 1928, tremendous progress began to take place under centralized state control of industry. "All of the country's resources were concentrated on certain objectives and their dissipation on other objectives, not conductive to rapid industrialization, was avoided."[22] This was clearly stated by Stalin himself, who said:

> ... it was necessary to accept sacrifices, and to impose
> the severest economy in everything. It was necessary to
> economize on food, on schools, on manufactured goods
> so as to accumulate the indispensable means for the
> creation of industry. This was the only way for over-
> coming the famine with regard to technical equip-
> ment.[23]

Thus the main target during the First and Second Five-Year Plans
was the development and expansion of heavy industry, with particular emphasis on the production of capital goods.

For the rapid development of industry, however, a concurrent
and equally rapid development of the agricultural sector was imperative. The introduction of large-scale farming on cooperative
lines was the cornerstone of the industrialization program: "This
transformation of the age-old basis of Russian agriculture was
adopted," writes Maurice Dobb, "as the 'missing answer' for which
the country was seeking: as the only solution to the riddle of how to
industrialize on the basis of NEP."[24]

The collectivization of Soviet agriculture was at first initiated by
Stalin on the principle of voluntary participation of small peasant
farms into large farms, organized around collective units. In his
report to the Fifteenth Congress of the CPSU, in which this policy
was enunciated, Stalin spoke as follows:

> The way out is to turn the small and scattered peasant
> farms into large united farms based on the common
> cultivation of the soil, to introduce collective cultiva-
> tion of the soil on the basis of new and higher technique.
> The way out is to unite the small and dwarf peasant
> farms gradually and surely, not by pressure but by
> example and persuasion, into large farms based on
> common, cooperative cultivation of the soil, with the
> use of agriculture. There is no way out."[25]

But as resistance grew, mainly among the *kulaks* (rich peasants),
against the state's collectivization efforts, the state found it necessary to exert force to overcome the obstacles to the advancement of
socialist industrialization. For, as Paul Baran points out, "The

collectivization of agriculture in Russia . . . was the only possible approach to a broad avenue of economic, social, and cultural progress."[26] And as the material performance of the agricultural sector was later to prove, "Collectivization was a tremendous, and, indeed, an indispensable step toward economic and social advancement";

> . . . in the final year of the Second Five-Year Plan, the grain harvest reached an all-time record, while the output of so-called technical crops (flax-fiber, cotton, sugar beet) more than doubled by comparison with 1928.
>
> Thus was solved not only the food problem, both in the collectivized village and the rapidly expanding city, but consumer's goods industries obtained the raw materials base indispensable for their growth, and the government came into a position of accumulating substantial food reserves for possible emergencies. . . . What is equally important is that the increased agricultural production was accompanied by a release of over 20 million people from agriculture—a migration from village to city that was indispensable for the growth of industry. It reflected a per capita increase of productivity in agriculture of as much as 60 percent between 1928 and the end of the 1930s. And this in turn was the result of a "proffer of social assistance" to agriculture on a tremendous scale. Having received in the course of the First Five-Year Plan nearly quarter of a million tractors, and almost twice as many by the end of the Second Five-Year Plan, Russian agriculture, [writes Baran, quoting Baylov] "previousiy one of the most backward . . . [was able] to accumulate in the space of a few years an enormous production capital—in agricultural machinery and buildings—and to mechanize the main branches of cultivation to a much greater extent than other countries have done in the course of a long period of history."[27]

In sum, the collectivization drive in Soviet agriculture achieved its major economic objective in serving as the *basis* for industrialization. And the tremendous growth of industrial production (over 18 percent per year from the beginning of the industrialization campaign in 1928, and an increase of approximately 16 percent per year in aggregate output during the same period) was an exceptional achievement. This is confirmed by the well-known developmentalist Alexander Gerschenkron's Rand Corporation study, which reports average annual rates of growth in Soviet heavy industry between 1928-29 and 1937 of 18.9 percent for machinery, 18.5 percent for iron and steel, 14.6 percent for coal, 11.7 percent for petroleum products, 22.8 percent for electric power, and 17.8 percent for all heavy industry.[28] Thus, as Dobb points out:

> Such a rate of growth represents a doubling each quinquennium, and is nearly twice as great as that found during exceptional boom periods in the capitalist world, such as the United States in the second half of the 1880s (8.6 percent), Russia in the 1890s (8 percent), or Japan between 1907 and 1913 (8.6 percent). With this may be compared a 5 percent rate of growth for manufacturing production in the United States between 1899 and 1929 and 3 percent in Britain between 1885 and 1913.[29]

Moreover, this unprecedented achievement in all the major fields of economic activity began gradually to improve the standard of living of the Soviet people: "By the end of the First Five-Year Plan," writes Baran, "the worst 'squeezing' of the consumer was over, by 1935 rationing could be abolished."[30]

> While the rise in living standards was interrupted by the threat of war, and in particular by the war itself, the postwar decade witnessed their rapid and consistent improvement. By the end of 1954 they were approximately 75 percent above those of the last year before the war.[31]

These achievements in the Soviet economy and society were made possible by the integration of both agriculture and industry into the mainstream of the Soviet economy. It was done by the socialization and collectivization of the means of production under state supervision and control, and the promotion of a major industrialization drive during the Stalin era.

The Post-Stalin Era to the Present

After Stalin's death in 1953, the Soviet Union embarked upon a cyclical path of centralized versus liberalized forms of economic organization and political rule—from Khrushchev and the Kosygin reforms to the centralist Brezhnev era to Gorbachev's reforms of *perestroika* and *glasnost*, and finally to Yeltsin's market reforms.

The coming to power of Khrushchev and the liberal technocratic forces signaled a shift toward greater managerial control of the production process and led to the reorganization of work at the point of production, thus providing the impetus for local control on the one hand, and weakening the grip of the Communist party over the structure of production at various levels. The power struggle that led to the ascendence of the technocratic forces led by Khrushchev at the same time brought about a split within the international communist movement and led to a rupture in relations with the People's Republic of China. The full-scale ramifications of the strained Soviet-Chinese relations did not become evident until the launching by Mao of the Great Proletarian Cultural Revolution in 1967, which, while domestic in nature, nevertheless was initiated to prevent developments in China similar to those underway in the Soviet Union at the time.

The interpretation of changes in the Soviet Union since Stalin's death and the rise to power of the Khrushchevite technocratic forces to the present has taken many twists and turns—sometimes guided by a genuine materialist analysis, but often through the dictates of the prevailing party line devised more for its propaganda value than for a clear understanding of the unfolding situation. Such was the case, for example, of the Chinese characterization of the Soviet state during the 1960s and 1970s as a "monopoly capitalist state of the fascist type," or the elevation of the Soviet Union to the level of a "superpower" that is "more dangerous" than the United States. The concept of "social imperialism" was thus devised during this period, corresponding to what the dominant forces within the Chinese Communist party viewed as allegedly taking place within the Soviet Union, that is, a capitalist counterrevolution. Hence, the struggle against "capitalist roaders" within the Chinese CP became the priority of the day.

Despite the dogmatic nature of the attacks on the Soviet state by ultra-leftist forces within the Chinese CP for the former's "deviation" from the principles of Marxism-Leninism, it is true that in the 1960s structural shifts did take place in the Soviet economy that can be construed as moving the country in a "capitalist direction" (i.e., shifts resulting from reforms initiated to increase efficiency and productivity). Although factional struggles within the Communist party have historically shifted the base of power in the Soviet Union through the 1980s, these changes represented variations in policy within the framework of a developing socialist state. However, the changes that took place during this period facilitated the spread of capitalist practices that worked to eventually undermine the further development of socialism in the Soviet Union in the subsequent period.

Developments in the former Soviet Union and Eastern Europe during the past decade do indicate a movement toward a market-oriented economy, where capitalist elements are integrated into a socialist base within the framework of multi-party politics. In Poland and Hungary such changes became institutionalized through a process of reform that preempted a mass uprising which later swept across Eastern Europe in 1989. But elsewhere, as in Czechoslovakia, the German Democratic Republic, Bulgaria, and, most violently, in Romania, mass protests and movements directed at the governments in power in these countries accelerated the pace of change, and in some cases unleashing the forces of counter-revolution which came to power following a violent confrontation between the army and the security forces, as in Romania. In contrast, the reform movement in the former USSR came from within the Communist party.

The monumental social, economic, and political transformations that took place in Russia under the Yeltsin regime, as well as in other former Soviet republics, in the period following the collapse of the Soviet Union in the early 1990s, do indicate a counterrevolutionary development that has had a major impact on Russia and many of the other former Soviet republics. Whether the transformations that are now taking place throughout the former Soviet Union and Eastern Europe will lead to the restoration of capitalism there, is still difficult to ascertain, especially since the greatest portion of productive resources, land, and capital remains in the hands of the state. Although such a situation can easily lead to the establishment of a form of bureaucratic state-capitalism that does not require the widespread conversion of state property into private capital, this has not yet (as of the late 2000s) developed to the extent that it would pose a threat to the prevailing social system.

Whether the market-oriented reforms introduced under the Yeltsin regime's counter-revolutionary agenda will lead Russia to a new era of "prosperity and democracy" as the West claims, or continue to sink the country deeper into the malaise of a deformed Mafia capitalism, only time will tell. It is clear, however, that at least as of this writing in late 2000, the dynamics of Russian society are moving that nation in the latter direction. Whatever the momentary detractions and reversals that Russia and the other former Soviet republics continue to face today, the dialectics of the class contradictions that are maturing under conditions of deformed capitalism in these countries, are bound to lead to further struggles for power among the contending class forces and open up new arenas of mass struggle that go beyond criticisms of exploitation and economic deprivation, and toward collective action to gain state power and effect change.

The Development of the Socialist State in China

The post-1949 revolutionary experience of China has in a number of ways been similar to that of socialist construction in Russia following the October Revolution. After the 1949 revolution, China went through several important stages in its political economic development: the three years immediately following the revolution (1949-52); the socialist transformation of the economy (1953-57); the Great Leap Forward (1958); the crisis years (1959-61); the New Economic Policy (1961-64); the Cultural Revolution (1966-69); the growth years of the early 1970s (1970-76); the great reversals of the late 1970s and 1980s (1976-89); and the expansion years of the 1990s (1990-99).

The First Three Years (1949 to 1952)

Before the revolution in 1949, China was a poor and backward country. The predominant mode of production was feudal; less than

10 percent of the population (made up of landlords and rich peasants) owned 70 percent of the land; about 80 percent of the population was employed in agriculture; disease, hunger, and mass starvation were not uncommon. The industrial sector was small and largely owned by foreign capitalists.

After the revolution, the immediate strategic objective of the socialist state was to bring order to the chaotic economic situation of the country. During the initial period (1949-52), economic control was secured over the major branches of the national economy, and a series of broad-based measures of land reform were put into effect, which redistributed the estates of landlords and rich peasants. The national bourgeoisie was viewed as a progressive force; hence, with the exception of the industrial assets belonging to those allied with foreign capital, no large-scale nationalization policy was initiated to confiscate private capital. Rather than a revolutionary transformation in the ownership of the means of production, the economic policy of the state during this period was one of gradualism.

The Socialist Transformation of the Economy (1953-57)

In 1953, China launched its First Five-Year Development Plan, the aims of which were to lay the foundations for a comprehensive industrial base as rapidly as possible. In the initial stage of this industrialization process, emphasis was placed on the production of capital goods (over 50 percent of the state's investment funds was tied to heavy industry) and agriculture remained in the background. By placing strong emphasis on industrialization, China's objective was to replicate the Soviet experience into the framework of a development strategy based on the particular historical context in which the country found itself. This was clearly stated by Mao:

> In order to turn our country into an industrial power, we
> must learn conscientiously from the advanced experi-
> ence of the Soviet Union. The Soviet Union has been
> building socialism for forty years, and its experience is
> very valuable to us. . . . It is perfectly true that we should
> learn from the good experience of all countries, socialist
> or capitalist, and there is no argument about this point.
> But the main thing is still to learn from the Soviet Union.

Now, there are two different attitudes towards learning from others. One is the dogmatic attitude of transplanting everything, whether or not it is suited to our conditions. This is no good. The other attitude is to use our heads and learn those things which suit our conditions, that is, to absorb whatever experience is useful to us. That is the attitude we should adopt.

To strengthen our solidarity with the Soviet Union, to strengthen our solidarity with all the socialist countries—that is our fundamental policy, this is where our basic interest lies.[32]

Following the post-1928 Soviet strategy, planning became highly centralized, and targets were fixed by the central government, which administered the various development programs through the ministries. Long-term loan agreements were set up with the Soviet Union to begin a large number of diversified modern industrial plants throughout the country.

Most industrial targets of the First Five-Year Plan were achieved and some surpassed. Heavy industry constituted 48 percent of industrial output by 1957. Over the period of the plan, crude steel output increased from 1.35 million metric tons to 5.35 million; coal from 66.5 to 130.7 million; petroleum from 0.44 to 1.46 million; cement from 2.9 to 6.9 million; sulfuric acid from 190 thousand metric tons to 632 thousand; and electric power from 7.3 billion kilowatt hours to 19.3 billion.

According to official figures, the gross output value of all industry, including handicrafts, increased by 128.4 percent during the plan, an annual average of 18 percent. . . .[33]

In the agricultural sector, the strategy was to extend collectivization gradually. This was done in several stages: (1) mutual aid teams were developed, especially during 1949-52; (2) the movement into cooperatives occurred in 1955-56; and (3) communes were introduced in rural areas by the end of the decade.

Significant advances were made both in industry and agriculture. Although the major emphasis was on the expansion of heavy industry, the gross output value of agriculture increased by 24.7 percent at 1952 prices, and the output of food grains increased by 19.8 percent. And as the movement toward cooperative (and in broader terms, the collectivization of agriculture) was speeded up in late 1955 through Mao's major policy intervention, by the end of the following year over four-fifths of peasant households had become members of higher cooperatives.[34]

Despite the relatively sizeable advances made in agriculture, the state's emphasis on heavy industry placed agriculture in the background; a mere 6.2 percent investment in the latter was nowhere near the level needed to generate the rapid production of food and agricultural goods crucial for maintaining a high level of heavy industrial productivity. The slow progress in agriculture, coupled with the relative neglect of light industry, created problems for peasant incentives:

> Just as in the Soviet Union in the 1920s, the encouragement of a marketable surplus in agriculture depended largely in investment in agriculture, and on making available supplies of light industrial goods for peasants to buy in exchange for their product, so in China it was found that, under conditions of only gradual collectivization, peasant productivity lagged as a result of lack of incentives. Without steadily growing surpluses of agriculture, not only were there problems in supplying food to urban areas, but the financial backing (derived from taxation on agriculture and state profits from resale of agricultural deliveries) for industrialization was not there. Lack of expert surpluses did not permit the alternative method of industrialization, of exporting grain to obtain imported machinery.
>
> In 1956-57 the State procurements of grain and taxation in kind fell to 25.1 percent of the value of all grain produced, compared to 29.1 percent in 1953-54.[35]

One method of dealing with the emergent problems of industrialization generated during the course of the First Five-Year Plan was, as pointed out above, the rapid growth of agricultural collectives in 1955-56. Two other methods, initiated by Mao, also were designed to overcome these problems: (1) the commune system in agriculture in 1958, and (2) the encouragement of the Great Leap Forward in industry in 1958-59.

Writing on the relationship between heavy industry, light industry, and agriculture, Mao, after pointing out that "heavy industry is the core of China's economic construction," stressed that "full attention must be paid to the development of agriculture and light industry." His message was clear: "Industry must develop together with agriculture,"

> for only thus can industry secure raw materials and market, and only thus is it possible to accumulate fairly large funds for building a powerful heavy industry. Everyone knows that light industry is closely related to agriculture. Without agriculture there can be no light industry. But it is not yet so clearly understood that agriculture provides heavy industry with an important market. This fact, however, will be more readily appreciated as gradual progress in the technical improvement and modernization of agriculture calls for more and more machinery, fertilizer, water conservancy and electric power projects and transport facilities for the farms, as well as fuel and building materials of the rural consumers. . . . As agriculture and light industry develop, heavy industry, assured of its market and funds, will grow faster.[36]

Hence, during 1958, the movement toward the communalization of agriculture occurred concurrently with the decentralization of light industry. Earlier, in *Report on the First Five-Year Plan of Development*, Chief Planner Li Fu-Chun had announced a policy of "appropriately locating new industries in different parts of the country so that industrial production will be close to the sources of raw materials and fuels as well as consumer markets."[37] And this policy was in line with the measures advocated later during the Great Leap Forward.

The Great Leap Forward (1958)

The decentralization of industry and the communalization of agriculture were the central aims of what came to be known as "the

Great Leap Forward." This period saw the creation of the communes and the industrial policy of "walking on two legs":

> The aim of the commune system was the intensification of agricultural socialism to increase the marketable agricultural surplus and widen local agricultural and other investment opportunities. The industrial policy of "walking on two legs" aimed to tap the sources of industrial growth inherent in widely spread, easily mined coal and iron ore deposits, and small-scale indigenous technology, by the rapid development of small and medium industry in the interior of the country, both within and without the communes. In this respect it can be viewed as a kind of "crash industrialization" program, but within the context of developing agrarian socialism, without large-scale labor transfers to the cities.[38]

The Great Leap Forward was thus designed to achieve industrialization in a rural setting that was both complementary to the agrarian sector and decentralized enough to meet local demand for industrial goods. The coordination of the agrarian and industrial sectors within the context of a developing socialist society was the key to the success of the Great Leap Forward and of Chinese socialism in general—one that was to take place within the framework of communal social relations.

The Crisis Years (1959-61)

While in 1958 the Great Leap Forward facilitated the development of industrial production within a rural communal setting, in 1959 China was on the eve of a major crisis that was to continue for the following two years. Two major developments were primarily responsible for the disastrous effects of the crisis years: (1) widespread natural disasters in agricultural regions, brought about by drought, typhoons, floods, and pests, destroyed more than half of the cultivated area, leading to a serious food shortage; and (2) the sudden withdrawal of Soviet economic aid in 1960 caused major disruptions in heavy industry, as some 150 enterprises (with over 1000 Soviet technicians) were stopped. These two problems not only slowed down growth in both the agricultural and industrial sectors but also had adverse effects on operations throughout the economy. The Chinese industrialization process, based largely on Soviet aid, came to an end. And these events gave rise to sharp political and ideological debates over China's future economic policy toward agriculture and industry.

The New Economic Policy (1961-64)

The economic crisis of 1959-61 led the state to adopt a new strategy of economic development and a new set of policies that would put such strategy into motion. The new course of development came to be known as the New Economic Policy (NEP).

The basic similarity between this and the Soviet NEP of 1921-28 was the granting of concessions for the expansion of free-market forces and the return of the profit motive in both agricultural and industrial production. As in the Soviet Union, of course, this was to take place within the framework of proletarian political leadership and the state's ownership of the major means of production and exchange.

In January 1961, an official declaration was made "to reinforce the agricultural front by making agriculture the foundation of the national economy and giving industry second priority":

> It was pointed out then, and later, that the Chinese countryside constituted eighty percent of the market of light industrial goods, as well as a large market for heavy industrial goods. It was proposed to adjust the rate of development of industry to the amount of raw materials and foodstuffs that agriculture could supply, and that industry should supply the flow of goods made necessary by agricultural development to help mechanize the rural sector.[39]

One of the first moves under the NEP was the gradual introduction of a free market in the countryside. Later, further concessions were made to the peasants through the adoption of the policy of *san zi yi bao*, which involved the restoration of private plots to peasants; the use of the household as the main accounting unit in communes; the assumption by enterprises in communes of sole responsibility for profit and output quotas. Although the implementation of these policies made it possible to increase agricultural production, it also meant widespread diffusion of private cultivation practices throughout China's rural interior. And this, in turn, gave rise to the formation of a *kulak* peasant class.

It is clear that many of the steps taken during China's New Economic Policy resembled closely the situation that existed in the Soviet Union during the 1920s. Lenin's plans under NEP were clear; it was a transitional policy that was necessary for the full-scale development of industry and agriculture to prepare the road for the transition to socialism. Was this also true in China? Certainly the parallel is clear; and while agriculture in China got the upper hand, it nonetheless was to be coordinated with the development of industry. But the important question is, Were the policies adopted under the NEP in China from the beginning regarded as temporary? Or was such a move a response to unexpected changes in material conditions at the time? The reason we raise these questions is that although things were clear in Lenin's mind with regard to the future transition to socialism when he introduced the New Economic Policy in 1921, the consistency of this policy was threatened after his death in 1924 by rightists within the Communist party under the leadership of Bukharin, who essentially wanted to change the transitional NEP into a permanent one. This was almost exactly the situation in which the Chinese Communist party found itself in the early 1960s; at the same, time capitalist forms of production and exchange (at least at the small-scale level) were in full swing throughout the rural areas. Moreover, this vigorous movement to the Right (led by Bukharin's Chinese counterpart, Liu Shao-chi, who had once strongly supported revolutionary policies), was multiplied by the growing emphasis on profitability, expertise, and bureaucratization, in addition to the reappearance of traditional patterns of industrial organization and ownership. Again, the question to be asked is whether the NEP was a transitional stage in Chinese socialist development or was it to become institutionalized into the mainstream of Chinese economy and society?

To clarify this point, and to place the post-1960 policy changes within the proper historical context, Wheelwright and McFarlane put it this way:

> Broadly speaking, Mao's technique in 1960-64 was to prepare and issue warnings about the implications of the "rightist" trend in economic policy and culture, and to counterpose "the revolutionary tradition of the masses," the need to train reliable successors to the revolution who would not follow the Soviet road,[40] the need for everyone to be a soldier, and the need to implement, wherever possible, the line of "from the masses to the masses," which had fallen into disarray with the "seventy points" in industry and the "san zi yi bao" policy in agriculture. Mao also took certain organizational steps, notably in obtaining the adherence of the People's Liberation Army and General Lin Piao. . . .
>
> By 1965 the tensions in Chinese Society were building up. The official ideology of the Chinese Revolution remained Maoist. But the State organizations and enterprises, and large sectors of cultural and ideological life, were governed by different rules. The years 1964 and 1965, in particular, saw the beginning of the struggle to resolve the question—"Which will transform which?" between State and Party practice, and Maoism? In this sense, 1965 marked the prelude to the Great Proletarian Cultural Revolution.[41]

The Cultural Revolution, which raised the crucial political issues confronting the Chinese state to the level of collective action, was intended to resolve this imbedded contradiction between theory and practice, ideology and practical politics—a contradiction that could be resolved, as it turned out, only through a mass action that the Cultural Revolution came to represent in the political uproar of the late 1960s.

The Cultural Revolution (1966-69)

Closely observing the changes brought about by the NEP and disturbed by the direction in which it was moving, Mao, by launching the Great Proletarian Cultural Revolution, once again brought China under revolutionary leadership guided by proletarian principles and strategies.

The Cultural Revolution was launched, above all, to end entrenched bureaucratization of political life at the highest levels of the Chinese state, including the political officialdom and the intelligentsia, in an effort to halt the development of bourgeois values and privileges among a cadre of self-serving "revisionist" bureaucrats who were "communist" in name only. The attack on bourgeois ideas and privileges within the party and the promotion of class struggle at the ideological level (between the communists and the "capitalist roaders" within the party) was an effort to halt the danger of capitalist restoration while at the same time consolidating the gains of socialism.

We cannot go into a detailed analysis of the Cultural Revolution here, but its main features can be summarized as follows: (1) in political terms, the Cultural Revolution meant a clear victory for the Maoists in the fierce struggle against the "revisionists," led by Liu Shao-chi; (2) by taking power away from the rightists, the Maoists were able to resume the strategy of economic development launched by Mao during the Great Leap Forward in 1958; (3) culturally, it was a campaign against Confucianism and tradition—the tradition based on bourgeois and feudal ideologies—in the process of which the supremacy of the Maoist ideology over "revisionism" was assured; (4) at the mass level, it was a major effort to involve the masses deeply in the revolutionary fervor, an exercise in reminding them of the central importance of the class struggle; (5) again at the mass level, it was an educational campaign directed at the younger generations—a learning process in the midst of the revolutionary experience of the masses. The Cultural Revolution thus opened up a new phase in China's development that was to continue to the end of the 1960s.

The Growth Years (1970-76)

During the 1970s, China made great advances in economic development and social progress. Production increased, exports grew, and industrialization forged ahead, with impressive rates of growth in major branches of industry, especially in crude oil production, machinery, and manufactured goods. By the mid 1970s, China was producing 259 million metric tons of grain, 24 million metric tons of steel, 655 million metric tons of crude oil, 25 million metric tons of chemicals and fertilizers, 133 thousand tractors, and 5 million bicycles.[42]

This period also saw a marked growth in small industries that produce many of the inputs required by agriculture (cement, steel, fertilizers, etc.) and process the sector's output of food, cotton, sugar, tobacco, and other commercial crops. Moreover, with its strides in rapid industrialization, China reached a position by the mid 1970s of exporting one-quarter of its oil production and a large volume of manufactured goods (including bicycles, sewing machines, cameras, watches, and radios) to countries around the world. At the same time, the planning authorities promoted greater intensity of land use, further mechanization, and other measures to keep food supplies ahead of population, including a nationwide effort to limit birthrates. All these policies were implemented within the framework of a revolutionary program of social transformation leading to the consolidation of socialism that guaranteed a higher standard of living for the people.

The Great Reversals (1976-89)

With the death of Mao in 1976, China entered another period of reversals and setbacks in socialist construction, as rightist forces within the Chinese CP, headed by Teng Hsiao-ping, took advantage of the advances made in the economic sphere and made a comeback, repositioning China on the "capitalist road" and away from the socialist programs of the previous period. As a result, China began moving during the 1980s in the direction of a process that would restructure its socialist economic base through superstructural reforms of a market-oriented nature.

The changes that China underwent during this period were the result of a new approach adopted by the Chinese CP toward private capital, including foreign capital, with which the state entered into joint ventures in various industries. While this approach facilitated the evolution of the Chinese economy along a development path that was export-oriented, the state's strong controls to curb the negative impact of the opening to foreign and domestic capital helped mediate the process whereby the central authority (the state) would retain its reign over the major means of production, while at the same time accelerate the development of the productive forces and increase China's position in world trade. China's decade-long drive for modernization of its economy through a tactical alliance with foreign capital for further domestic growth and diversification in the direction of consumer goods production for export thus fed into its rising prospects for international trade—one that necessitated changes in the domestic economic structure, affecting the social-economic position of millions of Chinese who more and more engaged in small-scale entrepreneurial activities, hence facilitating the expansion of the private sector.

The changes China underwent in its domestic and global economic relations during this period inevitably necessitated a fundamental change in its foreign and domestic policy in the political sphere that was far more significant than the reversals of the early 1960s and comparable in magnitude to the Cultural Revolution, but in the opposite direction.[43]

China's opening to the West and increasing collaboration with foreign capital during the 1980s not only led to the further reversals of the policies promoted during the Cultural Revolution, but was an extension of the economic progress made during the growth years of the 1970s and set the stage for China's fuller participation in the world economy beyond the 1980s and well into the 1990s.

The Expansion Years (1990-99)

With the emergence of Li Pang and the opposition forces within the Chinese CP in the late 1980s, the new party leadership began to tighten China's "pragmatic" economic policies that it had embarked on earlier, and led the country in a direction that placed the economy under greater state control. Thus, during the 1990s, the market reforms of the previous period evolved within the framework of an expanded role for the state—a role that complemented the enormous economic gains of the 1980s.

However, China's continued integration into the world economy during this period, through joint-ventures with foreign capital, increased trade with the advanced capitalist countries, especially the United States, and pending membership in international financial and trade organizations, which regularly impose stringent economic conditions for compliance with regulations concerning international capital flows, global financial transactions, and social policy, have had a serious negative effect on the Chinese state, economy, and society. While such an outcome has come as a surprise to the pragmatic leadership of the Chinese CP during this latest phase of China's economic development tied to the world economy, the process in place during this period has generated a new set of problems for the Chinese state.

The contradictions imbedded in this process, subjecting the state to the dictates of the global political-economic structure and its institutions, has had a heavy toll on the evolution of Chinese socialism, forcing on the state setbacks and distortions that it has so far been unable to avoid. The effects of global political economic relations on China and its role in the world economy in this and the coming period have thus become hot topics for discussion and debate—topics that are of critical importance for China's further development in the years ahead.

What the final outcome of this evolving situation will be in the next stage of the development process in China in the 21st century, only time will tell. But it is clear that the process of socialist construction in China, as in the former Soviet Union, has been a cyclical and contradictory one with many setbacks along the way—a process that is characteristic of the transition from capitalism to socialism throughout the world.

Conclusion

We have seen that the experiences of the Soviet Union and China in socialist construction were the result of social and historical conditions that set the boundaries in which the development process was to proceed. The circumstances that shaped the policies set forth and implemented by the state in both countries were beyond the control of any individual(s); they required the concerted effort of the working class allied with the peasant masses and led by a vanguard political organ, the Communist party, which assured its control and domination of the state and formulation of state policy favorable to the laboring masses.

Both countries took measures to offset any damaging effects on the socialist order. These measures, such as the ones taken during the 1920s in the Soviet Union and in the early 1960s in China, affected the course of socialist development in a big way, sometimes arresting its progress and even forcing tactical retreats. Nevertheless, it can be argued that, except for the turn of events in China in the early 1960s and more recently in the post-1976 period, the policies implemented in both countries during the early stages of postrevolutionary construction were seen as necessary for the survival of the socialist state. No amount of high-sounding pronouncements would have corrected the situation in favor of the proletariat when the balance of class forces, domestically and internationally, especially in the Soviet Union, was stacked decisively against it. Clearly, it was the relentless efforts of a committed revolutionary leadership imbedded in the struggles of the time that made it possible to safeguard, defend, and advance the interests of the proletarian state, in spite of the concessions they were forced to make to the enemies of the revolution and of the socialist state.

In retrospect, it should be pointed out that while it is easy to wish for a smooth and linear progression of socialist construction following a proletarian revolution, the realities of the capitalist dominated world economy force us to see that the transition from capitalism to communism is anything but a smooth and linear process. It is, in fact, a conflicting and contradictory process of development that both the Soviet Union and China went through to safeguard socialism in the various stages of socialist construction that they initiated to promote their development during the course of the twentieth century.

Notes

1. Karl Marx, *Critique of the Gotha Programme*, in Karl Marx and Frederick Engels, *Selected Works* (New York: International Publishers, 1972), p. 331; emphasis in the original. For an extended discussion on the concept of the "dictatorship of the proletariat" in the context of the debates on the left, see Etienne Balibar, *On the Dictatorship of the Proletariat* (London: NLB, 1977).

2. V.I. Lenin, *The State and Revolution*, in V.I. Lenin, *Selected Works in One Volume* (New York: International Publishers, 1971), p. 281; emphasis in original.

3. Ibid., p. 288; emphasis in original.

4. Ibid., p. 327; emphasis in original.

5. F. Engels, *Anti-Duhring* (New York: International Publishers, 1976), p. 307.

6. Lenin, *The State and Revolution*, pp. 327–28.

7. During the 1970s, a variety of political positions characterized the Soviet Union as capitalist or socialist across the political spectrum on the left. See for example *On the Transition to Socialism*, eds. Paul Sweezy and Charles Bettelheim (New York: Monthly Review Press, 1971); Charles Bettelheim, *Class Struggles in the U.S.S.R.* 2 Vols. (New York: Monthly Review Press, 1976 and 1978); Martin Nicolaus, *Restoration of Capitalism in the U.S.S.R.* (Chicago: Liberator Press, 1975); Revolutionary Union, *How Capitalism Has Been Restored in the Soviet Union* (Chicago: The Revolutionary Union, 1974); Tony Cliff, *State Capitalism in Russia* (London: Pluto Press, 1974); Michael Goldfield and Melvin Rothenberg, *The Myth of Capitalism Reborn: A Marxist Critique of Theories of Capitalist Restoration in the U.S.S.R.* (San Francisco: Line of March Publications, 1980); Sam Marcy, *The Class Character of the U.S.S.R.* (New York: World View Publishers, 1977); Erwin Marquit, *The Socialist Countries* (Minneapolis: M.E.P. Publications, 1978). Also see Albert Szymanski, *Is the Red Flag Flying? The Political Economy of the Soviet Union* (London: Zed Press, 1979).

8. The most bizarre of these positions, that the Soviet state was a "monopoly capitalist state of the fascist type," was advanced by China and the Maoists in the late 1960s and throughout the 1970s for propaganda purposes, who argued: "The Soviet Union today is under the dictatorship of the bourgeoisie, a dictatorship of the big bourgeoisie, a dictatorship of the German fascist type, a dictatorship of the Hitler type." *Peking Review*, January 30, 1976. Also see *How the Soviet Revisionists Carry Out All-Round Restoration of Capitalism in the U.S.S.R.* (Peking: Foreign Languages Press, 1968) and Yenan Books (ed.), *Social Imperialism: The Soviet Union Today* (Berkeley: Yenan Books, 1977) (reprints from the *Peking Review*).

9. Maurice Dobb, *Soviet Economic Development Since 1917* (London: Routledge & Kegan Paul, 1948), p. 88, 92.

10. V.I. Lenin, *Selected Works in Three Volumes*, vol. 2 (Moscow: Progress Publishers, 1975), p. 634.

11. Dobb, *Soviet Economic Development*, p. 93.

12. Ibid., pp. 95–96.

13. See Barrington Moore, Jr., *Soviet Politics: The Dilemma of Power* (Cambridge, Mass.: Harvard University Press, 1950); E.H. Carr, *History of Soviet Russia*, vol. 2 (New York: Macmillan, 1952); Dobb, *Soviet Economic Development*.

14. Dobb, *Soviet Economic Development*, p. 96.

15. Lenin, *Selected Works*, 3, p. 537.

16. Quoted in Alexander Erlich, *The Soviet Industrialization Debate* (Cambridge, Mass.: Harvard University Press, 1960), p. 3.

17. Moore, *Soviet Politics*, p. 93.

18. Quoted in Erlich, *Soviet Industrialization*, p. 6.

19. Ibid., p. 10.

20. Ibid., pp. xvi–xvii.

21. Carr, *History of Soviet Russia.*

22. Charles K. Wilber, *The Soviet Model and Underdeveloped Countries* (Chapel Hill: University of North Carolina Press, 1969), p. 59.

23. J.V. Stalin, *Questions of Leninism* (Moscow: Foreign Languages Publishing House, 1939), p. 487.

24. Dobb, *Soviet Economic Development*, p. 222.

25. Stalin, quoted in ibid.

26. Paul Baran, *The Political Economy of Growth* (New York: Monthly Review Press, 1957) p. 297.

27. Ibid., p. 280.

28. Alexander Gerschenkron, *A Dollar Index of Soviet Machinery Output, 1927– 28 to 1937* (Los Angeles: The Rand Corporation, 1951); and idem, *Economic Backwardness in Historical Perspective* (New York: Praeger, 1965), p. 247.

29. Maurice Dobb, "The Soviet Economy: Fact and Fiction," *Science and Society*, Spring 1954.

30. Baran, *Political Economy of Growth*, p. 282.

31. Ibid.

32. Mao Tse-Tung, "China's Path to Industrialization," Part 12 of "On the Correct Handling of Contradictions Among the People," *Selected Readings from the Works of Mao Tse-Tung* (Peking: Foreign Languages Press, 1971), pp. 477–78.

33. E.L. Wheelwright and B. McFarlane, *The Chinese Road to Socialism* (New York: Monthly Review Press, 1970), p. 36.

34. Higher cooperatives were large units that embraced whole villages, containing from 100 to 300 households, whereas lower cooperatives consisted of from 20 to 40 households. The former became the basic economic unit in the countryside during this period. For the nature, size, extent, and central importance of cooperatives in the early phase of China's collectivization of the agricultural sector, see Mao Tse-Tung, "On the Question of Agricultural Cooperatives," *Selected Readings*, pp. 389–420.

35. Wheelwright and McFarlane, *The Chinese Road to Socialism*, p. 40.

36. Mao Tse-Tung, "Correct Handling of Contradictions," p. 476.

37. Li Fu-Chun, *Report on the First Five-Year Plan of Development* (Peking: Foreign Languages Press, 1950), p. 50.

38. Wheelwright and McFarlane, *The Chinese Road to Socialism*, p. 43.

39. Ibid., p. 66.

40. The reference here is to the "revisionist" policies of the Soviet leadership following Stalin's death and the "restoration of the capitalist road" by the Khrushchev forces.

41. Wheelwright and McFarlane, *The Chinese Road to Socialism*, p. 93.

42. John Gurley, *Challengers to Capitalism* (San Francisco: San Francisco Book, 1976), pp. 136–37.

43. Charles Bettelheim, "The Great Leap Backward," *Monthly Review* 30, no. 3 (July–August 1978).

CHAPTER 8

CONCLUSION

CLASS, STATE, AND POWER:
THE POLITICS OF CHANGE

We can draw a number of conclusions from the analysis presented in this book. First, it is clear that the state has come to play an increasingly important role in a large number of societies around the world over an extended historical period that spans many centuries. Indeed, in class societies, the state has played a central role not only as the prime superstructural institution but also as the organ reinforcing the class rule of the dominant class, hence the dominant mode of production. Moreover, its monopoly of force and violence has, in certain periods, given the state considerable independence, thus giving it extraordinary powers over society.

Three major perspectives in political sociology—pluralism, elite theory, and Marxism—have provided alternative answers on the nature and role of the state in society and have attempted to develop a theory of the state and politics that would explain the form and content of the state as one of the key institutions of modern society. We have in this book examined the fundamental arguments of each perspective and their variants at length, and provided a critique of their formulations on the nature and role of the state.

We have argued that both pluralism and elite theory fall far short of providing a complete and accurate analysis of the *real* nature of the state and its relation to class forces in society, although elements of their approach correspond to *appearances* of power relations in the multiparty polity and the bureaucratic organizations of society. In fact, the pronouncements of both perspectives are highly ideological and end up being not much more than an apologetic theoretical rationalization for "pluralistic" and authoritarian forms of the capitalist state, respectively.

In contrast to these dominant theoretical positions in political sociology, we have counterposed classical and more recent Marxist theories of the state and their neo-Weberian variants, and have provided a critique of the deficiencies prevalent in most of these recent reformulations, opting instead for an historical-materialist approach based on the concepts and analyses provided by the Marxist classics.

In line with this approach, we have argued that the state is a product of class divisions and class struggles lodged in the dominant mode of production, which, once articulated through the state, become politicized and take on the form of political struggles (i.e., struggles for state power). Moreover, under capitalism, the state as a rule remains the organ of the dominant capitalist class and represents the interests of that class, except when such rule is challenged by forces whose interests run counter to the interests of this class and the state that it controls. Thus, short of a major shift in the balance of class forces and centers of political power effected through a social revolution, which would bring about a major restructuring of the state apparatus and dominant class linkages to the state, the "relative autonomy" of the state must be seen within the context of its ultimate control by the dominant capitalist class, which, by necessity, gives the state a degree of independence to serve its class interests and the interests of capitalism in general. As such, the state in this context cannot be viewed as having a "codeterminant" role so that its actions are free of dominant class sanctions; rather, the dialectics of the political superstructure must be seen as a reaction to (but not against) the prevailing social-economic order, which in turn places the ultimate limits to such actions. Any deviation from such conception of the base-superstructure problematic, as in the case of the neo-Weberian and Hegelian-Marxist formulations of state autonomy, leads one in a pluralist or elitist direction, such that the arena of power struggles becomes the state and state alone, independent of the mode of production and the class struggles, which in the end are manifested in full force at the level of the state. For this reason, not only pluralism and elite theory but also their neo-Marxist variants influenced by Hegelian and Weberian formulations are rejected in favor of the historical materialist approach that I feel best explains the logic and structure of relations between class, state, and power in society and accounts for the process of change as based on class relations and class struggles as the major determinants of social transformation. Indeed, following all the analyses and debates on the state during the 1970s and 1980s, this approach once again became the dominant mode of Marxist theorizing on the state during the 1990s, extending its influence further into the field of political sociology as we enter the twenty-first century.

Applying the historical-materialist approach to the study of the state, we have examined the origins and development of the state from its early beginnings to the most recent period—tracing its history through Oriental despotism, slavery, feudalism, capitalism, and socialism. We have found that the state has not always existed; its prevalence is a recent occurrence, going back only a few thousand years out of the entire history of human society. In fact, only in the past few hundred years has the state, as the supreme superstructural institution in society, become prevalent throughout the world. A few societies still exist, in isolated parts of the world, that govern themselves without a state. But the growth and expansion of capitalism over the past two hundred years has led to the expansion of the capitalist state across national boundaries, claiming for itself the "exclusive right" to dictate its terms to the world community.

The origins of the capitalist state go back to the transition from feudalism to capitalism in Western Europe during the sixteenth to the eighteenth centuries, when a dual process of capital accumulation, aided by overseas trade, led to the establishment of the great commercial and manufacturing firms that gave rise to the industrial capitalist class throughout the Continent by the late eighteenth century. Evolving at a different pace in different parts of Europe and later in the United States, this class acquired state power to serve and expand its class interests. Across the Continent and throughout the colonies, bourgeois revolutions took hold of the state machine and turned it into an instrument of capital accumulation that consolidated capitalist class rule over large portions of the world, in time giving rise to monopolies, cartels, and trusts. Thus was established the mass-scale exploitation of labor across continents that fostered the capital accumulation process—a process that could not have been fully realized without the active participation of the state.

We have seen this in our analysis of the formation of the U.S. state in the late eighteenth century, and the subsequent development and consolidation of capitalist rule nationwide following the Civil War. Since then, U.S. capitalism has developed beyond its territorial boundaries, and with it the U.S. capitalist state has extended its power and dominance throughout the world. As U.S. capitalism reached its postwar prominence and brought forth greater demands on the state, this led to increased conflicts and crises that have become ever more difficult to resolve within the framework of the prevailing economic and political structure. The increasing dominance of the monopoly fraction within the state has made matters worse, as the U.S. state has lost all semblance of relative autonomy from capital as a whole and has turned into a direct tool of monopoly capital to protect the latter's narrow interests.

The crisis of the U.S. state in the late twentieth century has in part emerged as a result of the challenge to its global dominance, where revolts and revolutions throughout the colonies and neocolonies of the imperial centers, together with a variety of protest movements in the heartland of imperialism, have set limits to U.S. capitalist domination of the world economy and polity, giving rise to counterforces in the global class struggle, leading to the establishment of various postcolonial and socialist states. This, in turn, has generated movements and struggles in the imperial centers, as the exploited and oppressed classes of advanced capitalist society have put up a determined and protracted struggle against capital and the capitalist state, a struggle that continues to intensify as the crisis of capitalism enters a new stage.

While contradictions of the newly formed capitalist states in Asia, Africa, Latin America, and the Middle East during this century are being manifested in conflicts and crises across the Third World and are leading to an intensification of the class struggle between the contending class forces and the state lined up on the side of the exploiting classes in society, the working class, the peasantry, and other popular sectors in the Third World are beginning to take things into their own hands and bring an end to capitalist exploitation and the rule of the local capitalist state.

Finally, in socialist societies, the trials and tribulations of the victorious laboring masses in constructing a new social order have given them new tools and methods of advancing toward an egalitarian society with the prospects of a future withering away of the state. In our analysis of the origins and development of the socialist state in the Soviet Union and China we concluded that the transition from capitalism to socialism and from socialism to full communism is anything but smooth and uniform. The historical experience of these two socialist states have demonstrated that the road to social progress, genuine democracy, and popular rule may be filled with problems and setbacks, which sometimes derail efforts in this collective project. In any event, they depend, in the final analysis, on the active role and participation of the laboring masses in all aspects of economic, social, and political life, including first and foremost the state.

The protracted class struggles of the working class under advanced capitalism, whatever their temporal intensity or form, together with the struggles of the laboring masses in the postcolonial states of the Third World and in the socialist states developing toward a more egalitarian state and society, indicate the march of history that indeed one day will yield results in favor of the laboring masses throughout the world in gaining full democracy and popular rule. They will make the monopoly of force and violence of the state over society obsolete, so society, organized "on the basis of a free and equal association of the producers," as one champion of the working class has proclaimed, "will put the whole machinery of state where it will then belong: into the museum of antiquities, by the side of the spinning-wheel and the bronze axe."

REFERENCES

Agh, Attila. 1998. *The Politics of Central Europe*. Thousand Oaks, Calif.: Sage Publications.

Alavi, Hamza. 1975. "India and the Colonial Mode of Production." *Economic and Political Weekly* (August).

———. 1982. "State and Class under Peripheral Capitalism." In *An Introduction to the Sociology of "Developing Societies"*, edited by H. Alavi and T. Shanin. London: Macmillan.

Alex-Assensoh, Yvette Marie and Lawrence J. Hanks (eds.). 2000. *Black and Multiracial Politics in America*. New York: New York University Press.

Althusser, Louis. 1971. "Ideology and Ideological State Apparatuses." In L. Althusser, *Lenin and Philosophy and Other Essays*. London: New Left Books.

———. 1976. *Essays in Self-Criticism*. London: New Left Books.

Althusser, Louis, and Etienne Balibar. 1968. *Reading Capital*. London: New Left Books.

Amin, Samir. 1974. *Accumulation on a World Scale*. New York: Monthly Review Press.

———. 1976. *Unequal Development: An Essay on the Social Formations of Peripheral Capitalism*. New York: Monthly Review Press.

———. 1990. *Delinking: Towards a Polycentric World*. London: Zed Books.

———. 1997. *Capitalism in the Age of Globalization*. London: Zed Books.

Anderson, Perry. 1974. *Lineages of the Absolutist State*. London: New Left Books.

———. 1974. *Passages from Antiquity to Feudalism*. London: New Left Books.

Aptheker, Herbert. 1960. *The American Revolution, 1763-1783*. New York: International Publishers.

———. 1976. *Early Years of the Republic*. New York: International Publishers.

Ashley, David and David Michael Ornstein. 1998. *Sociological Theory: Classical Statements*. 4th ed. Boston: Allyn and Bacon.

Balibar, Etienne. 1977. *On the Dictatorship of the Proletariat*. London: New Left Books.

Baran, Paul. 1957. *The Political Economy of Growth*. New York: Monthly Review Press.

Baran, Paul, and Paul M. Sweezy. 1966. *Monopoly Capital*. New York: Monthly Review Press.

Batatu, Hanna. 1978. *The Old Social Classes and the Revolutionary Movements of Iraq*. Princeton: Princeton University Press.

Beard, Charles. 1962. *An Economic Interpretation of the Constitution of the United States*. New York: Macmillan.

Beard, Charles, and Mary Beard. 1930. *The Rise of American Civilization*. New York: Macmillan.

Beinin, Joel. 1982. "Egypt's Transition under Nasser." *MERIP Reports*, no. 107 (July-August).

Belov, Gennady. 1986. *What Is the State?* Moscow: Progress Publishers.

Bentley, Arthur. 1967. *The Process of Government*. Cambridge, Mass.: Belknap Press of Harvard University.

Berberoglu, Berch. 1977. "The Transition from Feudalism to Capitalism: The Sweezy-Dobb Debate." *Revista Mexicana de Sociologia* 39, no. 4 (October-December).

———. 1980. "Pre-Capitalist Modes of Production: Their Origins, Contradictions, and Transformation." *Quarterly Review of Historical Studies* 19, nos. 1-2.

———. 1986. *India: National Liberation and Class Struggles*. Meerut: Sarup & Sons.

———. 1987. *The Internationalization of Capital: Imperialism and Capitalist Development on a World Scale*. New York: Praeger.

———. 1989. *Power and Stability in the Middle East*. (London: Zed Books.

———. 1992. *The Legacy of Empire: Economic Decline and Class Polarization in the United States*. New York: Praeger.

———. 1992. *Class, State, and Development in India*. Delhi: Sage Publications.

———. 1992. *The Political Economy of Development: Development Theory and the Prospects for Change in the Third World*. Albany: State University of New York Press.

———. 1993. *The Labor Process and Control of Labor*. New York: Praeger Publishers.

———. 1993. *Critical Perspectives in Sociology*, 2nd ed. Dubuque, Iowa: Kendall-Hunt Publishing Co.

———. 1994. *Class Structure and Social Transformation*. Westport, Conn.: Praeger Publishers.

———. 1995. *The National Question: Nationalism, Ethnic Conflict, and Self-Determination*. Philadelphia: Temple University Press.

———. 1999. *Turmoil in the Middle East: Imperialism, War, and Political Instability*. Albany: State University of New York Press.

Bettelheim, Charles. 1976. *Class Struggles in the USSR: First Period, 1917-1923*. New York: Monthly Review Press.

———. 1978. *Class Struggles in the USSR: Second Period, 1923-1930*. New York: Monthly Review Press.

———. 1978. "The Great Leap Backward." *Monthly Review* 30, no. 3 (July-August).

Block, Fred. 1977. "The Ruling Class Does Not Rule: Notes on the Marxist Theory of the State." *Socialist Review*, no. 33 (May-June).

———. 1978. "Class Consciousness and Capitalist Rationalization: A Reply to Critics." *Socialist Review*, no. 40-41 (July-October).

———. 1996. *The Vampire State*. New York: The New Press.

Bluestone, Barry, and Bennett Harrison. 1982. *The Deindustrialization of America*. New York: Basic Books.

Bookman, Ann and Sandra Morgen (eds.). 1987. *Women and Politics of Empowerment*. Philadelphia: Temple University Press.

Borón, Atilio. 1995. *State, Capitalism, and Democracy in Latin America*. Boulder, Colo.: Lynne Rienner Publishers.

Bose, Sugata and Ayesha Jalal (eds.). 1997. *Nationalism, Democracy, and Development*. New York: Oxford University Press.

Bottomore, T.B. 1966. *Elites and Society*. Baltimore: Penguin.

Boyer, Richard O., and Herbert M. Morais. 1980. *Labor's Untold Story*. 3rd ed. New York: United Electrical, Radio and Machine Workers of America.

Brenner, Johanna. 2000. *Women and the Politics of Class*. New York: Monthly Review Press.

Buechler, Steven M. 1999. *Social Movements in Advanced Capitalism*. New York: Oxford University Press.

Cameron, Kenneth Neill. 1977. *Humanity and Society: A World History*. New York: Monthly Review Press.

Camilleri, Joseph A. et al. (eds.). 1995. *The State in Transition: Reimagining Political Space*. Boulder, Colo.: Lynne Rienner Publishers.

Carnoy, Martin. 1984. *The State and Political Theory*. Princeton: Princeton University Press.

Carr, E.H. 1952-58. *History of Soviet Russia* Vols. 2, 4, 5. New York: Macmillan.

Castells, Manuel. 1980. *The Economic Crisis and American Society*. Princeton: Princeton University Press.

Chatterjee, Partha (ed.). 1997. *State and Politics in India*. New York: Oxford University Press.

Chattopadhyay, Paresh. 1992. "India's Capitalist Industrialization." In *Class, State and Development in India*, edited by Berch Berberoglu. Delhi: Sage Publications.

Childe, V. Gordon. 1971. *What Happened in History*. Baltimore: Penguin.

Choueiri, Youssef M. (ed.). 1994. *State and Society in Syria and Lebanon*. New York: St. Martin's Press.

Clarke, S. 1977. "Marxism, Sociology and Poulantzas's Theory of the State." *Capital and Class* 2.

Clawson, Dan, Alan Neustad, and Mark Weller. 1998. *Dollars and Votes: How Business Campaign Contributions Subvert Democracy*. Philadelphia: Temple University Press.

Cockcroft, James D. 1999. *Mexico's Hope: An Encounter with Politics and History*. New York: Monthly Review Press.

Cooper, Mark. 1983. "Egyptian State Capitalism in Crisis." In *The Middle East*, edited by Talal Asad and Roger Owen. New York: Monthly Review Press.

Cox, Ronald W. and Daniel Skidmore-Hess. 1999. *U.S. Politics and the Global Economy: Corporate Power, Conservative Shift*. Boulder, Colo.: Lynne Rienner Publishers.

Croetau, David. 1994. *Politics and the Class Divide: Working People and the Middle Class Left*. Philadelphia: Temple University Press.

Dahl, Robert. 1961. *Who Governs?* New Haven: Yale University Press.

———. 1967. *Pluralist Democracy in the United States: Conflict and Consensus*. Chicago: Rand McNally.

Dahms, Harry F. (ed.). 2000. *Transformations of Capitalism: Ecomony, Society, and the State in Modern Times*. New York: New York University Press.

Davidson, Basil. 1961. *The African Slave Trade*. Boston: Little, Brown.

Devine, Jim. 1982. "The Structural Crisis of U.S. Capitalism." *Southwest Economy and Society* 6, no. 1 (Fall).

Dobb, Maurice. 1948. *Soviet Economic Development Since 1917*. London: Routledge & Kegan Paul.

———. 1954. "Soviet Economy: Fact and Fiction." *Science and Society* (Spring).

Domhoff, G. William. 1967. *Who Rules America?* Englewood Cliffs, N.J.: Prentice-Hall.

———. 1970. *The Higher Circles*. New York: Vintage.

———. 1979. *The Powers That Be*. New York: Random House.

Draper, Hal. 1977. *Karl Marx's Theory of Revolution: State and Bureaucracy*. Parts 1 and 2. New York: Monthly Review Press.

Earle, E.M. 1966. *Turkey, The Great Powers, and the Baghdad Railway: A Study in Imperialism*. New York: Russell and Russell.

Easton, David. 1971. *The Political System*. New York: Knopf.

Eisenstadt, S.N. 1966. *Modernization: Protest and Change*. Englewood Cliffs, N.J.: Prentice-Hall.

Eldersveld, Samuel J. and Hanes Walton Jr. 1999. *Political Parties in American Society*. New York: St. Martin's Press.

Eliasoph, Nina. 1998. *Avoiding Politics: How Americans Produce Apathy in Everyday Life*. Cambridge: Cambridge University Press.

Engels, Frederick. 1972. *The Origins of the Family, Private Property and the State*. In Karl Marx and Frederick Engels, *Selected Works*. New York: International Publishers.

———. 1972. *Ludwig Feuerbach and the End of Classical German Philosophy*. In Karl Marx and Frederick Engels, *Selected Works*. New York: International Publishers.

———. 1973. *The Peasant War in Germany*. New York: International Publishers.

———. 1976. *Anti-Duhring*. New York: International Publishers.

Erlich, Alexander. 1960. *The Soviet Industrialization Debate*. Cambridge, Mass.: Harvard University Press.

Ersson, Svante O. 1998. *Politics and Society in Western Europe*. Thousand Oaks, Calif.: Sage Publications.

Esping-Andersen, Gosta, Roger Friedland, and Erik Olin Wright. 1976. "Modes of Class Struggle and the Capitalist State." *Kapitalistate*, nos. 4-5 (Summer).

Evans, Geoffrey (ed.). 1999. *The End of Class Politics?* New York: Oxford University Press.

Ewen, Lynda Ann. 1998. *Social Stratification and Power in America*. New York: General Hall.

Faulks, Keith. 2000. *Political Sociology: A Critical Introduction*. New York: New York University Press.

Flammang, Janet A. 1997. *Women's Political Voice: How Women Are Transforming the Practice and Study of Politics*. Philadelphia: Temple University Press.

Foran, John (ed.). 1994. *A Century of Revolution: Social Movements in Iran*. Minneapolis: University of Minnesota Press.

Frank, Andre Gunder. 1967. *Capitalism and Underdevelopment in Latin America*. New York: Monthly Review Press.

Fu-chun, Li. 1950. *Report on the First Five-Year Plan of Development*. Peking: Foreign Languages Press.

Gandy, D.R. 1979. *Marx and History*. Austin and London: University of Texas Press.

Gerschenkron, Alexander. 1951. *A Dollar Index of Soviet Machinery Output, 1927-28 to 1937*. Los Angeles: Rand Corporation.

———. 1965. *Economic Backwardness in Historical Perspective*. New York: Praeger.

Gold, David, Clarence Y.H. Lo, and Erik Olin Wright. 1975. "Some Recent Developments in Marxist Theories of the Capitalist State," parts 1 and 2, *Monthly Review* 27, nos. 5 and 6 (October and November).

Gramsci, Antonio. 1971. *Prison Notebooks*. New York: International Publishers.

———. 1978. *Selections from Political Writings 1921-26*. London: Lawrence & Wishart.

Grillo, R. D. 1999. *Pluralism and the Politics of Difference*. New York: Oxford University Press.

Gurley, John G. 1976. *Challengers to Capitalism*. San Francisco: San Francisco Book Company.

Halebsky, Sandor and Richard L. Harris (eds.). 1995. *Capital, Power, and Inequality in Latin America*. Boulder, Colo.: Westview Press.

Hamilton, Clive. 1983. "Capitalist Industrialization in East Asia's Four Little Tigers." *Journal of Contemporary Asia* 13, no. 1.

Hamilton, Richard. 1972. *Class and Politics in the United States*. New York: Wiley.

Harris, Richard, ed. 1975. *The Political Economy of Africa*. Cambridge, Mass.: Schenkman.

Harrison, Bennett, and Barry Bluestone. 1988. *The Great U-Turn: Corporate Restructuring and the Polarizing of America*. New York: Basic Books.

Hilton, Rodney, ed. 1976. *The Transition from Feudalism to Capitalism*. London: New Left Books.

Hinton, William. 1966. *Fanshen: A Documentary of Revolution in a Chinese Village*. New York: Vintage.

Hirsh, Joachim. 1979. "The State Apparatus and Social Reproduction: Elements of a Theory of the Bourgeois State." In *State and Capital: A Marxist Debate*, edited by John Holloway and Sol Picciotto. Austin: University of Texas Press.

Hobsbawm, Eric. 1995. *The Age of Extremes, 1914-1991*. New York: Pantheon.

Holloway, John, and Sol Picciotto. 1977. "Capital, Crisis and the State." *Capital and Class*, no. 2.

———. 1979. "Introduction: Towards a Marxist Theory of the State." In *State and Capital*, edited by John Holloway and Sol Picciotto. London: Edward Arnold.

Hooglund, Eric J. 1982. *Land and Revolution in Iran, 1960-1980*. Austin: University of Texas Press.

Hoogvelt, Ankie. 1997. *Globalization and the Postcolonial World*. Baltimore: The Johns Hopkins University Press.

Hunter, Floyd. 1953. *Community Power Structure*. Chapel Hill: University of North Carolina Press.

————. 1959. *Top Leadership U.S.A..* Chapel Hill: University of North Carolina Press.

Hurrell, Andrew and Ngaire Woods (eds.). 1999. *Inequality, Globalization, and World Politics.* New York: Oxford University Press.

Hussain, Mahmoud. 1973. *Class Conflict in Egypt, 1945-1970.* New York: Monthly Review Press.

Ismael, Tareq Y. and Jacqueline S. Ismael (eds.). 1994. *The Gulf War and the New World Order: International Relations in the Middle East.* Gainesville: University Press of Florida.

Jayal, Niraja Gopal. 1999. *Democracy and the State.* New York: Oxford University Press.

Jenkins, J. Craig and Bert Klandermans (ed.). 1995. *The Politics of Social Protest: Comparative Perspectives on States and Social Movements.* Minneapolis: University of Minnesota Press.

Jessop, Bob. 1982. *The Capitalist State.* New York: New York University Press.

Katz, Richard S. 1997. *Democracy and Elections.* New York: Oxford University Press.

Kaufman, Michael and Haroldo Dilla Alfonso (eds.). 1997. *Community Power and Grassroots Democracy.* London: Zed Books.

Key, V.O. 1964. *Public Opinion and American Democracy.* New York: Knopf.

Kidron, Michael. 1970. *Western Capitalism Since the War,* Harmondsworth, England: Penguin.

Kimmel, Michael S. and Charles Stephen. 1998. *Social and Political Theory.* Boston: Allyn and Bacon.

King, Roger. 1986. *The State in Modern Society.* Chatham, N.J.: Chatham House.

Kourvetaris, George A. 1997. *Political Sociology: Structure and Process.* Boston: Allyn and Bacon.

Krader, Lawrence. 1975. *The Asiatic Mode of Production.* Assem: Van Gorcum.

Laclau, Ernesto. 1971. "Feudalism and Capitalism in Latin America." *New Left Review* 67 (May-June).

Lenin, V.I. 1947. *Works.* Vol. 31. Moscow: Foreign Languages Publishing House.

————. 1971. *Selected Works.* New York: International Publishers.

————. 1971. *The State and Revolution.* In V.I. Lenin, *Selected Works.* New York: International Publishers.

————. 1974. *The State.* In Karl Marx, Frederick Engels, and V.I. Lenin, *On Historical Materialism.* New York: International Publishers.

————. 1975. *Selected Works in Three Volumes.* Vol. 2. Moscow: Progress Publishers.

Levine, Rhonda F. (ed.). 1998. *Social Class and Stratification.* Boulder, Colo.: Rowman & Littlefield Publishers.

Levkovsky, A.I. 1966. *Capitalism in India.* Delhi: People's Publishing House.

Lewis, Cleona. 1938. *America's Stake in International Investments.* Washington, D.C.: Brookings Institution.

Leys, Colin. 1976. "The 'Overdeveloped' Post-Colonial State: A Reevaluation." *Review of African Political Economy,* no. 5.

Linklater, Andrew. 1998. *The Transformation of Political Community.* Columbia: University of South Carolina Press.

Lipset, Seymour Martin. 1960. *Political Man*. Garden City, N.Y.: Doubleday Anchor.

Lloyd, David and Paul Thomas. 1998. *Culture and the State*. New York: Routledge.

Longuenesse, Elizabeth. 1979. "The Class Nature of the State in Syria." *MERIP Reports* 9, no. 4 (May).

Luger, Stan. 2000. *Corporate Power, American Democracy, and the Automobile Industry*. Cambridge: Cambridge University Press.

MacEwan, Arthur. 1999. *Neo-Liberalism or Democracy?* London: Zed Books.

Mandel, Ernest. 1975. *Late Capitalism*. London: New Left Books.

———. 1979. *From Class Society to Communism*. London: Ink Links.

Manza, Jeff and Clem Brooks. 1999. *Social Cleavages and Political Change*. New York: Oxford University Press.

Mao Tse-tung (Zedong). 1971. "On the Question of Agricultural Cooperatives." *Selected Readings from the Works of Mao Tse-tung*. Peking: Foreign Languages Press.

———. 1971. "China's Path to Industrialization," Part 12 of "On the Correct Handling of Contradictions Among the People." *Selected Readings From the Works of Mao Tse-tung*. Peking: Foreign Languages Press.

Marger, Martin N. 1987. *Elites and Masses: An Introduction to Political Sociology*. 2nd ed. Belmont, Calif.: Wadsworth.

Markoff, John. 1996. *Waves of Democracy: Social Movements and Political Change*. Thousand Oaks, Calif.: Pine Forge Press.

Marquit, Erwin. 1978. *The Socialist Countries*. Minneapolis, Minn.: MEP Press.

Martinussen, John. 1997. *State, Society and Market*. London: Zed Books.

Marx, Karl. 1963. *The Poverty of Philosophy*. New York: International Publishers.

———. 1964. *Selected Writings in Sociology and Social Philosophy*. New York: McGraw-Hill.

———. 1965. *Pre-Capitalist Economic Formations*. New York: International Publishers.

———. 1967. *Capital*. 3 vols. New York: International Publishers.

———. 1968. *The Eighteenth Brumaire of Louis Bonaparte*. In Karl Marx and Frederick Engels, *Selected Works*. New York: International Publishers.

———. 1972. *The Civil War in France*. In Karl Marx and Frederick Engels, *Selected Works*. New York: International Publishers.

———. 1972. *Critique of the Gotha Program*. In Karl Marx and Frederick Engels, *Selected Works*. New York: International Publishers.

———. 1972. *Preface to a Contribution to the Critique of Political Economy*. In Karl Marx and Frederick Engels, *Selected Works*. New York: International Publishers.

———. 1972. *Marx to L. Kugelmann in Hanover*. In Karl Marx and Frederick Engels, *Selected Works*. New York: International Publishers.

Marx, K. and F. Engels. 1969. *The German Ideology*. New York: International Publishers.

———. 1972. *Manifesto of the Communist Party*. In Karl Marx and Frederick Engels, *Selected Works*. New York: International Publishers.

McConnell, Grant. 1966. *Private Power and American Democracy*. New York: Knopf.

McCrone, David. 1998. *The Sociology of Nationalism: Tomorrow's Ancestors.* London: Routledge.

McNeely, Connie L. (ed.). 1998. *Public Rights, Public Rules: Constituting Citizens in the World Polity and National Policy.* New York: Garland Publishers.

Michels, Robert. 1968. *Political Parties.* New York: Free Press.

Miliband, Ralph. 1969. *The State in Capitalist Society.* New York: Basic Books.

———. 1970. "The Capitalist State—Reply to Nicos Poulantzas." *New Left Review,* no. 59.

———. 1973. "Poulantzas and the Capitalist State." *New Left Review,* no. 82.

———. 1975. "Political Forms and Historical Materialism." In *Socialist Register, 1975,* edited by R. Miliband and J. Saville. London: Merlin Press.

———. 1977. *Marxism and Politics.* London: Oxford University Press.

———. 1982. *Capitalist Democracy in Britain.* London: Oxford University Press.

Mills, C. Wright. 1956. *The Power Elite.* New York: Oxford University Press.

———. 1959. *The Sociological Imagination.* New York: Oxford University Press.

Moaddel, Mansoor. 1993. *Class, Politics, and Ideology in the Iranian Revolution.* New York: Columbia University Press.

Moghadam, Valentine M. (ed.). 1994. *Identity Politics and Women: Cultural Reassertions and Feminisms in International Perspective.* Boulder, Colo.: Westview Press.

Mollenkopf, John. 1975. "Theories of the State and Power Structure Research." *Insurgent Sociologist* 5, no. 3.

Moore, Barrington, Jr. 1950. *Soviet Politics: The Dilemma of Power.* Cambridge, Mass.: Harvard University Press.

———. 1968. *The Social Origins of Democracy and Dictatorship.* London: Penguin.

Morais, Herbert M. 1944. *The Struggle for American Freedom.* New York: International Publishers.

Mosca, Gaetano. 1939. *The Ruling Class.* New York: McGraw-Hill.

Newman, Bruce I. 1999. *The Mass Marketing of Politics.* Thousand Oaks, Calif.: Sage Publications.

Nikolas, Rose S. 1999. *Powers of Freedom: Reframing Political Thought.* Cambridge: Cambridge University Press.

O'Connor, James. 1973. *The Fiscal Crisis of the State.* New York: St. Martin's.

———. 1984. *Accumulation Crisis.* New York: Basil Blackwell.

O'Donnell, Guillermo. 1973. *Modernization and Bureaucratic Authoritarianism: Studies in South American Politics.* Berkeley: Institute of International Studies, University of California at Berkeley.

———. 1979. "Tensions in the Bureaucratic-Authoritarian State and the Questions of Democracy." In *The New Authoritarianism in Latin America,* edited by David Collier. Princeton: Princeton University Press.

Offe, Claus. 1974. "Structural Problems of the Capitalist State." In *German Political Studies,* edited by K. Von Beyme. Vol. 1. London: Sage.

———. 1975. "The Theory of the Capitalist State and the Problem of Policy Formation." In *Stress and Contradiction in Modern Capitalism,* edited by L. Lindberg et al. Lexington, Mass.: Heath.

———. 1980. "The Separation of Form and Content in Liberal Democratic Politics." *Studies in Political Economy* 3.

————. 1981. "Some Contradictions of the Modern Welfare State." *International Praxis* 1, no. 3.

Olsen, Marvin E. and Martin N. Marger (eds.). 1993. *Power in Societies*. Boulder, Colo.: Westview Press.

Opello Jr., Walter C. and Stephen J. Rosow. 1999. *The Nation-State and Global Order*. Boulder, Colo.: Lynne Rienner Publishers.

Owen, Roger. 1992. *State, Power, and Politics in the Making of the Modern Middle East*. London: Routledge.

Panitch, Leo. 1980. "Recent Theorizations of Corporatism." *British Journal of Sociology* (June).

Panitch, Leo and Colin Leys (eds.). 1999. *Global Capitalism Versus Democracy*. New York: Monthly Review Press.

Parenti, Michael. 1970. "Power and Pluralism: The View from the Bottom." *Journal of Politics* 32 (August).

————. 1994. *Democracy for the Few*. 6th ed. New York: St. Martin's.

————. 1994. *Land of Idols: Political Mythology in America*. New York: St. Martin's Press.

————. 1995. *Against Empire*. San Francisco: City Lights Books.

————. 1997. *America Besieged*. San Francisco: City Lights Books.

————. 1999. *History as Mystery*. San Francisco: City Lights Books.

Pareto, Vilfredo. 1935. *The Mind and Society*. 4 vols. London: Jonathan Cape.

————. 1969. "Elites and Their Circulation." In *Structured Social Inequality*, edited by C.S. Heller. New York: Macmillan.

Parsons, Talcott. 1960. *Structure and Process in Modern Societies*. New York: Free Press.

————. 1966. *Societies: An Evolutionary Approach*. Englewood Cliffs, N.J.: Prentice-Hall.

————. 1967. "On the Concept of Political Power." In T. Parsons, *Sociological Theory and Modern Society*. New York: Free Press.

Paul, T.V. and John A. Hall (eds.). 1999. *International Order and the Future of World Politics*. Cambridge: Cambridge University Press.

Petras, James F. 1978. *Critical Perspectives on Imperialism and Social Class in the Third World*. New York: Monthly Review Press.

————. 1981. *Class, State and Power in the Third World*. Montclair, NJ: Allanheld, Osmun.

————. 1983. *Capitalist and Socialist Crises in the Late Twentieth Century*. Totowa, NJ: Rowman & Allanheld.

Petras, James, with Todd Cavaluzzi, Morris Morely, and Steve Vieux. 1999. *The Left Strikes Back: Class Conflict in Latin America in the Age of Neoliberalism*. Boulder, Colo.: Westview Press.

Picciotto, Sol. 1979. "The Theory of the State, Class Struggle, and the Rule of Law." In *Capitalism and the Rule of Law*, edited by Ben Fine et al. London: Hutchinson.

Polsby, Nelson. 1963. *Community Power and Political Theory*. New Haven: Yale University Press.

Poulantzas, Nicos. 1969. "The Problem of the Capitalist State." *New Left Review*, no. 58.

———. 1973. *Political Power and Social Classes*. London: Verso.

———. 1974. *Fascism and Dictatorship*. London: New Left Books.

———. 1975. *Classes in Contemporary Capitalism*. London: New Left Books.

———. 1976. *The Crisis of the Dictatorships*. London: New Left Books.

———. 1976. "The Capitalist State: A Reply to Miliband and Laclau," *New Left Review*, no. 95.

———. 1978. *State, Power, Socialism*. London: Verso.

———. 1979. "The Political Crisis and the Crisis of the State." In *Critical Sociology: European Perspectives*, edited by J.W. Freiberg. New York: Irvington Publishers.

Przeworski, Adam. 1979. "Economic Conditions of Class Compromise." University of Chicago. Mimeo.

Przeworski, Adam, and Michael Wallerstein. 1982. "The Structure of Class Conflict in Democratic Capitalist Societies." *American Political Science Review* 76, no. 2.

Rahnema, Saeed and Sohrab Behdad (eds.). 1995. *Iran After the Revolution: Crisis of an Islamic State*. London: I. B. Tauris.

Reed, Adolph L. 1997. *W.E.B. Du Bois and American Political Thought*. New York: Oxford University Press.

Roelofs, H. Mark. 1998. *The Poverty of American Politics: A Theoretical Interpretation*, 2nd ed. Philadelphia: Temple University Press.

Rose, Arnold. 1967. *The Power Structure*. New York: Oxford University Press.

Rose, Nikolas. 1999. *Powers of Freedom: Reframing Political Thought*. Cambridge: Cambridge University Press.

Roy, Ash Narain. 1999. *The Third World in the Age of Globalization*. London: Zed Books.

Saville, John. 1995. *The Consolidation of the Capitalist State, 1800-1850*. London: Pluto Press.

Sassen, Saskia. 1998. *Globalization and Its Discontents*. New York: The New Press.

Schatzki, Theodore R. and Wolfgang Natter (eds.). 1996. *The Social and Political Body*. New York: Guilford Press.

Schmitter, Phillippe. 1974. "Still the Century of Corporatism?" In *The New Corporatism*, edited by Frederick Pike and Thomas Stritch. Notre Dame, Ind.: University of Notre Dame Press.

Sen, Anupam. 1982. *The State, Industrialization, and Class Formations in India*. London: Routledge & Kegan Paul.

Shivji, Issa G. 1976. *Class Struggles in Tanzania*. New York: Monthly Review Press.

Shklar, Judith N. 1998. *Political Thought and Political Thinkers*. Chicago: University of Chicago Press.

———. 1998. *Redeeming American Political Thought*. Chicago: University of Chicago Press.

Skocpol, Theda. 1979. *States and Revolutions: A Comparative Analysis of France, Russia and China*. Cambridge: Cambridge University Press.

Smelser, N. 1963. "Mechanisms of Change and Adjustment to Change." in *Industrialization and Society*, edited by B. Hoselitz and W. Moore. New York: Mouton.

Stalin, J.V. 1939. *Questions of Leninism*. Moscow: Foreign Languages Publishing House.

Stein, Stanley J., and Barbara H. Stein. 1970. *The Colonial Heritage of Latin America*. New York: Oxford University Press.

Stepan, Alfred. 1978. *The State and Society: Peru in Comparative Perspective*. Princeton: Princeton University Press.

Stork, Joe. 1981. "Iraq and the War in the Gulf." *MERIP Reports*, no. 97 (June).

Street, John. 1998. *Politics and Popular Culture*. Philadelphia: Temple University Press.

Sutcliffe, R. B. 1971. *Industry and Underdevelopment*. London: Addison-Wesley.

Sweezy, Paul M., and Charles Bettelheim (eds.), 1971. *On the Transition to Socialism*. New York: Monthly Review Press.

Szymanski, Albert. 1978. *The Capitalist State and the Politics of Class*. Cambridge, Mass.: Winthrop.

———. 1979. *Is the Red Flag Flying? The Political Economy of the Soviet Union*. London: Zed Press.

———. 1981. *The Logic of Imperialism*. New York: Praeger.

———. 1983. *Class Structure: A Critical Perspective*. New York: Praeger.

Therborn, Goran. 1976. *Science, Class and Society*. London: New Left Books.

———. 1977. "The Rule of Capital and the Rise of Democracy," *New Left Review*, no. 103.

———. 1978. *What Does the Ruling Class Do When It Rules?* London: New Left Books.

———. 1980. *The Ideology of Power and the Power of Ideology*. London: New Left Books.

———. 1986. "Neo-Marxist, Pluralist, Corporatist, Statist Theories and the Welfare State." In *The State in Global Perspective*, edited by A. Kazancigil. Aldershot, UK: Gower and UNESCO.

Thompson, E.P. 1963. *The Making of the English Working Class*. New York: Vintage.

Tigar, Michael. 2000. *Law and the Rise of Capitalism*. New York: Monthly Review Press.

Tillman, Ray M. and Michael S. Cummings (eds.). 1999. *The Transformation of U.S. Unions*. Boulder, Colo.: Lynne Rienner Publishers.

Tocqueville, Alexis de. 1945. *Democracy in America*. New York: Knopf.

Tornquist, Olle. 1998. *Politics and Development*. Thousand Oaks, Calif.: Sage Publications.

Townsend, Janet et al. 1999. *Women and Power*. London: Zed Books.

Trimberger, E.K. 1978. *Revolution from Above: Military Bureaucrats and Development in Japan, Turkey and Peru*. New Brunswick, N.J.: Transaction Books.

Truman, David. 1964. *The Government Process*. New York: Knopf.

United States Congress. 2000. *Economic Report of the President, 2000*. Washington, D.C.: Government Printing Office.

United States Department of Commerce. 1999. *Statistical Abstract of the United States, 1999*. Washington, D.C.: Government Printing Office.

———. 1999. *Survey of Current Business* (August).

United States Office of Management and Budget. 2000. *Budget of the United States Government, 2000*. Washington, D.C.: Government Printing Office.

Wallerstein, Immanuel. 1974. *The Modern World System*. New York: Academic Press.

———. 1979. *The Capitalist World Economy*. Cambridge: Cambridge University Press.

———. 1984. *The Politics of the World Economy. The States, The Movements and the Civilizations*. Cambridge: Cambridge University Press.

Warren, Bill. 1980. *Imperialism, Pioneer of Capitalism*. London: Verso.

Weber, Max. 1967. *From Max Weber. Essays in Sociology*. Translated, edited and with an introduction by H.H. Gerth and C. Wright Mills. New York: Oxford University Press.

———. 1968. *Economy and Society*. New York: Bedminster Press.

Wheelwright, E.L., and McFarlane, B. 1970. *The Chinese Road to Socialism*. New York: Monthly Review Press.

Wilber, Charles K. 1969. *The Soviet Model and Underdeveloped Countries*. Chapel Hill: University of North Carolina Press.

Williams, Eric. 1944. *Capitalism and Slavery*. Reprint. New York: Capricorn (1966).

Wolfe, Alan. 1977. *The Limits of Legitimacy: Political Contradictions of Late Capitalism*. New York: Free Press.

Wolff, Jonathan and Michael Rosen (eds.). 1999. *Political Thought*. New York: Oxford University Press.

World Bank. 1999. *World Development Report, 1999*. Washington, D.C.: The World Bank.

Wright, Erik Olin. 1974-75. "To Control or To Smash Bureaucracy: Weber and Lenin on Politics, the State, and Bureaucracy." *Berkeley Journal of Sociology* 19.

———. 1978. *Class, Crisis and the State*. London: New Left Books.

———. 1985. *Classes*. London: Verso.

———. 1994. *Interrogating Inequality*. London: Verso.

———. 1997. *Class Counts*. London: Verso.

Zeitlin, Maurice. 1980. *Classes, Class Conflict, and the State*. Cambridge, Mass.: Winthrop.

ABOUT THE AUTHOR

Dr. Berch Berberoglu is Foundation Professor and Chairman of the Department of Sociology at the University of Nevada, Reno, where he has been teaching and conducting research for the past 23 years.

Dr. Berberoglu has written and edited 17 books and many articles on topics related to political sociology. His most recent books include *The Legacy of Empire: Economic Decline and Class Polarization in the United States*; *The Political Economy of Development*; *Class Structure and Social Transformation*; *The National Question: Nationalism, Ethnic Conflict and Self-Determination in the 20th Century*; *Turmoil in the Middle East: Imperialism, War, and Political Instability*; and *An Introduction to Classical and Contemporary Social Theory* (also published by General Hall).

Dr. Berberoglu's areas of specialization include political economy, class analysis, development, political sociology, and comparative historical sociology. He is currently working on a new book, *Class, State and Nation: The Class Nature of Nationalism and Ethnic Conflict*, which will be published by Greenwood Press in 2001.

Dr. Berberoglu received his Ph.D. in Sociology from the University of Oregon in 1977 and his B.A. and M.A. from Central Michigan University in 1972 and 1974, respectively. He also did graduate studies at the State University of New York at Binghamton in the early 1970s.

Index